ASYLUM SEEKERS' POLICY v INTEGRATION POLICY

Case study of Kosovan Families in the East End of London
(2003-2005)

Janusz Balicki
Anne Wells

ASYLUM SEEKERS' POLICY

V

INTEGRATION POLICY

Case study of Kosovan Families
in the East End of London
(2003-2005)

Political Science Institute
Cardinal Sefan Wyszynski University in Warsaw

Review:
Siew-Ean Khoo
The Australian National University

Andrzej Ochocki
Cardinal Sefan Wyszynski University in Warsaw

Note for Librarians: A Cataloguing record for this book is available from Library and Archives
Canada at www.collectionscanada.ca/amicus/index-e.html
ISBN 1-4120-7403-7

*Printed in Victoria, BC, Canada. Printed on paper with a minimum 30% recycled fibre. Trafford's print shop
runs on "green energy" from solar, wind and other environmentally-friendly power sources.*

This book was published *on-demand* in cooperation with Trafford Publishing. On-demand
publishing is a unique process and service of making a book available for retail sale to the
public taking advantage of on-demand manufacturing and Internet marketing. On-demand
publishing includes promotions, retail sales, manufacturing, order fulfillment, accounting and
collecting royalties on behalf of the author.

Book sales for North America and international*:*
Trafford Publishing, 6E-2333 Government St.,
Victoria, BC v 8T 4P4 CANADA
Phone 250 383 6864 (toll-free 1 888 232 4444)
Fax 250 383 6804; email to orders@trafford.com
Book sales in Europe
Trafford Publishing (UK) Limited, 9 Park End Street, 2nd floor
Oxford, UK 0X1 1HH UNITED KINGDOM
Phone 44 (0) 1865 722 113 (local rate 0845 230 9601)
Facsimile 44 (0) 1865 722 868; info.uk@trafford.com
Order online at:
trafford.com/05-2298

10 9 8 7 6 5 4 3

TABLE OF CONTENTS

ABBREVIATIONS

ACPO - Association of Chief Police Officers
AIT - Asylum and Immigration Tribunal
ARC - Application Registration Card
BBC - British Broadcasting Corporation
CAIT - Child Assessment and Investigation Team
DU - Depleted Uranium
DWP - Department of Works and Pensions
ECRE - European Council on Refugees and Exiles
ELR - Exceptional Leave to Remain
EU - European Union
HEP - Humanitarian Evacuation Programme
HPU - Homeless Persons Unit
ICAR - Information Centre about Asylum and Refugees
ICG - International Crisis Group
IND - Immigration and Nationality Directorate
IVD - International Volunteers for Development
KFOR - Kosovo Force (NATO-led international force responsible for establishing
      and maintaining security in Kosovo)
KLA - Kosovan Liberation Army
LSC - Local Service Centre
NASS - National Asylum Support Service
NATO - North Atlantic Treaty Organisation
NGO - Non-Governmental Organisation
NHRT - Non-Habitual Resident Team
OFSTED - Office for Standards in Education
RAMP - Renewal Refugee and Migrant Project
RC - Roman Catholic
SEF - Statement of Evidence Form
STAR - Student Action for Refugees
TOL - Transitions on line
UK - United Kingdom
UN - United Nations
UNEP - United Nations Environment Program
UNHCR - United Nations High Commissioner for Refugees
UNMIK - United Nations Interim Administration in Kosovo

ACKNOWLEDGMENTS

We are deeply indebted to all those who made possible the interviews which constituted our core research, especially Harmony House, RAMP and Sure Start, not forgetting the invaluable support and expertise offered by the staff of the Shpresa Group in Manor Park. Our particular gratitude is owed to the fifty asylum seeking families who so generously shared their often extremely painful experiences with us.

We are especially grateful to:
- Luljeta Nuzi who initially put us in touch with many of the Kosovans and whose support was invaluable to us in the writing of this book
- Flutra Shega who gave a great deal of her time to helping with interviews as a translator and also following up interviews for us with dedication and enthusiasm
- Clare O'Regan and Margaret Gallagher SHJM for their help in securing interviews with asylum seekers at Harmony House
- Maire O'Donnell RSHM for her careful and painstaking proof reading, her patience and encouragement
- Elane Heffernan, a Refugee support worker in the East End of London for her invaluable expertise and support, her reading and clarification of the text
- Moya Hamilton for her encouragement and suggestions
- The priests and religious of the Newham Deanery – Fathers Denis Hall, Ray Collier SSC, Sisters Monica Butler RSM, Joyce Bell FMM and Mary Barrow RSCJ for sharing their personal experiences of working with asylum seekers and whose interviews provided a detailed picture of the involvement of the Roman Catholic Church in helping asylum seekers to integrate
- Siew-Ean Khoo and Andrzej Ochocki for reviewing our publication and their helpful suggestions for editing the text

Special thanks to the Sisters of the Sacred Heart of Mary and Father Denis Hall. Their generosity made this publication possible.

Finally grateful thanks to our families, our friends and all those who encouraged and supported our publication.

INTRODUCTION

After the Second World War thousands of displaced people came to Britain. At the beginning the influx caused a few problems but with the growth of industrialism in the 1950s and 1960s, the UK needed more workers and even appealed to its colonies for help. Many people from the Caribbean and the Indian subcontinent took up the offer. However after the Suez crisis in 1973 the UK Government closed its doors to economic migrants and encouraged the migrant workers to return to their home countries. Many were reluctant to do so as they had become settled. The government could not force them to leave as many were British Citizens. Consequently the government continued to allow family members of existing immigrants to enter the UK and immigrant workers were in the UK to stay.

From the mid 1980s a large proportion of the immigrants who arrived in the UK were undocumented economic migrants and asylum seekers. In the ten years between 1989 and 1998, over four million people applied for asylum in Europe. Pressure mounted on the Western European governments, including the UK, to reduce the numbers of immigrants entering their territories illegally.

The UK Government constantly changed its immigration laws to make it more difficult for people to settle in the UK. Between 1993 and 2002 there were approximately 526,000 applications for asylum (not counting dependants) in the UK. Although the majority received refusals only 31,565 were deported. By October 2003 the Government realized that it had to solve the growing problem and announced an asylum Amnesty in October 2003 thereby allowing 15,000 families to stay in the UK. Most of the asylum seekers affected lived in London and the South East.

One of the greatest problems for any receiving State is connected with the integration of newcomers into its society. In order to solve this problem it is necessary firstly to consider how immigrants and more specifically refugees access their immediate needs such as housing, welfare, work and education (Home Office 2003f).

The Integration policy in the UK is aimed specifically at refugees not asylum seekers. Asylum seekers while encouraged to integrate are not encouraged to integrate fully until they have Refugee Status. Therefore the UK integration policy is not particularly helpful for the many asylum seekers, who after a few years of living in limbo, will get permission to stay in the UK. The issue of integration is especially important regarding asylum seekers' families. They are very vulnerable, after traumatic experiences in their home countries and they usually have young children. Every family in the world needs stability and a feeling of security, and this is no less true regarding families of asylum seekers. As Maeve Sherlock of the Refugee Council declared: 'It is utterly unfair on families - and especially children - to leave them in limbo, unable to rebuild their lives for years on end. Now the government must focus on getting decisions right much earlier, so people are not left in years of uncertainty.'

The purpose of our publication is to consider the compatibility of asylum seekers' family policy in the UK with the UK's integration policy, in the light of the experiences of asylum seekers' families (Kosovan/Albanian) in the East End of London.

The Kosovan families studied were a part of the huge group of refugees who came to the UK as a result of the conflict in Kosovo. Many of them had been part of a great exodus of Kosovan-Albanians from the province of Kosovo prior to and during the Kosovan conflict and NATO bombing campaign of March - June 1999 when ninety percent of Kosovan Albanians were actually displaced. The United Kingdom had recognised and accepted them as refugees since 1996, on account of their ethnicity and the fact that they had a history of persecution, and from the start of NATO's bombing the Home Office had been processing all Kosovans without a great deal of consideration of the individual cases. However, after the bombing campaign the Kosovans were no longer granted Refugee Status but rather granted automatically twelve months Exceptional Leave to Remain (ELR). By December 1999 the Province of Kosovo was considered secure and the Home Secretary declared that Kosovans would no longer automatically be granted ELR but should return to Kosovo. However as the Home Office was experiencing administration difficulties, they were not immediately returned and thousands of Kosovan Albanian families found themselves left awaiting the decision of the Home Office regarding their status. Many of those families were included in the Amnesty mentioned above.

The fifty families we interviewed came to the UK between 1997 and 2003. Twenty-three families arrived before the intervention or during the intervention of NATO. Seventeen families came to the UK in the second part of 1999 after the bombing campaign while only six arrived in 2000, one in 2001, two in 2002 and one in 2003. In our survey approximately three quarters of the families interviewed had entered the UK by chance and the majority had arrived illegally. Almost four fifths of the group had registered for asylum within two days of their arrival.

At the time of the first interviews in the Spring of 2003 only three of the respondents had received Refugee Status, another three had received Permanent Residence and three Exceptional Leave to Remain. One respondent had her case closed and two respondents claimed that they had received other documents but the language barrier made it impossible for them to be more specific. One respondent had Discretional Leave to Remain. Of the group of fifty an astounding thirty-six had no status whatsoever and were in a state of limbo awaiting a decision from the Home

Office. Two respondents' husbands had been deported while their wives and children were left behind.

By early November 2004, twenty-eight of the fifty families had some form of status: five had been granted Refugee Status; nineteen in all had been granted the Amnesty, that is they were allowed to stay in the UK indefinitely, outside the normal rules of immigration; two had been granted Exceptional Leave to Remain; one had been granted Discretionary Leave and one had been granted Humanitarian Protection until 2006. One had been refused the Amnesty and was appealing against the decision, while ten were still awaiting the decision of the Home Office. The remaining eleven families were no longer in any contact and had either been relocated or deported.

In order to consider the compatibility of the UK asylum seekers' family policy with the UK integration policy we used the 'snowballing' method to find interviewees. Starting with Kosovan families we already knew and various NGO Support Centres: Sure Start, Shpresa, Harmony House and the Renewal Refugee and Migrant Project (RAMP) in the East End of London, we relied on these contacts to put us in touch with other Kosovan asylum seekers. We interviewed fifty people, who responded on behalf of their families, between January 2003 and October 2004, pre-Amnesty and post-Amnesty and we held a limited number of in-depth interviews. With the help of a questionnaire and interpreter we covered the following topics:

- Profile of family: age, marital status, children, household, education and occupation in country of origin, affiliation to any Faith group
- Choice of the UK, way of arrival legally/illegally, application processes for asylum
- Integration: English lessons, children's education, accommodation, medical and legal care, present status in the UK, permission to work, help from Christian communities/faith groups, treatment received from other people in London
- Well-being, health, material situation, help from voluntary and state groups
- Links with home country and future plans, hopes regarding a future Immigration policy
- Affects of the Amnesty on status, well-being and occupation

The book has nine chapters. Chapter One presents the immigration policy in the UK. It contains the following topics: immigration trends in the UK; asylum trends in the UK; numbers of asylum seekers in the EU and UK; asylum decisions taken by the UK Government. It looks at the policy in the UK before April 2002; from May 2002 until October 2003; and after October 2003 when the Amnesty was announced. It concludes with a few facts about asylum in 2005 in the UK.

Chapter Two covers the background of the respondents. It begins with a brief early history of Kosovo from 700 until 1988. It looks at the distribution of Kosovo's population in 1991 and goes on to consider its history from 1989 until 23 March 1999 when NATO intervened. It describes in some detail what happened in Kosovo during the NATO bombing campaign and immediately afterwards, covering the period 24 March - December 1999. It concludes by looking at the Kosovan refugees in Europe firstly from 1995-99 then in 2000. Finally it considers the situation in Kosovo from 2000-02, 2003-05 and its future.

Chapter Three introduces the Survey. It contains a description of the questionnaires used; sources of information/respondents, NGO's - Sure Start; Shpresa Programme; RAMP and Harmony House. It presents the family profiles; country of origin and whether the families came from a rural or urban area; the sex and age of the respondents; their religion and marital status; the number of children per family; the ages and sex of the children; the respondents' education and occupation in their home country. Lastly it looks at the number of family members the respondent left in their home country and the number who fled abroad and the year the respondent arrived in England.

Chapter Four looks at becoming asylum seekers. It contains the motivation to leave their country of origin; any family members reunited in England and their reasons for choosing the UK. It asks if they considered other destinations. It looks at their status on entry to the UK, whether they arrived legally and whether they held a passport. It considers the route and transport they used to reach the UK, looking at their port of entry and where the respondent first set foot in the UK. The respondents were asked if they had needed to make an application for asylum and about the place and time of their registration. Finally the respondents describe what they were given on registration, their destination after registration and the treatment they received from the authorities (police, Home Office).

Chapter Five shows the initial process of integration as seen through the types of assistance received by asylum seekers on their arrival in the UK. It considers the following issues: the papers the respondents had received from the Home Office; the support offered by Christian communities/Faith groups and the treatment received from other people in London. It looks at whether the respondents required English lessons and how they acquired lessons. It considers how easy or difficult it was for the children to get places in the local schools. It looks at the respondents' accommodation; length of time in and condition of present accommodation; time spent living in hotel accommodation; number of properties lived in since arrival in the UK; benefits in general; benefits for asylum seekers awaiting the decision of the Home

Office; immigration solicitors; quality of advice given by immigration solicitors; how respondents obtained their immigration solicitors and housing solicitors.

Chapter Six deals with the asylum seekers' views of their current situation in the UK regarding their well-being and integration. It contains the following subjects: links with home country and future intentions; contact with people from the same ethnic group in the UK; contact with own country; desire to return to home country and reasons given; reasons respondents cannot return to their own country to live; comparison of how respondent's family lived five years ago in their home country to how they live now. It looks at asylum seekers' thoughts about future living conditions; their attitudes towards England; the greatest problems experienced by respondents in the UK; time it took respondents to access medical care; health problems in the UK; description of health problems; respondents' greatest fears; permission to stay in England indefinitely; National Insurance Numbers; permission to work and type of job held; preferred job; contact with any asylum seekers or refugee state/voluntary or Christian community groups; desire to be a British citizen. It concludes with respondents' suggestions regarding an immigration policy and how the Christian communities could help immigrants.

Chapter Seven contains six short case studies and one long study, entitled 'Snapshots of Asylum.' The first six studies look at aspects of life for asylum seekers' families: being pregnant and alone; housing fears; having to move at Christmas; nightmares; emergency accommodation with a handicapped child; detention caused by a solicitor's mistake. The main case study looks at a Kosovan family's experiences from the moment the family arrived in the UK until early 2005. It includes: destination safety; commencement of integration; housing problems; redundancy; a new home – more housing problems; problems with status and Amnesty granted.

Chapter Eight shows some of the challenges the Christian communities face as they try to help asylum seekers to integrate. It attempts to answer the question what they can do to help genuine asylum seekers.

Chapter Nine presents some of the dilemmas regarding the UK integration policy and asylum seekers. It contains the following issues: integration – basic concepts; immigration and refugees' integration policy; asylum seekers' integration policy. Finally there is a review of the UK integration policy in the light of the Kosovan families' experiences.

The Conclusion looks at the results of our survey regarding the compatibility of asylum seekers' family policy in the UK with the UK integration policy and the UN Convention on the Right of the Child.

The book contains an Appendix with copies of the questionnaires we used for the survey.

CHAPTER ONE
ASYLUM SEEKERS' POLICY IN THE UK

In this chapter we begin by looking at the immigration and asylum trends in the UK. We go on to compare the numbers of Asylum Seekers in the EU and UK. We consider the total number of asylum applications (excluding dependants) submitted to the five top countries of destination between 1998 and 2003, plus the eight top countries of origin, from which asylum seekers came to the UK between 2001-03 including those who came from the Federal Republic of Yugoslavia, of which Kosovo is a part. We look at the decisions taken by the UK Government and the number and outcome of initial decisions on applications for asylum in the UK, excluding dependants, in the years 2000-03. We go on to look at the immigration policy in the UK in recent years; before April 2002; between May 2002 and October 2003; after October 2003, plus the financial support available to asylum seekers during those periods. Finally we look very briefly at a few facts regarding asylum in the UK at the beginning of 2005.

1.1. IMMIGRATION TRENDS IN THE UK

Although the UK had had a long history of immigration nothing could prepare it for the scale and impact of immigration after the Second World War when thousands of displaced people came to Britain. One of the largest groups to enter the UK as refugees or displaced persons was the Poles (Elkes 2003).

More than a 100,000 Poles had fought with British forces during the Second War World while the Polish Government-in-Exile operated from London. After the war they were reluctant to go back to Poland because of the Yalta agreement, drawn up between Stalin, Roosevelt and Churchill, which had once again redrawn Poland's borders. Poland lost the eastern part of its territory where most of the displaced Poles had originally come from. Moreover the whole country was placed under Soviet Union control. The Poles were seen as a 'special case' by the British. Consequently they were given special treatment differing from that afforded to other refugee groups. On 22 March 1947, in an effort to provide help and support to the 190,000 Poles who wished to settle in the UK, the Polish Resettlement Act was passed and approximately two hundred camps, many situated in rural areas, were set up to help the Poles to settle.[1] In all approximately 210,000 Poles arrived between 1940-50 and they were followed in 1957 by 20,000 Hungarians (Wright 2004:18). The many Poles who found it difficult to obtain work, even though they had permission to work and were willing,

---

[1] Polish Community http://www.multicultural-matters.com/polish_community.htm.

were given unemployment assistance. Despite a difficult start and the spread of unfounded rumours that the Poles were being supported by British tax payers and taking British jobs, they managed to come to terms with their exile and integrated successfully into the British community (Elkes 2003).

While the Poles and Hungarians did not choose to leave their countries as a consequence of World War Two, many Europeans did choose to emigrate in search of a better life away from the extreme austerity of Europe in the 1950s. Even in the UK immediately after the War and throughout the 1950s and 1960s many poor families were encouraged by the UK government to send their children to a supposedly better life in Australia, Canada and South Africa under the Child Migrants Programme. Few European Governments actually encouraged emigration, since the war had cost 7.8 million lives but eventually the reconstruction of Europe brought an economic boom that created a demand for new labourers.

In the 1950s and 1960s, the UK found it needed to look further afield for workers and naturally looked first towards its colonies—the Caribbean and the Indian subcontinent. According to Stalker (2001) in 1951 this non-European minority ethnic population was growing steadily, and in the ten years between 1950 and 1960 net immigration for Western Europe reached around 10 million.

Most immigrant groups on arrival had to live with hostility and discrimination, whether it was racial harassment or religious intolerance. By the late 1960s opposition (fired by the media) was growing in the UK towards large numbers of immigrants, stemming from fears of being swamped, with not enough jobs or housing for those born in the UK, due to the steady arrival of more and more immigrants. The Suez crisis in 1973 brought the whole situation to a head and the UK Government closed its doors to economic migrants, terminated the labour recruitment programmes and encouraged the migrant workers to return to their home countries. Naturally these people had already become settled. Many were citizens and wished to stay in the UK, so the government continued to allow family members of existing immigrants to enter the UK and attempts to repatriate them were largely unsuccessful. In particular the arrival of the migrants' families, in spite of the restrictive admission policies, within not only the UK but the whole of Western Europe, confirmed that immigrant workers were here to stay (Hailbronner 2000).

The UK Government felt increasingly under pressure and during the thirty years (1973-2003) constantly changed its immigration laws to make it more difficult for people to settle in the UK. As Madeleine Bunting wrote in her special report for the Guardian: 'Throughout the Twentieth Century, government policy has been torn between two conflicting pressures: on the one hand, a passionate and proud tradition of Britain as a country that offered asylum and, on the other hand, a strong belief that the national identity could not accommodate ethnic diversity' (Bunting 2001). Some groups like the Poles and Hungarians had been more readily welcomed into the UK than others as they were considered more likely to be assimilated. However the arrival of the Ugandans in 1972-74 brought about a lengthy debate regarding the asylum policy of the UK and multi-culturalism. Surprisingly the Thatcher government in 1979 agreed to take 2,500 Vietnamese displaced persons without any apparent concerns regarding multi-culturalism (Bunting 2001).

From the early 1970s on, the non-European minority ethnic population in the UK grew from about 50,000 in 1951 to just over 4.6 million (7.9% of the total population) by 2001 of whom about 50% were from South Asia with the largest group - Indians numbering just over 1 million, Pakistanis about 747,000, Bangladeshis 283,000, and other Asian groups 247,000. Other non-European groups included Black Caribbeans numbering about 565,000, Black Africans 485,000 and other Black groups 97,000 with approximately 247,000 Chinese, and 230,000 declaring they were none of the above. About 677,000 declared they were of mixed race (National Statistics 2001b). This meant that in 2001 about one person in fifteen in the UK was from an ethnic minority group. Since 1989 there has been a large influx of asylum seekers so it follows that while the majority of adults from ethnic minority groups were born overseas the majority of their children are British born. This is particularly the situation among Indians. Only one in fifty Indian adults aged 35 or over was born in the UK compared to over nine in ten Indian children under the age of 16 (Home Office, date unknown). The total UK population was 58,789,194 and the total ethnic minority population was 4,635,296 (National Statistics 2001b). It would be impossible to estimate how many of this immigrant population initially came as asylum seekers. Many, naturally, were economic migrants and many skilled immigrants had been invited to the country to aid the ailing, ageing work force.

Since the mid 1980s a large proportion of the immigrants who arrived in the UK and other Western European countries has been undocumented economic migrants and asylum seekers (Hailbronner 2000:14). The fact that it was also a time of political upheaval in Eastern Europe with the collapse of Communism, meant that many people from Eastern Europe joined the thousands of people seeking safety from conflict by moving to Western Europe. As the UK governments made it harder for people to enter the UK legally as contract workers many had no option but to try to enter illegally or through seeking asylum.

The 2001 census showed that the minority ethnic groups were more likely to be living in England than in other parts of the UK. They accounted for 9% of the total population of England, while 2% lived in Scotland and Wales and 1% in Northern Ireland. The largest minority group was the Indians, followed by the

Parkistanis, those of mixed ethnic backgrounds, Black Caribbeans, Black Africans and Bangladeshis. The majority of the ethnic population was situated in London where 45% of the total ethnic groups reside. The Home Office 2001 Census showed that while many ethnic groups were fairly widely dispersed, 78% of black Africans, 61% of black Caribbeans and 54% of Bangladeshi were living in London in 2001.

1.2. ASYLUM TRENDS IN UK

Actual asylum trends in the UK can be differentiated from immigration trends. Although the Jews and the Poles among other displaced people came to the UK after the Second World War, as asylum seekers, as did the Hungarians, most of the immigrants during the period 1950-80 were economic migrants. However since the early 1990s more and more people have fled to the EU directly seeking asylum. In the ten years between 1989 and 1998, over four million people applied for asylum in the EU (Hailbronner 2000:15), and of those 7.7% (311,565) applied in the UK. In the following five years 1999-2003, 358,125 people applied for asylum in the UK, 18.9% of the total 1,888,675 who applied in the EU (Home Office 2005a).

According to Hailbronner (2000:8) in 1997 the study of migration statistics did 'not lead to the conclusion that migrants aim for the EU, but rather for specific EU states.' He said that some countries within the EU which offer a higher standard of living and a better job prospect are naturally more attractive to migrants and are therefore more favoured as destination countries than countries with a poorer economy (Hailbronner 2000:8).

Obviously if one is trying to enter a country illegally it is less risky by land than by sea or air. One would therefore expect that the prospect of a slightly safer journey would play a part in the asylum seekers' destination, but it seems that geographical proximity has little bearing on any decision and the price of transport isn't a significant factor. Unlike the majority of European destinations, Great Britain and Ireland can only be reached by ship or plane or through the Channel tunnel. However, while in the nineteen European countries with available data, the number of monthly asylum applications fell by an average of 13% in February 2003 compared to Jan/Feb 2002, the number in the UK dropped only by 3% from 8,495 to 8,256 (UNHCR 2003). It appears that many asylum seekers chose the UK, not for ease of access, for the benefit system or because they think it will be easy to obtain asylum but because the UK is known as a tolerant and law abiding society. In fact it is not only difficult to get to the UK but it is becoming increasingly more and more difficult to obtain financial support, to claim asylum and also to receive Refugee Status in the UK. A person has to prove that one is personally persecuted not just a victim of general hostilities such as a war, as we will see when we look later at the UK asylum policies.

Many of us would expect the majority of asylum seekers to have come from outside Europe but an incredible 43% came from within Europe, while only 35% came from Asia and 19% from Africa (Stalker 2001). As the numbers seeking asylum grew the Western European governments once more felt pressurized into tightening their regulations regarding asylum. People who formerly could have entered legally as asylum seekers or even as contract workers now found themselves with no choice but to seek alternative, illegal ways of entering Western Europe and many took to availing of the services of people smugglers. Illegal immigrants have become a major problem in many EU states and this situation has not been aided by the fact that the EU does not have a common immigration policy. Often European states react to the phenomenon of illegal immigration by legislation to regularize the status of their illegal immigrants thus allowing them to work (Hailbronner 2000:15). Some EU countries will not recognize a person as an asylum seeker if they have crossed their borders from a 'safe third country' (Goble 2002). Until recently it appeared that migration encourages migration. People choose their host country according to where others have gone before them. The most important factor for immigrants appeared to be the desire to join people of their own language and religion (Hailbronner 2000:8). Other factors included the host country's reputation towards asylum seekers regarding support and hospitality and the nature of the economy, as well as the country's laws and the time it took to process an asylum claim (Goble 2002).

Nevertheless in 1999 a change seemed to come about in the attitudes of asylum seekers. No longer did they appear to be seeking a host country where others had gone before them but now they fled their own countries and sought only a host country that would be safe. This is clearly seen in the huge number of Kosovan Albanians who fled the civil war in Kosovo, seeking shelter all over Europe regardless of whether anyone spoke their language or shared their culture. In fact many who entered into deals with people smugglers had no idea of their final destination. However the political aspects and economic aspects cannot be clearly separated. They are not distinct unconnected issues, since the refugees were trying to escape political suppression and also terrible living conditions.

1.3. NUMBERS OF ASYLUM SEEKERS IN EU AND UK

Many assume that applications for asylum rise each year in Europe but the figures in Table 1.1 show that this is not true. In fact having reached a peak of 675,455 in 1992 the numbers are now falling and have halved.

Table1.1 shows that 381,623 people applied for asylum in the EU in 2002 - a decrease of 1.7% (6,749) in applications on 2001 when there were 388,372 applications in the EU (UNHCR 2002). In 2003 the numbers dropped even further with 331,668 people applying for asylum in the European Union - a decrease of 13% (49,955) in applications on 2002.

Table 1.1 Number of asylum applications in EU

Asylum applications in the EU 1990 –2003						
1990	1991	1992	1993	1994	1995	1996
400,315	509,493	675,455	516,398	309,722	274,951	233,460
1997	1998	1999	2000	2001	2002	2003
251,762	311,408	396,737	391,275	388,372	381,623	331,668

Source: UNHCR (2002) Asylum Applications Lodged in Industrialised Countries: Levels and Trends, 2000-2002, UNHCR (2001) Statistical Yearbook 2001 Annex C.1 and C.2, UNHCR (2004a) Asylum Applications Lodged in Industrial Countries: Levels and Trends Jan - Jun 2004

Table 1.2 Number of asylum applications in UK (excluding dependants) 1980- 2004

1980	1981	1982	1983	1984	1985	1986	1987
2,352	2,425	4,223	4,296	4,171	4,266	4,256	3,998
1989	1990	1991	1992	1993	1994	1995	1996
11,640	26,205	44,840	24,625	22,345	32,830	43,925	29,640
1997	1998	1999	2000	2001	2002	2003	2004
32,500	46,015	71,145	80,315	71,370	85,890	49,405	33,930

Source: Total Number of Asylum applications submitted by country of destination (United Kingdom) 1980-2001 www.migrationinformation.org/GlobalData/countrydata/data.cfm; Home Office (2005a) Asylum Statistics 4th Quarter 2004

Until the year 2000 the top receiving country in the EU for refugees was Germany (Figure 1.1). From that time (with the exception of 2001) the UK has been the top receiving country, with 80,315 in 2000, 85,890 in 2002 and even with a significant drop of 24,000 to the figure of 61,100 in 2003 with Germany respectively 78,564, 71,127 and 50,600 in 2003. France, ranking third in Europe's asylum applications, had a steady growth, with 22,375 in 1998 rising to 59,800 in 2003. Sweden's numbers had also been steadily rising with 12,844 in 1998 to 33,106 in 2002 but showed a slight drop in 2003 to 31,300 while Austria's numbers almost trebled in the five years, from 13,805 in 1998 to 39,395 in 2002 before dropping by 7,000 in 2003 to 32,400 (UNHCR 2004b).

Figure 1.1 Total number of asylum applications (excluding dependants) submitted to five top countries of destination, 1998-2003

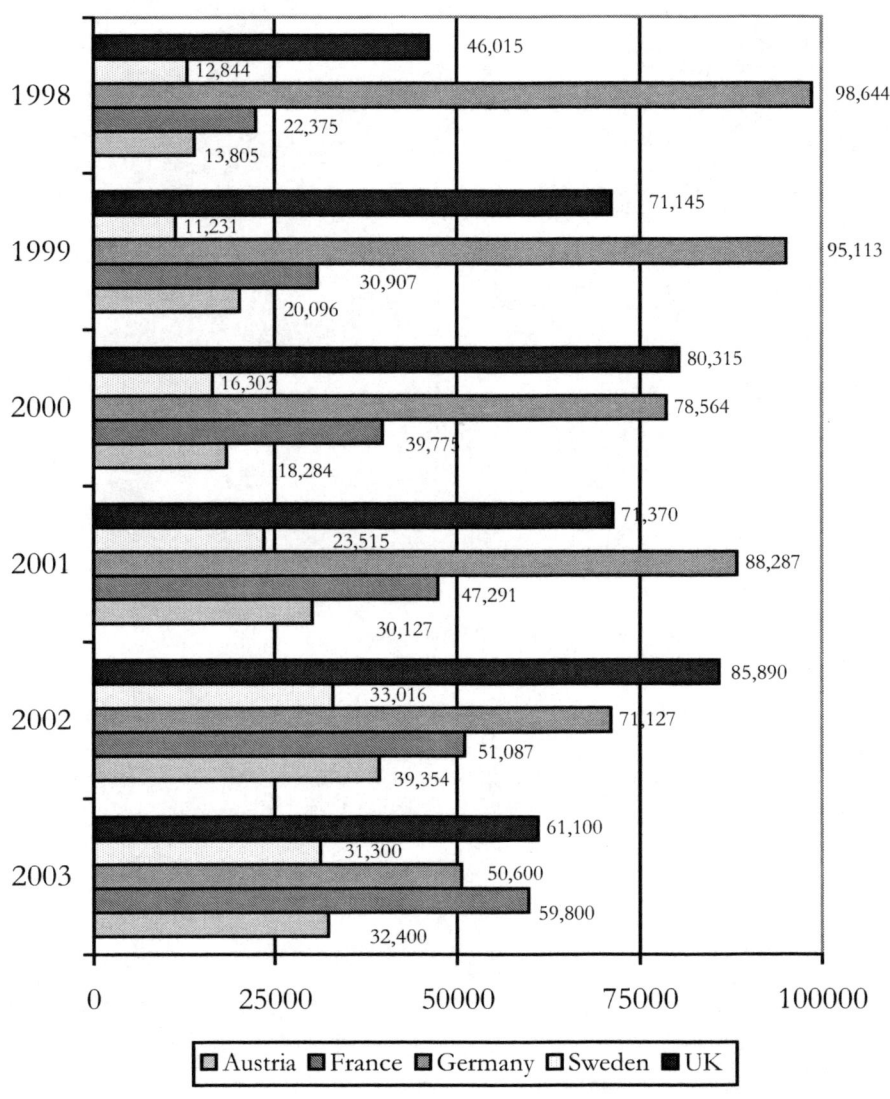

Source: UNHCR Population Data Unit
http://www.migrationinformation.org/DataTools/asylumresults.cfm;
Basic information about UNHCR (2004c) - Refugees by numbers (2004 edition)

Figure 1.2 The top eight asylum countries in the UK 2001-03 plus FRY/SAM

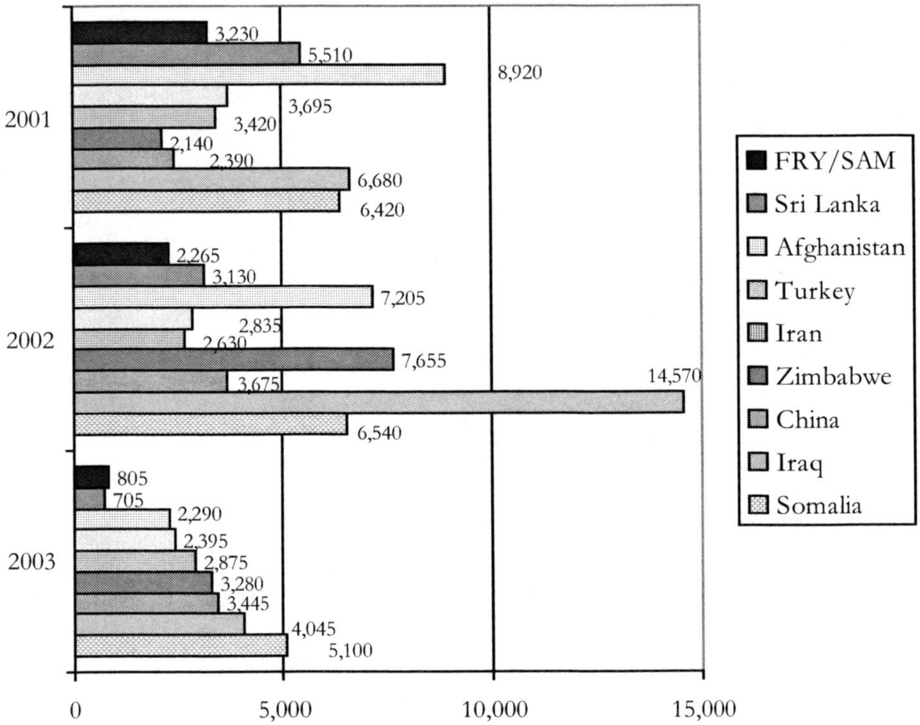

FRY/SAM = Serbia and Montenegro (SAM) replaced Federal Republic of Yugoslavia (FRY) from 5 February 2003 SAM comprises the Republic of Serbia, the Republic of Montenegro, and the Province of Kosovo (administered by the UN on an interim basis since 1999)

Source: Home Office, Asylum Statistics: 4th Quarter 2003 in United Kingdom

During 2001 the majority of people who applied for asylum in the UK were from Afghanistan (8,920), Iraq (6,680) Somalia (6,420) Sri Lanka (5,510) and Turkey (3,695). The following year 2002 the majority of people who applied were from Iraq (14,570) with Zimbabwe second (7,655) Afghanistan (7,205) third, China fourth with 3,675 and Sri Lanka fifth (3,130). During 2003 the majority came from Somalia (5,100), Iraq (4,045), China (3,445), Zimbabwe (3280) and Iran (2,875). SAM/FRY have been included in this table as our survey was based on asylum seekers from that region. As we can see although only 805 applied from there in 2003, there had been many more in the preceding years with 2,265 in 2002 and 3,230 in 2001. In 2000 there had been

6,070 applications for asylum to the UK from citizens of FRY, with 11,465 in 1999 and 7,395 in 1998.

1.4. ASYLUM DECISIONS TAKEN BY UK GOVERNMENT

During the four years 2000-03 as seen in figure 1.3, it is obvious that the majority of people who applied for asylum in the UK were refused after full consideration. The largest number to be refused was 66,070 in 2001, with 50,145 refused in 2000, while 41,710 were refused in 2002 and 42,345 in 2003. A smaller but still significant number were refused on the grounds of non-compliance. In 2000 that number was 24,290; in 2001 it was 21,220; in 2002 the number refused was 12,120 while in 2003 the number had dropped considerably from the year 2000 to 9,590. In the four years just over 4,500 people were refused on the grounds that they had passed through a safe third country. Approximately 1,240 were refused on this basis in 2000, 700 people in 2001, 1,305 in 2002 and 1,575 in 2003. Over the four years a total of 272,310 people were refused asylum in the UK.

In the same four years (2000-03) just 33,705 people were granted Refugee Status; 55,446 had been refused Refugee Status but granted Exceptional Leave to Remain – permission to reside in the UK for a temporary period; 135 people had been granted Humanitarian Protection for a number of years and 3,105 had been granted Discretionary Leave to Remain. Of those granted Refugee Status 10,375 had been granted Status in 2000, a slightly larger number 11,180 in 2001. In 2002 the number dropped to 8,270 and in 2003 there was a 50% drop to 3,880. At the end of September 2003 there were 33,895 asylum seekers in the UK in receipt of subsistence-only support and 51,810 supported by NASS (National Asylum Support Service) with subsistence and accommodation. Consequently in September 2003 a total of 85,705 people were supported by NASS in the UK, of whom 27,730 were supported in the Greater London area (Home Office 2003a).

According to Seddon et al (2002) these figures did not account for asylum seekers not supported by NASS and all the asylum seekers who applied for asylum before 3 April 2000 and were awaiting Home Office decisions on their cases. Those people were supported by the 'interim asylum support scheme' and received support from their local authority.

These figures do not take into account the number of clandestine migrants in the UK. Exact clandestine statistical material does not exist so the Home Office is unable to say exactly how many illegal immigrants are actually present in the UK. However in June 2005 the Home Office published a research report, 'Sizing the unauthorized (illegal) migrant population in the United Kingdom in 2001,' in which it stated that there was an estimated 430,000 unauthorized migrants living in the UK-0.7 % of the population (Home Office 2005b).

Figure 1.3 Number and outcome of Initial Decisions on application for asylum in the UK, excluding dependants in the years 2000-03

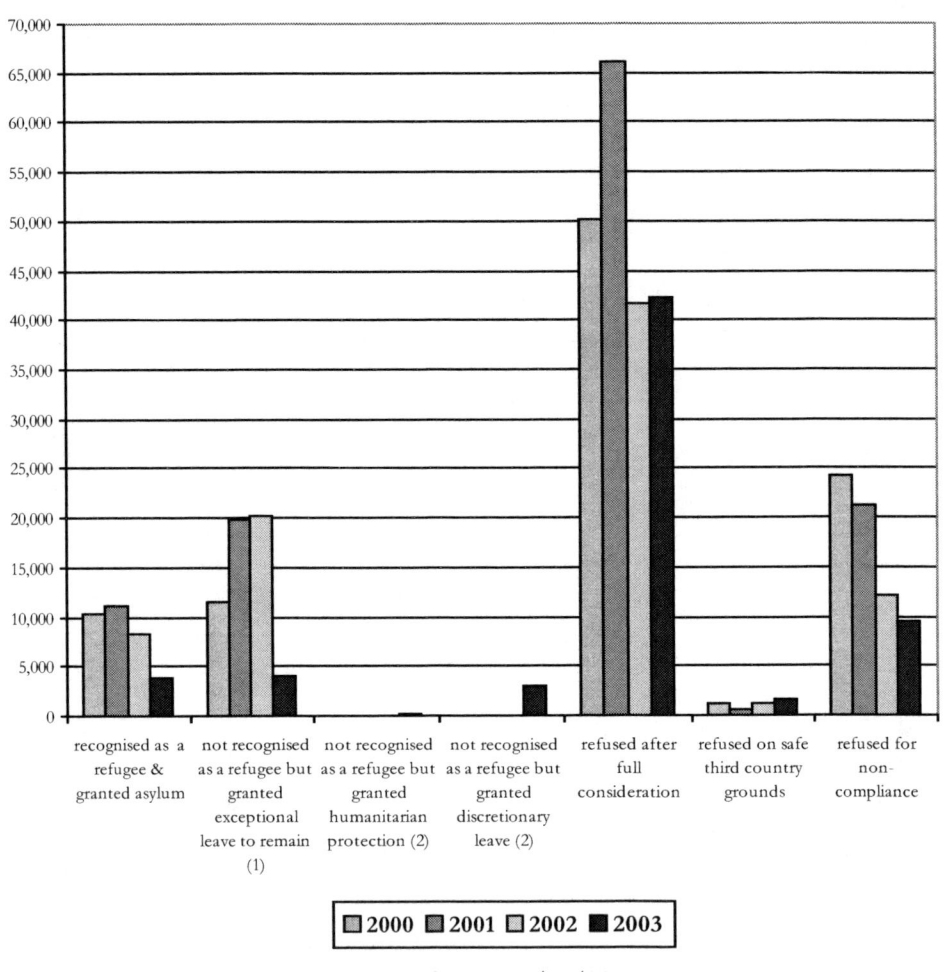

(1) granted up to 31/03/03
(2) granted from 01/04/03

Sources: Home Office, Control of Immigration Statistics UK 2001, Nov 2002.
Tina Heath, Richard Jeffries, Adam Lloyd, Asylum Statistics 2002, 28 Aug 2003.
Home Office, Asylum Statistics: 4th Quarter UK 2003 United Kingdom

1.5. POLICY IN UK BEFORE APRIL 2002

Before April 2002 applicants who applied for asylum in the UK were granted residency if their situation met with the 1951 UN Convention's definition of refugees and its 1967 Protocol (Home Office 2003c). In other words they had to have a 'well founded fear of persecution' on the grounds of 'race, religion, nationality, membership of a particular social group or political opinion.' There were exceptions to this rule. If the Home Office believed that the asylum seekers would be in danger if returned to their place of origin, even though the full conditions were not met, persons could be granted 'Exceptional Leave to Remain', usually for a period of four years. When the time expired they could apply for permanent residence.

Under the immigration rules it was impossible to apply for entry clearance to come to the UK as a refugee (Seddon et all 2002). Refugee Status was the best possible status that an asylum seeker could be granted in UK law. Anyone granted Refugee Status was immediately entitled to social assistance benefits equal with those available to British and EU citizens. Refugee Status also allowed for immediate family reunions with spouses and children and there was a sympathetic approach to parents wishing to be reunited with their adult children. It included access to nondiscriminatory education, equal economic rights and a right to permanent residence (Guild 2000:78). However in 1998, while 17% of asylum applications were given Refugee Status, another 12%, whose return to their home country was considered a real risk, were granted Exceptional Leave to Remain (ELR) but for only a limited period. These applicants' asylum decision was effectively put on hold and while they were entitled to social assistance benefits they were not considered eligible for family reunion (Guild 2000:78).

Asylum applications could only be made on arrival to an immigration officer either at the port of entry (sea or air), or 'in-country' that is after entering the UK. On application most asylum seekers were given 'Temporary Admission'. They were allowed to live in the UK with few restrictions provided the immigration authorities knew where they were living and they reported either weekly or monthly to a police station. The majority of applicants applied for asylum 'in-country' at a police station or at the Home Office. In 2001, 46,200 people applied for asylum after entry and only 25,500 asked for asylum at the port of entry (Goble 2002).

The UK Government had already taken tough measures to tackle illegal immigration. The UK border controls had been moved to France in an attempt to stop undocumented people travelling to the UK and lorries were being screened by specialist high tech equipment at French and Belgian ports in an attempt to prevent illegal trafficking of asylum seekers (Home Office 2003b).

On application the asylum seeker was put through a screening process in an effort to establish identity and nationality. The applicant had an interview with a member of the immigration team, finger prints were taken (with the intention of preventing multiple applications for asylum by the same person across the EU), and the applicant had to complete in English, a Statement of Evidence Form (SEF) which gave the applicant's reasons for seeking asylum. The initial decision was based on that interview, the SEF plus the Home Office's knowledge of the country of origin and whether the applicant could be returned to a safe third country where he/she could have the asylum claim processed. If the applicant missed the interview or failed to complete the form on time he could be refused asylum or even be taken into detention. Between April 2001 and September 2001 over a third of initial refusals were based on this non-compliance. The Home Office was taking an average of nine months to process the initial claims.

In 2000-01 the SEF procedure experienced difficulties. Due to errors at the Home Office many SEFs, although submitted on time, were not considered and many asylum seekers received refusals. Once the Home Office became aware there was a problem, the refusals were withdrawn and the claims were reconsidered but the Home Office did not agree to the actual decision recording the claim as determined, being withdrawn with the result that the asylum seekers involved could not access social security benefits and were not allowed to work even though they were entitled to benefit as pre-April 2001 transitionally protected 'on arrival' asylum seekers (Seddon et al 2002). The Home Office agreed to change its practice after it was challenged by the High Court and as long as the applicants concerned requested that the decision was withdrawn within three months of receiving the decision, they could continue to receive social benefits.

Any applicants, whose claims were thought to be 'straightforward' or thought unlikely to be successful were detained in the Oakington Immigration Centre in Cambridgeshire and in theory their applications were processed within 7-10 days (Goble 2002).

Any asylum seeker whose application was initially refused had the right to appeal to an independent adjudicator at the Immigration Appellate Authority, as long as he or she did so within ten days of the initial refusal. Asylum seekers who failed to appeal within the given time could be removed from the UK. If the application was still refused it was possible to re-appeal on a point of law to the Immigration Appeals Tribunal. Sometimes the Home Office 'certified' the asylum seeker's claim, refusing them the right to appeal. The only way that a certified asylum seeker could challenge the Home Office's decision was by a legal process called 'Judicial Review'(Goble 2002).

The asylum processing system was generally thought, before April 2002, to be inefficient. By early 2000, due to the rising number of asylum seekers, the move of the Immigration and Nationality Directorate's headquarters and the fact that the new computerized system for applications had failed, there was a backlog of over 100,000 asylum cases. Jack Straw (Home Secretary) admitted that the Home Office had lost contact with thousands of failed asylum seekers (Seddon et al 2002).

The following problems were identified regarding the decision process:
- Inadequately trained junior officials making the initial decisions.
- Assessments of countries of origin were sometimes inaccurate or misleading without adequate consideration given to the personal circumstances of the applicant.
- The system was unfair—many applicants did not speak good English, did not understand what was required of them, were exhausted and traumatized and did not have access to good legal advice or even translators.
- Some of the advocates were 'naive' and thereby prevented a fair decision.

The process for detaining asylum seekers could be arbitrary. From February 2002 only asylum seekers who had committed a crime could be detained in prison but there was an increase in the use of detention or removal centres (Seddon et al 2002). On 30 March 2002 there were 1,370 detainees of whom 170 were in prison (Goble 2002).

Before April 2000 the various local authorities were responsible for providing all asylum seekers who had children, or who were elderly, sick or disabled with temporary accommodation. However in April 2000 the Home Office set up a new department – NASS (National Asylum Support Service) to be responsible for looking after all asylum seekers' basic needs, including accommodation. In order to relieve London and the South East from some of the expense and responsibility, it became a policy to disperse asylum seekers to one of the many 'cluster regions' in the country. In theory asylum seekers were to be housed in suitable areas where there were already existing support services and multicultural communities (Goble 2002). In practice this rarely happened and the system of dispersing of asylum seekers to specific cluster areas meant that they rarely had adequate access to community support or appropriate legal advice. Often the cluster areas were inexperienced in hosting minority ethnic groups and were unfortunately more likely to be racist. In October 2001 one hundred and twelve incidents of racial harassment were reported to NASS by asylum seekers. Often the accommodation given to asylum seekers was sub-standard (Seddon et al 2002).

The financial support was an unjust system of vouchers whereby asylum seekers were given vouchers for food and clothes and only a little cash for bus fares, telephone calls etc. This method meant that if their shopping cost £3.50 they would be given no change from a £5.00 voucher. The voucher system was abolished in April 2002 but the level of benefits remained very low, only 70% of a British citizen's income support (Goble 2002). Levels of support in 2002 were as seen in Table 1.3. At that time asylum seekers were not allowed to work for the first six months, while their claims were being processed (Goble 2002).

Table 1.3 Financial support offered to asylum seekers in 2002

	Amount per week in 2002
Couple	£59.26
Lone parent 18 or over	£37.77
Single person aged 25 or over	£37.77
Single person aged 18-25	£29.89
Person aged 16-17	£32.50
Children under 16	£33.50 (to be increased to 100% of income support)

Source: National Asylum Support Service http://www.getrights.co.uk/nass_support.htm

1.6. POLICY IN UK - OCTOBER 2003

On 7 February 2002 the Government brought out a number of proposals to reform the asylum system in the UK. These proposals were contained in the Immigration and Asylum White Paper called *Secure Borders, Safe Haven – Integration with Diversity in Modern Britain* and then in April 2002 *The Nationality and Asylum Bill*. The main aim of the White Paper and the Bill was to create 'an end-to-end process for dealing with asylum seekers, in which applicants are tracked and supported from induction, through new accommodation and reporting centres, to integration or removal' (Home Office 2002a). The Government hoped that the White Paper would reform the asylum system so that the UK would have in place 'measures to produce a coherent strategy' (Home Office 2003d). In the words of the Home Office: 'The reform is based on the principle that we should have a humanitarian process which honours our obligations to those fleeing persecution while deterring those who have no right to asylum, from travelling here' (Home Office 2003d).

The White Paper also contained procedures:
- to streamline the appeals process to ensure applicants and their advocates have less opportunity to delay cases and obstruct removal of those who have failed in their claim' (Home Office 2002a);
- to penalize people smugglers and people traffickers;

- to tighten border controls. This included a scheme to give airlines an 'authority to carry' whereby carriers are allowed to check the details of passengers against Home Office databases to see if they pose an immigration threat;
- to crackdown on illegal workers;
- to take a tougher attitude towards any criminal offence committed by asylum seekers.

Naturally it was recognized that it would take a number of years for the above measures to be fully implemented (Home Office2002a).

While Human Rights groups and refugee organizations recognized that there was a need to revise the asylum system, the system proposed in 2002 was only cautiously welcomed. While the recognition of the contribution of refugees to society; the acknowledgment of the failure of the voucher system; the decision to detain refugees in refugee centres rather than prisons had been welcomed, other aspects of the scheme were viewed with a certain amount of concern. The proposal seemed to ignore the real purpose of the system which was surely to protect genuine asylum seekers and it did 'not adequately address the shortcomings in the asylum decision procedure' (Home Office 2002a). Instead it concentrated on deterring and removing asylum seekers. Despite commitments made in the White Paper the Bill did not guarantee access to legal advice for asylum seekers nor give any provision to challenge the detention of asylum seekers through automatic bail hearings, although provision for this had been included in the 1999 Immigration and Asylum Act.

Before April 2002 asylum seekers received their health care in the local community and their children attended mainstream schools. The only exception to this was children accommodated in the Oakington Immigration Centre. However in the 2002 Bill the Government proposed to make it the norm for asylum seekers' children to be educated in the trial accommodation centres, where they would also receive their health care, in order to relieve pressure on local services. To allay fears that the education would be sub-standard they promised that it would be equivalent to the education provided in main stream schools and open to OFSTED inspection, complying with the European Convention on Human Rights, the UN Convention on the Rights of the Child and the Race Relations Amendment Act. If the occasion arose that any child's educational needs could not satisfactorily be catered for in the accommodation centre then the child could attend a local school. While some working with refugees actually thought it would be less traumatic for children to be removed from a specialist education school than from mainstream schooling if their parents proved to be failed asylum seekers, others were not so sure that this proposal was a good idea (Home Office 2002a).

A short time after the White paper was published the Government put forward plans to follow the current practice of a number of European countries, by deporting failed asylum seekers back to their country of origin after the initial refusal and allowing only appeals from outside the UK. Asylum seeker support groups criticized that suggestion as unfair and potentially very dangerous (Home Office 2002a).

On 8 January 2003 the Government implemented Section 55 of the 2002 Act which legislated against all in-country asylum-applicants, depriving them of the right to food and shelter. On 1 April 2003 another new legislation came into force. The Home Office decided that Exceptional Leave would no longer be granted. Two forms of limited leave would replace it – Humanitarian Protection and Discretionary Leave, both to be used only sparingly. Humanitarian Protection could be granted to persons who had been able to show they had a need of protection in the UK but had failed to be granted asylum. Discretionary Leave would only be granted in exceptional circumstances to someone who had not been granted Asylum or Humanitarian Protection. Any asylum seeker who had been granted Refugee Status would be granted Indefinite Leave to Remain in the UK. The refugee would be guaranteed help to build a new life in the UK, would be entitled to the same social and economic rights as all other UK citizens, could be joined by family members and would be entitled to apply for a Convention Travel Document. They would naturally have to obey the laws of the UK. The Home Office set up an Integration Project that would be funded by the Home Office Challenge Fund to support refugees in this integration (Home Office 2003c).

Table 1.4 Financial support available to asylum seekers from 7 April 2003

	Per week
Couple	£60.03
Lone parent aged 18 or over	£38.26
Single person aged 25 or over	£38.26
Single person aged 16-27	£30.28
Person aged 16 or 17	£32.60
Person aged under 16	£38.50

Source: The Asylum Support (Amendment) (N.2) Regulations 2003 as quoted in Annelise Baldaccini, Providing Protection in the 21st Century, ARC 2004: 63

Asylum seekers, however, would be still eligible for only 70% of the Income Support available to other UK citizens. The financial support available to asylum seekers was based on the size of the family and the age of each person in that family. NASS also provided fully furnished accommodation paid for centrally and including payment of

Council Tax and utility bills. Asylum seekers could not choose where their accommodation would be and could be sent anywhere in the UK. Those asylum seekers who did not wish to move to other areas had to make their own arrangements regarding accommodation. They received only financial support as stated in Table 1.4 and usually stayed with relatives or friends.

1.7. POLICY IN UK AFTER OCTOBER 2003 AMNESTY ANNOUNCED

As we can see the UK Government found itself with a huge problem regarding asylum issues. Between 1993 and 2002 there were approximately 526,000 applications for asylum not counting dependants. Although the majority received refusals only 31,565 were deported. By October 2003 the backlog had reached such a colossal size that the Government was desperate to solve the problem. Mr. Justice Maurice Kay in the High Court criticized the way Mr. Blunkett handled the asylum system, saying: 'The lack of an efficient decision-making procedure is the main reason why courts are flooded with an almost unmanageable number of asylum support cases' (Ford 2003).

On 23 October 2003 the Immigration and National Directorate Department for Constitutional Affairs sent out a consultation letter on the new legislative proposals on asylum reform. Referring to the Nationality, Immigration and Asylum Act of 2002 the Home Office declared that the Act had:

> 'enabled us to make significant progress in reforming the UK's nationality, immigration and asylum systems. For asylum this has meant that the number of claimants has halved, removals are at record levels and the number of claims awaiting an initial decision is at the lowest for a decade. The Government is determined that there should be a balanced approach in asylum and immigration policy, so that we bear down on those who would seek to enter the UK illegally and who make unfounded claims, whilst ensuring effective help for refugees who need our protection. Our policy on asylum has to be seen in the wider context of managed migration, through which we are opening up routes for people to enter the UK legally. That is why we are committed to continued reform, as necessary, of the asylum system to ensure that those in need of protection are identified quickly and those who try to exploit the system are prevented from doing so' (Home Office 2003b).

In an attempt to seek an answer to the growing problem David Blunkett announced on 24 October 2003 an Asylum Amnesty for 15,000 asylum seeking families (approximately 50,000 asylum seekers), mainly from Kosovo, the former republic of Yugoslavia and Turkey, allowing them to stay in the UK. Most of the families affected lived in London and the South East. These families had suffered from the historic delays in the system and although they had exhausted the appeals system the Government had not managed to deport them (Ford 2003). Under the Amnesty families who had sought asylum before 2 October 2000 would be eligible for Indefinite Leave to Remain in the UK and in five years time would be eligible to apply for British Citizenship (The cut off date was not chosen at random but marked the introduction of new legislation preventing rejected asylum seekers from making multiple appeals against being removed from the country). Many of the asylum seekers' families covered by the Amnesty had already been in the UK for seven years and yet under human rights legislation were still entitled to challenge official removal directions in the High Court therefore they could remain in the UK until 2008 even without the Amnesty. The Home Office claimed it would save the taxpayer money as the country was supporting 12,000 families who were not allowed to work, costing the tax payers £180 million a year. However it stated that another 3,000 families already allowed to work would also be eligible for the Amnesty (Ford 2003).

The Home Office also announced new laws preventing failed asylum seekers from receiving benefits if they refused to leave Britain on the voluntary return programmes. To safeguard their children's well being, their children would be put into local authority care (Ford 2003). Two groups would be excluded from the Amnesty – those who had committed a criminal offence and any asylum seeker who had lodged multiple asylum applications to the UK or previously made an asylum claim in any other European country.

Any family who had been granted Leave to Remain in the UK automatically would be eligible for mainstream benefits. The spokeswoman for the Home Office declared that all those eligible for the Amnesty would receive a questionnaire and the majority would be assessed within six months. Some people did not welcome the news of the Amnesty. However Maeve Sherlock of the Refugee Council declared: 'It is the right and moral thing to do. It is utterly unfair on families - and especially children - to leave them in limbo, unable to rebuild their lives for years on end. Now the government must focus on getting decisions right much earlier, so people are not left in years of uncertainty.' Oliver Letwin, the Shadow Home Secretary, was gravely concerned that news of the Amnesty would attract even more asylum seekers to the UK and said that the Conservative Government would scrap the current system completely, replacing it with a system of quotas for all genuine refugees while processing applications offshore to deter all but genuine asylum claims. It is interesting to note that the Conservatives actually applied a similar Amnesty ten years previously allowing approximately 32,000 adults to stay in the UK (Travis 2003).

Other supporters of the Amnesty included Nick Pearce, director of the progressive think-tank, the IPPR, who stated: 'This is a difficult decision for any politician to make, but it's the right one. It's sensible and pragmatic, and fair to the families concerned, who can now plan a settled future in the UK with confidence.'

Keith Best speaking on behalf of the Independent Immigration Advisory Service added:

> 'We have long said that the only way to make a fresh start is to grant a kind of Amnesty for people already in the country. This is the inevitable humanitarian response to an increasing number of people who may not fit the strict definition of persecution under the Refugee Convention, but nevertheless are unable to return home because of conflict or other difficulties' (Press Assoc. 2003a).

On 23 November 2003 the Home Office released a document entitled *'Fairer, Faster and Firmer — An Introduction to the UK Asylum System'* where it endeavoured to explain the main features of the asylum system as follows:

- 'All claimants have a responsibility to co-operate with the authorities considering their claim. They must:
  - Tell the truth about their circumstances;
  - Obey the law. It is a criminal offence to submit a claim involving deception, the maximum penalty for which is two years' imprisonment
  - Keep in regular contact with the authorities considering their claim;
  - Leave the country if their claim is ultimately rejected.

- Support is provided to asylum seekers who are destitute whilst their claims for asylum are being considered. Accommodation is provided on a "no choice" basis in parts of the UK where there is less pressure on accommodation than in London and other parts of the South East. Asylum seekers are given subsistence payments in order that they may purchase food and other goods. This "dispersal" of asylum seekers and their support is provided by the National Asylum Support Service (NASS).

- Some claimants are removed to another EU member state in order to pursue their claim there, if that member state is responsible for the claim under the terms of the Dublin Convention. Some other claimants are removed in order to pursue their claim in a safe country outside the European Union.

- Those who are recognized as refugees will be granted immediate settlement in the UK and will be helped to build a new life' (Home Office 2003d).

The document went on to explain the procedures any asylum seeker would need to complete. Firstly the applicant would be screened to establish his/her identity and nationality. Interpreters would be present and finger prints taken to prevent multiple applications. All claimants would then go through an induction process where they would have their rights and responsibilities explained to them. Until November 2003 all asylum seekers used to receive a piece of paper (IND) with their claimed name, age and nationality plus their photograph. In November 2003 a single file number for each asylum seeker was introduced, to prevent duplication of costs, to provide more secure evidence of identity, and to make it more difficult to forge documents. All claimants would be given an Application Registration Card (ARC) containing their details—name, date of birth and nationality. They would use this document to access support services. During their induction the Voluntary Assisted Return Programme would be explained to them. Anyone who still had a pending claim, a refused claim or had been granted Exceptional Leave to Remain could apply for this scheme, which would assist the claimant in returning to their own country (Home Office 2003d). The Assisted Return Programme was put into place in the hope that some applicants would change their mind about wanting to remain in the UK and knowing they would be helped to return to their country of origin, do so. All claimants who required support would be eligible for support by NASS but would have no choice of location. They would be obliged to remain at the address allocated them by NASS until IND permitted them to move either to another location or to an accommodation centre. All claimants would eventually be called to attend an interview and their claim would be assessed, based on their SEF form plus an analysis of their home country's present situation. They would be notified of the result in writing. If the decision was a refusal the claimant would also receive notification on whether they would be allowed to appeal. Any person who was refused Refugee Status or Exceptional Leave to Remain was expected to leave the UK. If they did not do so of their own accord they would be detained until the authorities removed them (Home Office 2003d).

On 24 November 2003, the day after the Home Office released the White Paper, the Home Office declared yet another major reform of the asylum system – with a series of sweeping changes to the legal and appeals system for which the declared intention was to crack down on 'unscrupulous' immigration advisers who encouraged clients to lodge multiple appeals, at the tax payers' expense, despite having no legal basis on which to argue the case for leave to remain.

There had been a multi-layered appeals system providing an appeal to an adjudicator with a further appeal, with permission, to the Immigration Appeals Tribunal which was open to abuse by unfounded claims for asylum so the Home Office decided to:

-    Introduce a new tribunal called the Asylum and Immigration Tribunal (AIT), with the new judiciary titled Immigration Judges or Senior Immigration

Judges, and headed by a president for the appeals process. Asylum seekers would be limited to only one appeal and would find it more difficult to access the higher courts. The aim was to judge each application fairly and speedily and thus remove failed asylum seekers more quickly from the UK. The Home Office hoped that faster processing of applications and subsequent appeals would mean that some claims could be dealt with in as little as four weeks, though claimants might be detained for part if not all of that time (Home Office 2003c).

- Give the Immigration Services Commissioner authority to enter solicitors' offices and examine documents, as well as investigate unqualified advisers, designating certain professional bodies such as the Law Society to assist in investigations.

- Legislate against advertising or offering immigration advice without appropriate qualifications, which could carry a fine of up to £2,500 (Press Assoc. 2003b).

- Make it a criminal offence if the asylum seeker fails to provide a good explanation for being without travel documentation or fails to co-operate with re-documentation.

- Require all travel operators to make copies of travel documents on all routes where there are problems regarding undocumented passengers travelling to the UK.

- Return as quickly as possible any asylum seeker who had already claimed asylum in a safe third country to that country. A safe third country is any country where the Home Office is satisfied that an individual will be neither persecuted nor subjected to torture or inhuman or degrading treatment or punishment, in breach of the principles of the Refugee Convention or the ECHR (Home Office 2003b).

- Withdraw support from families who have exhausted all appeal routes and been offered a paid, voluntary route home but choose not to avail of this offer as well as families who already have had their support withdrawn because they failed to turn up for their flight once enforced removal arrangements had been made. If asylum support is withdrawn from a family in this way, other forms of support would no longer be available, including that provided under section 2 of the Local Government Act 2000. However it would still be available to the children under Section 20 of the Children Act 1989 (Home Office 2003b).

By introducing the measures above it was made more difficult for asylum claims to succeed especially if applicants had travelled through a safe third country or did not claim asylum on arrival. The Government introduced sanctions for those who had destroyed or thrown away their documents and made more considered assessments of claimants' credibility (Home Office 2003c). Following an investigation of 145 claims for asylum by the Home Office, 9% of applicants were discovered not to be from the countries that they claimed to be from. It is popular for asylum seekers not to have travel documents because the Home Office has difficulty removing them if their claims fail (Ahmed 2003).

Proposals were made by the Secretary of State for Constitutional Affairs regarding the considerable rise in the cost of asylum legal aid and expressing concerns about the variable quality of legal work. At present the response to the consultation on the following proposals is under consideration:

- introducing accreditation for solicitors working on asylum cases which will be independently assessed;
- introducing thresholds to restrict the advice available for asylum seekers, thereby limiting incurred costs.

The Home Secretary David Blunkett stated in the Home Office Press release on 24 November 2003:

> 'Our strategy is not anti-immigration. I have greatly expanded the opportunities for hard-working immigrants to come to the UK through legal routes. But the asylum system cannot work in the interests of genuine refugees if it is widely abused and open to exploitation by criminal gangs and the so-called legal advisers who help them. Some people will call these measures controversial. But to me, facing up to the real challenges posed by the changes in global migration is vital to building tolerance and understanding in our diverse communities' (IND 2003).

On 21 May 2004 the Court of Appeal made a judgment that the Home Office was in breach of Article 3 of the European Convention of Human Rights because it had denied three asylum seekers access to basic state support. This came about because Section 55 created conditions in which asylum seekers (with cases still not determined) had found themselves unable to find shelter and food free of charge. The Home Office announced that it would significantly revise its process for determining eligibility for NASS support under Section 55 (Refugee Council 2004b: 4). One of the three asylum seekers involved had applied for asylum the day after arriving in the UK but was refused NASS support and while sleeping rough outside a police station, went without food for two days (Inexile 2004b: 2). The Court also ruled that even the mere threat of no shelter in the future was sufficient to prove a breach of Article 3. It was also recognized that the charitable sector was stretched to full capacity and could not help to support anyone who had been refused NASS support (Refugee Council 2004b: 2).

From 12 April 2004 the financial support available to asylum seekers was still only 70% of the total entitlement for British citizens (Table 1.5).

Table 1.5 Financial support available to asylum seekers from 12 April 2004

	Per week
Couple	£61.11
Lone parent aged 18 or over	£38.96
Single person aged 25 or over	£38.96
Single person aged 16-24	£30.84
Person aged 16 or 17	£33.50
Person aged under 16	£42.27 (100% of Income support

Source: Refugee Council Info Centre: Support and entitlement
www.refugeecouncil.org.uk/infocentre/entit/sentit001.htm

On the 8 June 2004 the UK Government put forward a number of amendments to the Asylum & Immigration Bill. One major change meant that unsuccessful asylum applicants whom the Home Office were unable to return to their home country would be required to undertake community activities before they received any basic support or lodgings. Other amendments to the Asylum and Immigration Bill included:

-   Section 123 of the Immigration and Asylum Act 1999—Asylum applicants granted Refugee Status will lose their eligibility for backdated payments of the difference between income support and asylum support from the date of their asylum application. The government intends to use the money saved to set up a loan scheme instead to assist refugees integrating.

-   Asylum & Immigration Bill - Anyone subject to immigration control will be allowed to marry only if they have a church licence or have been allowed into the UK for the purpose of getting married.

-   Nationality, Immigration & Asylum Act 2002 – a new clause which removes the right of appeal to anyone who is refused entry after trying to enter the UK as a student, without having a place in their stated college.

- Section 96 of the Nationality, Immigration & Asylum Act 2002 — which prevents appeals against an immigration decision, if the appellant is trying to rely on an argument that could have been raised earlier in their case.

- The Home Secretary can order the removal of an individual's British citizenship if they have dual nationality and have acted in a way that seriously prejudices the interests of the UK (Refugee Council 2004b: 3).

1.8. A FEW FACTS ABOUT ASYLUM IN THE UK IN 2005

The UK Refugee Council in partnership with the Scottish and Welsh Refugee Councils and the Refugee Action and Student Action for Refugees (STAR), published in February 2005 a document entitled *Tell it like it is: The Truth About Asylum*, a pocket guide for anyone who wants to have the facts about asylum at their fingertips during the election campaign. It included the following facts (STAR 2005):

- Britain's asylum system is strictly controlled, multifaceted and therefore it is very difficult for anyone to gain asylum.

- Asylum applications have more than halved over the last two years (Home Office 2003).

- Home Office initial decision-making is not adequate. Nine out of ten are initially refused but 20% of those who are initially refused and go to appeal win the appeal.

- Less than 2% of the world's refugees live in the UK.

- In the league table of European countries for the number of asylum applications per head of population, the UK ranks ninth.

- Asylum seekers are not allowed to work and therefore they rely on state support set at 30% below the normal state benefits.

- Asylum seekers cannot choose where they live and the accommodation is nearly always property that no one else wants to rent. It is not owned or paid for by the local Council.

- According to organizations working with asylum seekers—the majority of asylum seekers are desperately poor, many experience hunger and are unable to afford to buy clothes or shoes (Oxfam, Refugee Council 2002).

- The UK police chiefs in a recent report came to the conclusion that the majority of asylum seekers are law-abiding citizens (ACPO 2000) and that asylum seekers are far more likely to be victims than perpetrators of crime. They are often victims of race-related crimes (ICAR 2004).

- Refugees can and do contribute a great deal to the UK as they are often highly educated (Kirk 2004). In fact there are over 1,000 medically qualified refugees recorded in the British Medical Association's database. However at present only sixty nine are employed by the health service. The BMA states that while it costs about £250,000 to train a new doctor, it costs only £10,000 to prepare a refugee doctor to practise in the UK (Refugee Council 2005).

- There are also many refugees who are qualified teachers. London based agencies have 754 refugee teachers registered with them (Employability Forum 2004). According to the OFSTED report of October 2003: 'Asylum-seeking children contribute very positively to schools across the country. This in turn enables more successful integration of families into local communities' (STAR 2005).

- Last but not least in 2001 the Home Office considered the net fiscal contribution to the UK economy made by migrants, including asylum seekers and refugees to the UK and declared that they contributed £2.5 billion (STAR 2005).

CHAPTER TWO
BACKGROUND OF RESPONDENTS:
KOSOVO

In Chapter Two we will consider the background of the respondents who took part in our questionnaire. First, we will look briefly at the early history of Kosovo (700-1988). We will go on to look at the distribution of the population of Kosovo in 1991 and then at some length the history of Kosovo between 1989-99 (23 March). We will then consider the History of Kosovo from 24 March 1999 until December 1999; Kosovan refugees in Europe 1995-99, taking into account the Asylum Applications from Serbia, Kosovo and Montenegro between 1996-98 in the UK including the Refugee Movements in early May 1999; spontaneous asylum seekers from former Yugoslavia in the UK, March-June 1999; humanitarian evacuations of Kosovans to Germany, France, Italy and the UK from Macedonia showing cumulative monthly totals from the period 5 April-1 July 1999. We will look at Kosovan Refugees in Europe in 2000 and then the situation of Kosovo in 2000-02 and in 2003-05 and finally the future of Kosovo

2.1. EARLY HISTORY OF KOSOVO (700-1988)

The Kosovo region has been an area of population movements and displacements for centuries. The fact is that Slavic and Albanian peoples have co-existed in Kosovo since the Eighth century (BBC 2004c). Under the Nemanjic dynasty in the twelfth century Kosovo was at the centre of the Serbian empire and many Serbian Orthodox churches and monasteries were built. The Serbians came to regard Kosovo as the birthplace of their state. However the Turks invaded in the fourteenth Century and in the epic Battle of Kosovo on the 28 June 1389 Kosovo became part of the Ottoman Empire. It remained part of that empire for 500 years and during that time many Christian Serbs left Kosovo. As the religious and ethnic balance shifted from being predominantly Serbian and Orthodox to Albanian and Muslim, Kosovo came to represent a Serbian golden age. During the Balkan wars of 1912 Serbia gained control of Kosovo and in 1918 Kosovo became part of Serbia. In 1941 much of Kosovo became part of an Italian–controlled greater Albania (BBC 2004d). During that time large numbers of Serbs were forced out of Kosovo.

The Second World War brought further changes. There is some dispute over numbers but the Serbs claim that approximately 100,000 ethnic Albanians moved into Serbia during and immediately after the Second World War and as many as 220,000 Serbs and Montenegrins abandoned their homes in Kosovo in the 20 years between 1968 and 1988. Others claim that there is no evidence of such massive movements in any of the documents of the occupying powers.

According to van Selm (2000a) in the 1960s many Kosovans entered Germany and Switzerland as 'guest workers' and later as rejected asylum seekers (those unable to return to Yugoslavia because the Belgrade Government was unwilling to cooperate, hinting that many were 'confirmed criminals'). In 1974 Kosovo became an autonomous State within the state of Serbia.

2.2. KOSOVO 1989 - 23 MARCH 1999

In 1989 Kosovo had an area of 10.9 km^2 with about 2 million inhabitants who were mainly Albanians (82%) with Serbians 10% and other ethnic groups 8%. Almost half of the population lived in cities including the capital Prishtina. Before 1999 no town inside the province of Kosovo ever had a population much over 100,000 which means that people were spread out quite evenly across the whole province

In 1989 the Serbian president S. Miloszewicz made the decision to strip Kosovo of its autonomy. This resulted in the Kosovan Albanians holding a referendum in 1991 asking for independence from Serbia and in 1992 they held free elections in which they elected their own parliament and a president - I. Rugova. Serbia refused to accept their independence and their decisions regarding their parliament and president were revoked by Serbia which began to oppress systematically the Albanian population in Kosovo while encouraging mainly reluctant Serbians to move into the province of Kosovo. During that time the Albanians' basic rights were often violated. Serbia closed all schools using the Albanian language, removed all Albanians from state-owned enterprises, and suspended Kosovo's legal parliament and government. At first the Albanians responded to the repression with passive resistance, using only peaceful means to achieve limited autonomy. They held Albanian language classes outside of state schools and provided their own health care system as most of the hospitals became Serbian controlled and Albanian doctors were dismissed (Albania news).

Over the next few years it became clear that peaceful resistance was ineffective and some of the Kosovan Albanians chose to fight for their freedom forming, in 1996, the Kosovan Liberation Army (KLA), a guerilla movement. The KLA had a number of temporary successes and the Serbian government reacted with a crackdown on the KLA. From January 1998 the Serbian security forces began a scorched earth policy in Kosovo. They burnt villages, removing them completely from the landscape and creating hundreds of refugees and internally displaced persons. The Serbians 'committed horrific atrocities against unarmed civilians, including women and children' (Albanian News 2003) and many Albanian Kosovans fled from the Federal Republic of Yugoslavia to other European states.

On 29 April 1998 an International Delegation came together in Rome to try to solve the Balkan crisis. When this delegation failed to come up with a solution acceptable to Serbia, the USA pressed for sanctions against Serbia and the UN put sanctions on Serbia. At the end of May 1998 thousands of Kosovans were forced to flee Kosovo because of a big offensive by Serbian forces. NATO started to prepare for intervention through International law. On 5 October the General Secretary of the UN presented to the Security Council a report about the situation in Kosovo. The Serbs reacted to this report by further ethnic cleansing of Albanians in Kosovo so the UN threatened military action.

In response to that threat, on 13 October 1998 Miloszewicz promised that the Kosovans could hold an election in the Autumn of 1999 under UN control. Miloszewicz accepted that the UN would send a party of international observers - Organization for Security and Co-operation in Europe (OSCE) to Kosovo. The observers were granted the status of diplomats with military air support. The Serbs agreed to withdraw their army from Kosovo and to allow 250,000 refugees to return to Kosovo and the Serbian forces began to leave on 25 October 1998.

Figure 2.1 UNHCR statistics show movements within and from Kosovo

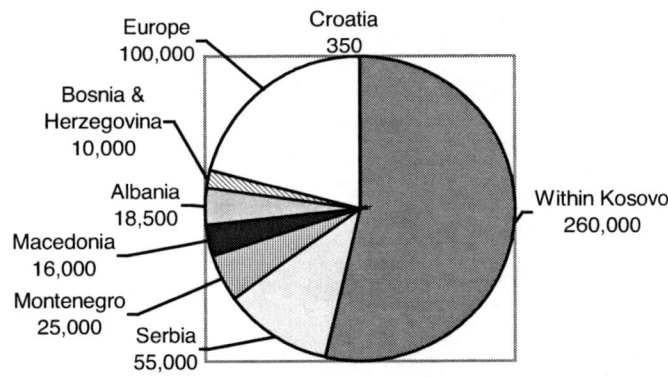

Source: UNHCR, 'Kosovo Crisis Update' February 1999 as cited in van Selm (2000b).

However in spite of the fact that the Serbian forces were withdrawing, the Serbs continued to burn Albanian property and kill civilians and by February 1999 several hundred thousand Kosovan Albanians had been displaced, many within Kosovo, while many others had fled to neighbouring or more distant countries (See Figure 2.1). The UN felt they had no choice but to threaten to begin military action (van Selm 2000a).

Under this threat in February 1999 both sides agreed to talk and a meeting was held in Rambouillet, Paris. The Albanians agreed to a ceasefire, having been assured of Kosovo's autonomy and the UN's inspection of the peace process, with NATO promising to send 28,000 soldiers. However both sides continued sporadic attacks, breaking the ceasefire, and Serbia continued its policy of ethnic cleansing. After two days of intensive attacks by the Serb security forces in northwest Kosovo the UN refugee agency UNHCR reported that approximately 20,000 ethnic Albanians had fled their homes. That followed a displacement of almost 40,000 people in the previous week and was one of the main reasons why NATO began air raids on 24 March 1999 on Belgrade and the Serb troops in Kosovo (van Selm 2000a).

2.3. KOSOVO 24 MARCH 1999-DECEMBER 1999

In early May 1999 the UNHCR was trying to persuade 30,000 refugees to move further south into camps in central and southern Albania (to relieve pressure on the border camps of Macedonia and Albania) See Map: 2.2 of Refugee Movements. The refugees were reluctant to move away from the border as they felt it lessened their chances of being reunited with family left behind in Kosovo (BBC NEWS 1999).

Map 2.1. Refugee movements in May 1999

Total refugees departed from Kosovo: 745,600
Total evacuated from the Balkans: 36,222
Estimated 260,000 refugees displaced within Kosovo.

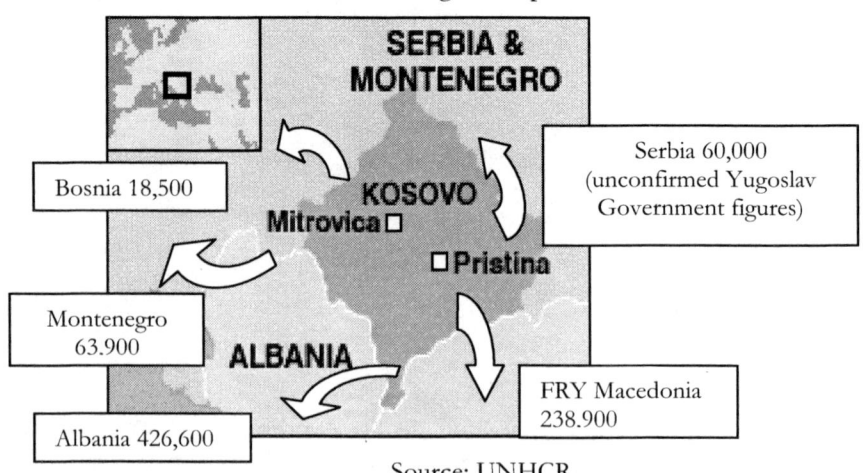

Source: UNHCR

According to a report by Human Rights Watch (HRW 2001) Serbian troops responded by sweeping through Kosovo's main towns chasing out ethnic Albanians, stripping them of their documents (their identity) and putting them on trains leaving Kosovo. The traumatized and exhausted refugees, on reaching safety, frequently spoke of the massacres they had witnessed, rape, burnt homes and abducted young men. According to the UNHCR in the Survey of November 1999 almost 40% of all homes in Kosovo were badly damaged or completely destroyed and of the 649 schools in the province over 390 were totally destroyed and approximately 130 were heavily damaged (HRW 2001). UNHCR's Kris Janowski told Out There News: 'all the testimonies of the refugees say the same thing: this is a one-way ticket and the Serbs do not expect the Albanians to come back' (Janowski 2004). While the Kosovan Albanians in the towns were chased out by the Serbs those in villages slipped away into the hills to hide. There were probably about 800,000 Kosovan Albanians trapped in a war zone, hungry and frightened, hiding in the hills inside Kosovo.

According to the UNHCR, after three weeks of bombing, 527,787 refugees had fled their homes and moved into adjoining countries. In total those who were displaced before and during the bombing amounted to approx 80% of the entire population, of whom 90% were Kosovan Albanians (HRW 2001). Areas known to have strong historical ties to the KLA suffered the most. Human Rights Watch reported that many Kosovan Albanians were being stripped of their identity documents that were then destroyed and they were even forced to discard their car and tractor licence plates before they were permitted to flee into Albania (HRW 2001). There were mass killings of civilians including women and children, forced expulsions, arbitrary detentions, torture and systematic destruction of property.

There appeared to be three main reasons for the killings:
  i.   to speed up the ethnic cleansing
  ii.   to target certain individuals who appeared to actively support the KLA. This included some human rights activists as well as political leaders and prosperous business men
  iii.   for revenge when the Serbian troops suffered losses by the KLA.

By July 2001 the International Criminal Tribunal for the former Yugoslavia reported that it had exhumed 4,300 bodies in Kosovo all believed to be unlawful killings by either Serbian or Yugoslavian forces. However this is unlikely to be the total number killed as Human Rights Watch found evidence of attempts to hide or dispose of bodies in some areas.

Rape had also been used to terrorize the civilians. Many ethnic Albanians had been raped by Serb or Yugoslav forces in attempts to terrify people into leaving their homes or in order to extort money from them. Human Rights Watch found credible accounts of 96 cases of sexual assault during the NATO bombing alone. These rapes happened either in women's homes, where women were often raped either in front of family members or elsewhere in their home, during flight from their homes or when they were stopped and robbed by Serbian forces under threat that their daughters would be taken away and raped in detention centres such as barns or abandoned homes (HRW 2001).

The ethnic Albanians were terrorized in many other ways. Human Rights Watch documented cases right across Kosovo of how Serbian and Yugoslav troops deliberately contaminated drinking water by dumping chemicals or dead animals into the villages' wells. In four villages murder victims were actually thrown into the wells. Human Rights Watch documented how many people were threatened with death if they did not hand over their money and many were robbed of their jewellery and cars even while they fled the country (HRW 2001).

The exodus of enormous numbers of refugees increased significantly after 24 March 1999 and it is unclear whether anyone realized that the bombing would have that effect. Certainly those charged with the protection of displaced people seemed to be totally unprepared for such a large exodus. It is estimated that the conflict and crisis in Kosovo and Yugoslavia (Serbia and Montenegro) resulted in the displacement of almost the entire Kosovan Albanian population (estimated at 1.8 million people). Although at least half remained within Kosovo the rest crossed Kosovo's borders (Guild 2000:73). March, when the seas are relatively calm, has always been

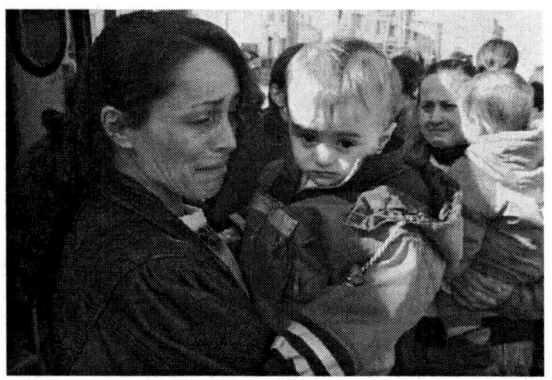

© AP/EMPICS 22.03.1999

the favoured time for asylum seekers to cross the Adriatic from Albania to Italy and March 1999, coinciding with the bombing in Kosovo, was an ideal time for Kosovans to leave their initial place of refuge in Albania and flee to Italy. Approximately 200 people left Albania by small boats (organized by smugglers) every night. Almost half the group (40%) were usually minors. The journey was hazardous. While many in danger of capsizing needed rescuing by Italian ships, other asylum seekers arrived in Italy with serious injuries or illnesses. The asylum seekers were totally dependent on the smugglers for their safe arrival in Italy and an unknown number never arrived as the smugglers were known to throw asylum seekers overboard if they saw an approaching vessel belonging to the Italian coastguard (Hein 2000: 150).

Other people in Yugoslavia were displaced as a direct result of the conflict and from mid-June 1999 onwards, some 170,000 Serbs from Kosovo were also displaced as they fled the revenge of returning ethnic Albanians.

During the first two weeks of the bombing by NATO forces there was considerable confusion regarding who was responsible for the protection of displaced people. Should it be the UNHCR? Eventually NATO took control. There was considerable speculation as to whether or not NATO's involvement in Albania was a way of amassing ground troops in the area in preparation for a land offensive. One major concern was the possibility that the Kosovan Albanians still in Kosovo were being used as 'human shields'. After the conflict Human Rights Watch found evidence that the Yugoslav Government had indeed used civilians as human shields to protect their troops from NATO attacks or from the KLA. The Yugoslav government had also placed a large number of antipersonnel mines or antitank mines along the borders with Albania and Macedonia probably because they feared a ground invasion by NATO forces (HRW 2001).

2.4. KOSOVAN REFUGEES IN EUROPE 1995-2000

Many Albanian Kosovans fled from the Federal Republic of Yugoslavia before 1995 but after that date the number increased with about 114,430 asylum applications being lodged between 1995 and 1997 in EU member states from citizens of FRY (van Selm 2000a). Citizens of FRY (Table 2.1) made 9,660 asylum applications in the UK between the beginning of 1996 and December 1998 (Guild 2000). However the processing of claims was slow and often occurred in a later year.

Table 2.1 Asylum applications from Serbia, Kosovo, Montenegro 1996-98 in the UK

Year	Applications	Decisions	Refugee Status	ELR	Refused
1996	400	555	70	40	445
1997	1865	1945	1355	210	380
1998	7395	1570	935	75	565

Source: Watson , M., McGregor, R., (1999) Asylum Statistics in the United Kingdom 1998 (London: The Stationery Office), issue 10/99, 27 May 1999

The UK Statistics Office has never included a separate category for Kosovans but includes Kosovans in FRY (nationals of Serbia, Kosovo and Montenegro). However the Statistics Office stated that the majority of asylum seekers from FRY at that time were thought to be Kosovan citizens. The Home Office processed less than half

(4,070), of whom, 2,360 were granted Refugee Status, 325 were given ELR and 1,390 received a refusal (Guild 2000).

As the UNHCR had a preference for keeping the refugees close to home, the neighbouring countries were put under increasing pressure and asked to offer support well above their means. On 2 April 1999 the president of the EU called on all States to accept a certain quota of Kosovan refugees and two days later the UNHCR also repeated this call (Guild 2000: 73). Some evacuations were arranged within Europe with the first airlifts on 6 April to Turkey and Norway. For many these evacuations appeared to be deportations, with frightened, confused refugees separated from their families and unaware of their destinations. While many EU countries were willing to offer financial aid to Kosovo's neighbouring countries, to aid refugees, there was considerable reluctance to actually accept refugees onto their territories and eventually the EU countries agreed to accept just 100,000 refugees (10% of the whole) between them. The British Home Secretary, Jack Straw was reluctant to agree to take a greater share of the Kosovan refugees claiming: 'We've already taken almost 10,000 refugees from Kosovo, the second highest number of any of our EU partners.' He seems to have reached this figure by counting all the FRY asylum applicants who had arrived in the UK from 1997 and over the first two months of 1999, a total of 10,520 people (Home Office 1999). There was some confusion as to whether the Kosovans were admitted to the UK as a direct result of the bombing or before the bombing actually commenced. However Jack Straw did promise to take further refugees under the EU quota scheme for resettlement.

For many months before the bombing commenced many Kosovans had been attempting to reach the EU through the Czech Republic, Hungary and Poland but had been unable to do so because they had no way of obtaining legal documentation. This highlighted the fact that many countries distinguished between the refugees who came within their acceptable quota and had somehow been legitimized by the selection process (all too often open to corruption), and spontaneous arrivals (those arriving illegally), even though they came from the same place of conflict. The UK was among those countries that appeared to favour the spontaneous arrivals above those who were potential arrivals under the quota system (Van Selm 2000a: 18-19).

Back in 1992 the UK had stated that all nationals of the former Yugoslavia could come to the UK only if they held visas. This meant that all applications for visas had to be made in Belgrade at the UK consulate. Naturally during the Kosovan crisis few people were either willing or able to approach Belgrade for a visa and could not legally leave their region. The problem was compounded by Kosovans whose documents had been either destroyed or confiscated by Serb forces. Consequently they had to look for alternative ways to flee and frequently arrived in the UK illegally, that is without visas or with false documents (Guild 2000: 70). Once at the UK border the person was free to apply for asylum but always ran the risk of being returned to a third country. During that time the UK admitted 4,346 Kosovan refugees, giving them a specific immigration status, under its resettlement plan. During the same period (Table 2.2) 3,230 asylum seekers arrived spontaneously from the former Yugolslavia (Guild 2000:68).

Table 2.2 Spontaneous asylum seekers from former Yugoslavia in the UK, March-June 1999

Month	Number of asylum requests	Decisions taken		
		Refugee Status	ELR	Refused any
March	755	10	50	
April	690	805	20	
May	755	2075	10	
June	1030	n/a	-	n/a

Source: Home Office Immigration Research and Statistics Service, RSD 31/08//99'. annex to letter from the service to Kingsley Napley, 7 September 1999 (as cited in Guild 2000: 68)

Note: ELR = Exceptional Leave to Remain, a national status less than that of refugee recognized under the Geneva Convention

As we can see in Table 2.2 the UK government at that time was inclined to give until May 1999, Refugee Status to spontaneous asylum seekers from Kosovo (Guild 2000:78). Until March 1999 this had been granted on an individual and quite random basis. This was due to the fact that the UK's Immigration and Nationality Directorate (IND) was experiencing serious problems. Having introduced a new computerized system they were struggling to maintain any system of processing applications and in desperation had introduced a special unit specifically to deal with Kosovan applications. It was felt that Kosovans could be processed quickly as a group and thereby clear some of the horrendous backlog. Albanian Kosovans had been recognized and accepted as refugees since 1996 on account of their ethnicity and the fact that they had a history of persecution, and few were ever put into detention.

So from the start of NATO's bombing the UK's Immigration and Nationality Directorate began processing all Kosovans without a great deal of consideration of the individual cases and delivering a fairer, faster and firmer system, as desired by the Government (Guild 2000: 69). However the Kosovans who were already in the UK due to the disaster in their province had their asylum applications dealt with far more quickly and generously than those who arrived as part of the UK quota. From June 1999 the Kosovans were not granted Refugee Status but rather granted automatically 12 months Exceptional Leave to Remain (ELR). On 13 December 1999 the Home

Secretary declared that Kosovans would no longer automatically be granted ELR as the KFOR (Home Office 1999b) had secured the Province of Kosovo and the Kosovan Albanians were no longer in danger of persecution (Guild 2000:79).

However, in December 1999 Amnesty International repeated its concerns at 'the on-going murder, abductions, violent attacks, intimidation and house burning [that] are being perpetrated on a daily basis at a rate which is almost as high as it was in June [1999] when the international UN civilian and security presence (KFOR) were initially deployed' (UNHCR 1999).

Figure 2.2 Humanitarian evacuations of Kosovans to Germany, France, Italy and UK from Macedonia showing cumulative monthly totals from period 5 April-1 July 1999

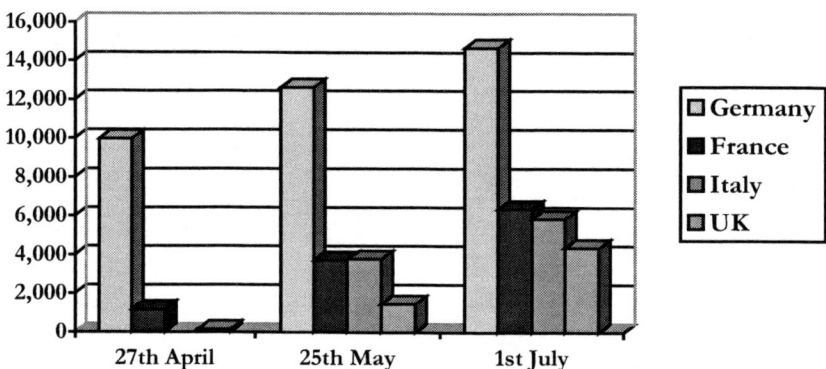

Source: UNHCR (1999) Kosovo Crisis Updates as cited in Kosovo's Refugees in the European Union ed J. Van Selm (2000b) Pinter, London, New York 2000, Appendix 2, 226

The Kosovan asylum seekers who had been temporarily in camps in Macedonia and Albania were far less likely to be offered the possibility of resettlement (Guild 2000: 69). On 18 April the UK was put under even greater pressure by the UNHCR to make a commitment to accepting more Kosovan refugees and a figure of 5,000 was suggested. Still the UK Government resisted (Guild 1999). The first group of only 161 refugees arrived on the 26 April. Jack Straw promised to accept 'significantly greater numbers' but apparently did nothing to fulfill that pledge. The UK was pressurized to fulfill its pledge of resettling more refugees from Kosovo and eventually in early May 1999 promised to accept 1,000 Kosovan refugees each week with the first group of 300 arriving in Scotland on 9 May. However by the end of the Resettlement

Programme, just four weeks later, the UK had only just managed to keep its promise and resettled 4,346 people (Guild 2000: 74).

During the period 5 April to 1 July a total of 52,853 people were evacuated under the Humanitarian Evacuation Programme (HEP) from Macedonia to EU states. Figure 2.2 shows the top three receiving countries in the EU – Germany accepting a total of 14,689 Kosovan asylum seekers, France accepting 6,339, Italy 5,829 as compared to the UK which accepted only 4,346 under the Resettlement Programme. Germany had begun immediately to receive large numbers of recipients of the Programme, receiving 9,974 within the first three weeks, while France received just 1,185 during that period and the UK only 330. Italy was even slower to start, not receiving anyone during the first month.

On the whole the British public and press looked favourably on the Kosovan refugees and welcomed them. This was due partly to the high involvement of the British army in the efforts at peace keeping in the province of Kosovo and the feeling that perhaps the bombing had actually aggravated the situation, causing many to flee unnecessarily. Through the media the situation was brought constantly to the attention of the British public who could relate easily to the Kosovans for they looked and dressed like them, had fled from Kosovo in cars and could articulate their sufferings in ways the public could relate to (Gibney 1999:29-30). For perhaps the first time the ordinary people had gained an insight into what it meant to be a refugee. The plight of the Kosovans had been given a very high profile and in the UK people genuinely deplored the situation the Kosovans found themselves in and wanted to help. However in August 1999, shortly after the end of the bombing campaign, Dover was among a number of towns on the south coast complaining of problems in coping with a large influx of Kosovan asylum seekers. There was serious concern that the UK's ethnic relations were being put under considerable stress.

When the war ended in Kosovo on 10 June 1999 the conflict had created over one million refugees and internally displaced persons. It left over 300,00 people without a home and an estimated 10,000 people had been killed including many civilians, women and children, 100 of whom had been discovered in mass graves, having been executed (Albania News).

In May 2000 the European Commission submitted a proposal[2] that would treat temporary protection as a prelude to asylum, an interim measure rather than a protective measure in its own right. It was not designed to deal with individual cases

---

[2] Comision of the European Communities, Proposal for a Council Directive for minimum standards in giving Temporary Protection in the event of a Mass influx of Displaced Persons and on measures Promoting a balance of Efforts between Member States in Receiving such Persons and Bearing the Consequences thereof, COM(2000) 303 final[2000/0127(CNS), Brussels 24 May 2000.

of humanitarian need but with multi cases such as those arising from a conflict situation. For a great many Kosovans the temporary protection in the EU was indeed only temporary. It is now clear that many other Kosovans received both initial short-term refuge in a neighbouring state and then a time of temporary protection in an EU state under the (HEP) Humanitarian Evacuation Programme (van Selm 2003:84).

During the course of 2001 a number of decisions were made by the EU with regard to Kosovans who had arrived on their territories under the temporary protection programmes of 1999.

In Germany Kosovan Albanians with 'tolerated Status' were given two six month extensions to their permission to stay in Germany. Those Kosovans who had not received a negative decision from the Home Office and who could prove they were employed, could support themselves financially and had suitable accommodation, were given a two year residence permit.

In France in 1999, the government established an assisted return programme, for refugees from Kosovo. By February 2001, 3087 persons had returned to their country. Under that same scheme 813 people were allowed to make an exploratory visit in order to look at the possibility of resettlement in Kosovo. However only six chose to stay in Kosovo while 807 returned to France.

In Italy from 12 May 1999, the Kosovan Albanians along with Serbs and Roma were granted a residence permit until 31 December 1999, later extended for six months until 30 June 2000. The Kosovan Albanians were also allowed to apply individually for asylum.

In the UK the Kosovans admitted under the HEP, at the request of the UNHCR, were granted the status of temporary refuge, permitting the individual to reside for one year in the UK, to work, have access to the NHS and to social services support. However the person was not eligible to be considered for Refugee Status under the Geneva Convention. The individual was also warned that to become involved in any criminal or terrorist activity would result in deportation. It was disputable as to whether this threat was in fact legal or would breach article 3 of the European Convention on Human Rights. The Kosovans who arrived in the UK under this Programme were placed outside of London, mainly in the Manchester, Leeds and Bradford areas (Guild 2000:82).

2.5. KOSOVO IN 2000-02

Post conflict attacks were made by the KLA on Serbs, Roma and many other non-ethnic Albanians as well as those ethnic Albanians who did not support the KLA or who were thought to have collaborated with the Serbian authorities. Even in early 2001 the violence was continuing, with NATO forces apparently unable to keep the peace between the KLA and Serbs with both sides suffering casualties (Shah 2001). Many of their homes were destroyed or looted and churches and monasteries were also destroyed. During that time many Serbs living in Kosovo fled their homes and by late 2001 over 210,000 Serbs had fled Kosovo. According to the Red Cross at least 3,525 people including many ethnic Serbs were still missing at the end of 2001. It appeared that the KLA acted not just out of revenge but had a political goal. They thought that they could justify an independent state more easily if they removed all non-ethnic Albanians from Kosovo. Even as late as 28 October 2000 attacks were continued against the Democratic League of Kosovo (HRW 2001).

In the aftermath of the war, Kosovo not only had to cope with continued ethnic tension but in addition faced serious environmental problems. Bekim Greicevci wrote in Pristina, Kosovo, in an article entitled '*Kosovo, My Home*' about some of the environmental problems that Kosovo faced at that time. Bekim wrote: 'Ethnic tensions aside, industrial and household waste and an at-best primitive environmental protection system make Kosovo less than a safe place to live.'

The Province of Kosovo is situated in a geographical basin at an altitude of about 500 metres and is surrounded by mountains. The whole area is divided in two by a north-south ridge and covers an area of approximately 5,000 square miles. About 40% is forest while 50% is agricultural land with 70% of this land arable and 30% pasture. On the plains the soil is fertile but unfortunately the muncipalities of Pristina, Mitrovica, Obiliq, Fushe Kosova, and Drenas have been contaminated by coal pits and the disposal of pit-waste - soot, slag, depleted soil and heavy metals plus the discharge of wastewater. Due to the lack of recent industrial activity the soil in those areas has not seriously degraded any further but as none of the industrial dumpsites have been protected or treated to prevent leakages, they continue to pollute the groundwater and therefore the surrounding agricultural land is dangerously contaminated.

Another problem recognized in 1999 was the fact that sewage pours untreated into the river systems along with household waste. Consequently downstream from cities and towns the rivers are heavily polluted (Greicevci 2003).

Before the armed conflict the environment in Kosovo was already under considerable strain, suffering from a lack of attention. Air pollution was among its problems. In Obiliq air pollution was fourteen times higher than average. However many of the factories closed during the conflict never to reopen and that lessened the effects of industrial waste. In 2001 air pollution was still a problem due to the inadequate disposal of both industrial and household waste. In 2001 Besim Dobruna senior adviser at the Environment and Spatial Planning Ministry declared: 'The greatest air pollution in Kosovo is from traffic. With proper management we could get rid of 30 percent of pollution.'

The conflict itself brought more serious environmental problems. The large number of military vehicles using diesel and leaded fuel also caused a rise in the levels of air pollution. A database of mine fields was drawn up in August 1999 which showed that although there were few mines in populated areas, unexploded mines were widespread in other areas. In the later months of 2000, health and environmental officials became aware of an even greater danger in the area – depleted uranium (DU) used in the bombs dropped by NATO. The United Nations Environment Program (UNEP) released a study of depleted uranium stating that DU had the potential to increase uranium concentrations in groundwater by a hundred times the natural level and that DU was suspected of being responsible for the increase in civilian deaths through cancer and leukaemia.

The local Government in Kosovo and the international community have been working to try and clean up the environment in Kosovo but this is a slow process (Greicevci 2003).

2.6. KOSOVO IN 2003-05

Since the Nato bombing campaign Kosovo had in practice been run by the UN although it still remained in theory a Province of Serbia. Many of the ethnic Albanians returned home in the intervening years only to find, that although Kosovo by 2003 was relatively peaceful, it was still in every way a rundown region with unemployment at 57%, daily power cuts, an unreliable telephone system and political parties frequently accused of corruption and involvement in crime. Some thought that former refugees would actually prove to be assets to Kosovo while others like Peggy Hicks at the UN office feared for those who had been or were being forcibly returned from the countries where they had sought refuge. She was only too aware of the fact that there was only one licensed Psychiatrist in Kosovo and yet many of the returnees were traumatised and had serious mental health problems. Moss (2003) said that it was important to remember that the UK and other Governments, in their efforts to bring peace to the region, invested vast sums of money and manpower and there was always a danger of putting the whole situation at risk by returning people too quickly and destabilising the region.

In April 2003 Amnesty International reported that 'Serbs and other ethnic minorities in Kosovo remained at serious risk of death or injury despite almost four years of peace and the presence of UN and NATO peacekeepers'. The report went onto say: 'Beatings, stabbings, abductions, drive-by shootings and the use of hand grenades to intimidate and kill members of these minorities are common in the province. As the vast majority of these crimes remain unsolved, perpetrators are free to commit further attacks contributing to a climate of fear and the denial of basic human rights' (Amnesty International 2003). The report outlines the fact that ethnic minorities make up just 8% of the population that is predominantly Albanian. The largest minority ethnic groups are the Serbs and Roma.

The UK director of Amnesty International, Kate Allen said that the international community's failures in Kosovo should serve as a lesson for other post-conflict situations such as that pertaining in Iraq:

> 'It is clear that the international authorities in Kosovo were unprepared for the massive abuses of human rights against minorities that accompanied the rapid return of the Albanian community. As the international community discusses the future of Iraq it is essential that we learn the lessons of the past and ensure that measures are put in place to protect the human rights of vulnerable groups. It must be ensured from the outset that there is no impunity for the perpetrators of human rights abuses.'

In the report of April 2003 Amnesty International expressed concern that there was still ongoing persecution of ethnic minorities in Kosovo which made it unsafe for minority refugees and internally displaced people to return to their homes. All minority ethnic groups were affected and depended largely on KFOR's presence in the Province for their protection. Amnesty International urged the international community not to forcibly return anyone from a minority community to Kosovo, while calling for the UN civilian police (UNMIK) to investigate all human rights abuses that were ethnically motivated and ensure that all witnesses to such crimes were protected. There was discrimination in healthcare and up to 90% unemployment among the Serb and Roma communities in Albanian areas while minority groups of ethnic Albanians living in Serb areas suffered from the same security restrictions and curbs on their freedom of movement. In July 1999 after the conflict over half of the pre-war minority population fled from Kosovo and sought protection in Serbia or Montenegro while others sought protection in Kosovo within ethnic enclaves guarded by KFOR and UNMIK. By April 2003 only 5,800 of the 230,000 Serbs and Romas who had fled Kosovo in 1999 had returned, and about a third of that group had chosen to live within the relative safety of three predominantly Serbian municipalities in the north of Kosovo. The others lived under the protection of KFOR in majority Albanian urban areas or in mono-ethnic villages (Amnesty International 2003).

However various hopeful initiatives are taking place. For example in October 2003 Zenit reported that the International Volunteers for Development (IVD), a nongovernmental organization linked to the Salesians (a Roman Catholic Order), had been requested by various Kosovan institutions and individuals to open an educational centre in Pristina to provide a source for local teachers to up-date their information and skills. Professional formation was offered in the use of modern technology in electronics, computer science, business, secretarial skills, languages and mechanics and educational material were made available.

The IVD carried out research revealing that there was a grave crisis in the educational system in Kosovo. They discovered that at elementary level there were few well trained teachers and a lack of books or educational materials. Just over a third of children had actually finished elementary school, two thirds leaving before the age of 15. There was little provision at secondary and tertiary levels. Only 17.3% had a secondary school diploma and only 3.3% had achieved a University degree.

The IVD president expressed hope that as the courses offered by IVD in Pristina would be open to both sexes and would accept young people from the Serbian minority, the multicultural ethos would help to lessen the ethnic tensions in the area (Zenit 2003).

Albanian News stated in 2003 that the Kosovans themselves, UNMIK, NATO and the international community were making every effort to rebuild Kosovo, by revitalizing its economy, establishing self-government, and bringing about healing and reconciliation.

In 2003 five years after NATO intervened in Kosovo the signs were hopeful that Kosovo could become a multi-ethnic, independent Province and that the various security agencies: the Kosovo Force (KFOR), the United Nations Civil Police and the Kosovo Police Service could somewhat relax their security arrangements although some of the minority groups still suffered from racial attacks. However, towards the end of 2003 the situation in Kosovo became less stable with an increase in serious crimes, in particular those committed against the Serb Minority community. Many of the ethnic minority groups were still fleeing from Kosovo. It was a region that struggled to maintain a fragile peace and where inter-ethnic crime was rarely investigated and often the less serious crimes were not reported for fear of reprisals from the majority community.

In March 2004 the situation became more insecure with an eruption of mass demonstrations spreading across the Province and leading to inter-ethnic violence and civil unrest. Although the majority of those attacked were Kosovan Serbs or from other ethnic minorities who had not been targeted before, some had been forced to flee their homes five years earlier and some Albanian communities in the northern regions asked to be evacuated to safer areas. The violence lasted three days and affected all ethnic groups, leaving 19 people dead and over 950 people injured, with

730 houses as well as religious and civic buildings burnt or destroyed and a total of 4,100 people displaced of whom 82% were Kosovan Serbs (UN 2004).

The northern area of Kosovo still required a strong KFOR presence to maintain security for the minority Kosovan Albanian community. The situation around Mitrovica continued to be very fragile and few had chosen to return there. Over a hundred people were temporarily displaced in March 2004 when property of the Kosovan Albanians was either damaged or occupied by Kosovan Serbs. The many surrounding villages found themselves cut off and short of supplies until KFOR could arrange support. Many Kosovan Albanians in the Serb majority Shterpc/Strpce region left their villages, fearing reprisals.

The UNHCR declared:

> 'The violent riots and the tense security environment following these events clearly demonstrate a continued threat to their security and Kosovo Albanians in an ethnic minority situation may face serious protection-related problems' (UN 2004).

The UNHCR listed other groups of Kosovan Albanians whom they considered to be at risk – people who
- are of mixed ethnicity
- are married to someone of another ethnicity
- have had any association with the Serbian regime since 1990
- are traumatized, particularly those who have been subject to serious persecution or torture
- are survivors of sexual violence
- witnessed crimes against humanity.

On 13 August 2004 the UNHCR went on to state that 'Kosovo Albanians originating from areas where they now are in a minority situation, should not be forced or compelled to return to Kosovo. There are also certain categories of the population, whether belonging to the majority or minority communities, who may face serious protection-related problems, including physical danger, were they to return home at this stage' (UNHCR 2004d).

On 23 October 2004 the Province of Kosovo held elections in order to choose its second parliament since it became a UN protectorate after the conflict in 1999. The Kosovans elected a 120-member assembly for a four-year term with one hundred seats distributed among all parties who contested the election, in proportion to their share of the vote. As the majority of Kosovans were Albanians, to ensure that the Serbs and minority ethnic groups were represented, ten seats had been reserved for parties representing the Serbs and another ten were set aside for smaller ethnic groups divided as follows: four seats for the Roma, Ashkali and Egyptian communities, three for the Bosniaks (Bosnian Muslims), two for the Turkish community and one for the Gorani (Muslim Serbs) community (BBC 2004b). The assembly was given the power to pass laws on internal affairs such as economic and financial policy (unemployment in Kosovo in Nov 2004 was 44%), education, trade and also health. The members of parliament could also propose the Prime Minister whose function was to represent Kosovo abroad (BBC 2004b).

The UN had hoped that the parliament would be representative of the ethnic groups in the Province and that the Government would establish a form of power sharing. The ethnic Albanians viewed the UN Interim Administration (UNMIK) as an obstacle to their aim of creating an independent state and were keen for the elections to be successful. However the Serb minority urged on by Serbian Prime Minister Vojislav Kostunica and the influential Orthodox Church chose to boycott the elections and this resulted in the Serbs' representation going down from the twenty-two in the outgoing assembly to ten in the new assembly (BBC 2004b).

The Democratic League of Kosovo (LDK) party gained the most seats but not enough to rule alone, with only 45% of the votes. The Democratic Party came second with 28.6% and the Alliance for the Future of Kosovo with 8% came in third place. The two largest Serbian parties the Return Coalition and the Serbian Resistance Movement, decided to boycott the election (BBC 2004b).

To add to problems in the eyes of the world, the Kosovan Parliament elected a former senior guerrilla commander in the Kosovo Liberation Army, Ramush Haradinaj as Prime Minister. He was a controversial figure questioned that November by investigators working for the International War Crimes Tribunal at The Hague (Partos 2004).

On *Tolerance Day*, 23 November 2004 KTV reported on a refugee camp in Plemetin whose residents are mainly Kosovo's Ashkalia and Roma minority. In their report *'Kosovo has not many reasons to be proud of Tolerance,'* KTV explained how since the end of the war, this group had no possibility of a normal life outside of the camp although some members declared that they had good relations with the majority Albanian population from whom they received social assistance. Others stated that they were afraid all the time and that little tolerance was shown for those with different opinions, values and behaviour (KTV 2004).

On the same day the UN Secretary General Koffi Annan stated that societies could only hope to make progress if they promoted key virtues such as tolerance, which he declared to be a condition for democracy, peace, and a sustainable development (KTV 2004).

On 25 January 2005 following a debate by the EU Committee on Foreign Affairs in Brussels, Doris Pack, president of the European Parliament Delegation for Relations with South-East Europe, declared that the Kosovo issue could not be resolved without Serbia or against Serbia. Ms Pack described the situation as very difficult and urged all parties to try to do all they could to improve the situation and make progress (Pack 2005).

The following day 26 January, Nebojsa Covic, head of Belgrade's Kosovo Coordination Centre addressed the Foreign Affairs Committee. He stressed that there could not be a lasting solution to the Kosovo issue unless Belgrade took an active role. He stated that Serbia was strongly opposed to any redrawing of borders and insisted on the territorial integrity and sovereignty of all countries in the region being honoured (ERP KIM 2005).

In February 2005 while UNMIK continued 'to be the good guys' and 'to publicly state that it respects human rights and the rule of law,' Marek Nowicki (2005a), Kosovan Ombubsperson declared that Kosovans needed more protection because there continued to be human rights issues in Kosovo due to the fact that Kosovans had no access to the European Court of Human Rights (ECRE) in Strasbourg. This was due to the fact that Kosovo had been a surrogate state run by the United Nations for five years and because human rights was the basis on which Kosovo had been governed, the people of Kosovo were not free to take their own government to court regarding human rights issues.

If Kosovans became the victims of human rights violations committed by UNMIK or its staff members, they had no recourse to any independent legal body that could intervene on their behalf and enable them to be granted reparation. Niowicki (2005a) declared in February 2005: 'The only legal instrument of human rights protection that exists in Kosovo at this point is my office.'

Nowicki explained that the 'chaotic legal and institutional environment' in Kosovo meant that the Ombudsperson was unable to give the required level of protection (Nowicki 2005a).

2.7. KOSOVO - THE FUTURE

In early 2005, realising that the present status quo in Kosovo was unsustainable the parties most interested in the outcome, including Belgrade, agreed that there needed to be a change even though they could not agree what the change should be. In mid-2005, the UN is planning to examine the Kosovo government's commitment to democracy, how it is actually governing Kosovo and its commitment to human rights. A Contact Group (America, France, Russia, Germany and Italy) has been set up, whose mandate is to decide whether to start a process to determine the province's final status (TOL 2005).

The ethnic-Albanian majority is strongly arguing for independence, firmly believing that only an independent Kosovo can deliver stability and the democratic standards demanded by the international community. The ethnic Albanians believe that independence would also protect the minority groups within Kosovo. However since the violent attacks on the Serbs in March 2004, the Kosovo Serb community has found its own position intolerable and is totally opposed to an Independent Kosovo. In a comprehensive report on Kosovo published on 24 January 2005, the influential International Crisis Group (ICG) think-tank argued that a process should begin whereby Kosovo could keep its present borders and become fully independent by the middle of 2006 (TOL 2005).

On 26 January Martin Schlesinger (political analyst from the Woodrow Wilson Centre) said that the International Crisis Group's proposal for independence for Kosovo was impossible and 'the only solution for Kosovo is European integration, not independence' (ERP KIM 2005).

It appears that no one can agree on how to resolve Kosovo's final status. There is no easy consensus among even the major international players let alone those immediately involved. The positions held by the Kosovan Albanians, Kosovan Serbs and Belgrade are at present irreconcilable. There is still incredible insecurity in the region mainly due to the levels of animosity between ordinary Kosovan Albanians and the Serbs, Roma, and other Slav minorities. As TOL reports: 'Their insecurity extends far beyond anything that can be addressed through better policing measures. This insecurity is, in fact, largely about their social exclusion and the political vacuum that surrounds them' (TOL 2005)

Perhaps the Albanian-led Government is willing to promote tolerance towards the ethnic minorities in Kosovo and to provide them with security but they will have to contend with deep-rooted tensions within their population. Perhaps the minority representatives and Belgrade are not being deliberately uncooperative but genuinely cannot accept an independent Kosovo. Who are we to judge? It is not a simple matter. It is within the mandate of the UN Security Council to come up with a legal credible solution. However, its Resolution 1244 which mandates the current UN administration in Kosovo, is contradictory about the province of Kosovo's status. Resolution 1244 calls for 'the commitment of all Member States to the sovereignty and territorial integrity of the Federal Republic of Yugoslavia [now renamed Serbia-Montenegro]' while also calling for 'a political process designed to determine Kosovo's future status' (TOL 2005).

All concerned parties realize that the insecurity and lack of a stable governance in Kosovo must be dealt with as quickly as possible. A process to determine the Province's final status must be put in place as soon as possible (TOL 2005).

On 22 February 2005, representatives from the US, NATO and the EU met in Brussels to discuss Kosovo and set some fundamental conditions for the future of Kosovo (ERP KIM 2005a).

Two days later, Gianfranco Fini Italy's foreign minister, visiting Kosovo, said that while Kosovo could never go back to the way it was in the former Yugoslavia, he cautioned against any hasty moves toward independence for the province stating: 'What is needed now is stability in the region. There are no existing conditions now to talk about independence for Kosovo' (ERM KIM 2004b)

A few days later, Marek Antoni Nowicki wrote on 25 February 2005 in *Taking a Hard Look* - his fortnightly article:

'Let's take an honest, hard look at Kosovo today: Poverty is widespread, and a considerable number of people endure difficult, even harsh, daily living conditions. There is a significant gap between those who are receiving meager social welfare assistance and those who are not, not to mention massive unemployment and a fast-growing youth population with few meaningful prospects' (Nowicki 2005b).

CHAPTER THREE

INTRODUCTION TO THE KOSOVAN FAMILIES SURVEY

In this chapter we describe the Questionnaire used in the Kosovan Families Survey. We go on to look at our Sources of information - our respondents and where we met them - Sure Start, Shpresa Programme, the Renewal Refugee and Migrant Project (RAMP) and Harmony House. We consider the respondents' family profiles, analysing the responses to the following questions: What was their country of origin? Did they live in a city/town or village? Was the respondent a man or woman? How old was the respondent? What was that person's marital status? Did they belong to any particular faith group? Had they any children and if so how many? What were their children's ages? Where were their children? How long were they in education in their country of origin? What was their occupation in their country of origin? Had the respondent left any family members in their home country or had any other family members fled abroad? Finally we asked which month and year the respondent arrived in England.

3.1. DESCRIPTION OF THE QUESTIONNAIRE[3]

In all there were seventy questions in the original Questionnaire (Spring 2003), with eight questions in the March 2004 update, and twenty-three in the October 2004 update for those granted the Amnesty and twenty-one for those who had not received the Amnesty but had been granted either Refugee Status or Exceptional Leave to Remain (ELR), Humanitarian Protection, Discretionary Leave or were either still awaiting the Home Office decision or were appealing against a refusal.

In the Original questionnaire the following topics were covered:
-   Profile of family: age, marital status, children, household, education and occupation in country of origin, affiliation to any faith group.
-   Choice of the UK, method of arrival legally/illegally, application processes for asylum.
-   Integration: English lessons, children's education, accommodation, medical and legal care, present status in the UK, permission to work, help from Christian communities/Faith groups, treatment received from other people in London.
-   Well-being, health, material situation, help from voluntary and state groups.

---

[3] See Appendix.

- Links with home country and future plans, hopes regarding a future immigration policy.

In the March 2004 update the questionnaire covered the following topics:
- Present Status.
- Changes to family's material situation since the Spring of 2003
  - Accommodation
  - Immigration lawyer
  - Children – another baby, school.
- Benefits/problems with benefits.
- Effects of the Amnesty on status, well-being and occupation.

In the October 2004 update the questionnaire covered the following topics:
- Present status, date of arrival in UK.
- Date granted Amnesty.
- Accommodation, condition, number of rooms, settled or required to move, any problems when moving from Social Services/NASS to housing provided by Local Council, emergency accommodation.
- Benefits.
- British citizenship, passport, travel documents.

3.2. SOURCES OF INFORMATION/RESPONDENTS

We interviewed fifty Albanian speakers (Table 3:1) of whom forty-four were Kosovans (one originally from Yugoslavia), five Albanians and one Montenegran. Our method of finding interviewees was 'snowballing'. Starting with Kosovan families we already knew, we relied on these contacts to put us in touch with other Albanian speakers and various NGO Support Centres in the East End of London, who could put us in contact with other Kosovan asylum seekers.

The first support Centres we became involved with were in the Borough of Newham where one of the authors lives. We discovered through one of the Kosovan asylum seekers that an Albanian speaking group was meeting once a week as part of the local Sure Start Programme and we went along to ask for permission to interview some of the participants. We were warmly welcomed and the majority of our respondents were members of the Sure Start and Shpresa groups.

3.2.1. SURE START

Sure Start is a Government initiative started in 1999 to work in the 20% most deprived wards in the UK. The aim of the Programme is to promote the health and well-being of children (under four years old) and their parents, by improving their social and emotional development; health and the children's ability to learn and by strengthening families and communities. The organisation is trying to ensure that all families living locally, in all sections of the community, have access to high quality services. It runs a number of successful support groups including a Roma Development Programme, Fathers' Project, Home Start Project, Asian Women's group, Keep Fit group, Parent and Toddler group. Sure Start offers advice also in welfare benefits, accommodation problems and special educational needs to support disabled children, to mention but a few programmes.

3.2.2. SHPRESA PROGRAMME

The Shpresa Programme began in 2000 to work with the Albanian speaking community in the UK, enabling them to participate fully in society by providing a range of services and activities. Shpresa is the Albanian word for 'hope' and the Programme works to enable the Albanian speaking community in the UK to settle, fully participate and gain in confidence and thereby make progress in their lives. The Programme is led by community members and in 2004 was working with 180 families and individuals. At that time the Programme ran two women's support groups, a youth project, a children's project and a volunteering project. The group ran dancing classes, Albanian language classes, Complementary Therapy, Sewing and IT classes as well as working in partnership with English classes and arranging cultural events and trips to places of interest. It can rightly be proud of what it has achieved so far and how beneficial it has been to many members of the Albanian speaking community. The Shpresa Programme has its offices and base in the Froud Center on the Romford Road, Manor Park although it also works through many other centres in Newham.

The Shpresa group put us in touch with the Renewal Refugee and Migrant Project from whom a number of our respondents were receiving support.

3.2.3. THE RENEWAL REFUGEE AND MIGRANT PROJECT (RAMP)

RAMP is a project of the Renewal Programme in the East London Borough of Newham. It is a registered charity whose mission is to enable refugees and migrants to realize their potential and facilitate their full participation in society. RAMP supports refugees, asylum seekers, migrants and members of the black and minority ethnic communities.

According to the RAMP brochure 2004, the project offers to individuals and families:
- advice, advocacy and support on Welfare, Housing, NASS, Immigration and Nationality, Race Equality and it provides emotional support for asylum seekers and refugees;

- mentoring – six months one to one volunteer mentor support for newly arrived refugees and migrants to enable them to settle in the unfamiliar environment;
- support for young refugees – after school and summer activities for children of refugees and asylum seekers, art therapy for children traumatized by their experiences;
- emergency food for people with no benefits;
- free clothing store;
- food for 'a penny'(weekly supply of fresh fruit and vegetables for eligible families not in receipt of benefits).

Support is also available to groups/refugee community organizations in the form of:
- advice and information on funding, constitutions, developing policy and services, planning, counselling and therapeutic services;
- office space which groups can use on a sessional basis.

3.2.4. HARMONY HOUSE

When we began our research we were desperately in need of translating our questionnaire into Albanian. We turned to a support centre in Dagenham for help as we were aware that they had been holding English classes for asylum seekers for many years and we knew that we would be able to access a good translation through their assistance. With the cooperation of the Harmony House staff we were able to carry out thirteen interviews of the Kosovans/Albanians who attend courses there and to follow up some of their experiences.

Harmony House is a project of the Sisters of the Sacred Hearts of Jesus and Mary. It began when asylum seekers came to the Sacred Heart Convent in Dagenham needing help with the basic necessities of life. The project has developed into an innovative model of working with asylum seekers and refugees while striving to integrate the refugees and asylum seekers into the local community. Harmony House today is a centre consisting of a wide range of statutory and voluntary organizations, providing education and training that is accessible to all. The Harmony House Newsletter in June 2004 stated: 'We have found that innovation springs from the connectedness between people and so we have sought to bring together a range of partners and ideas to explore the common ground that leads to solutions.'

The Harmony House Mission Statement is:
- to encourage and promote recognition of the richness and diversity of our multi-cultural society;
- to encourage and promote a willingness to learn from each other, whatever our ethnic origin, for the benefit of the whole community.

The aims of Harmony House are:
- to provide opportunities for asylum seekers and refugees and the local community;
- to experience quality courses in education and training;
- to ensure that services offered reflect priority needs and help towards entry into employment and other levels of training and education;
- to provide a child care service of the highest quality as part of the response to priority needs.

Harmony House seeks to complement its mission and aims through a holistic approach of on-site statutory and voluntary services (Regan 2004).

Among the many courses offered in Harmony House are the following: ESOL (English for Speakers of Other languages) classes, Child Care courses, Hairdressing, Needlework, Pottery and Horticulture classes. There are also many support groups and advice surgeries dealing with immigration issues, health problems, disability information, help in preparing a CV and for a job interview.

3.3. FAMILY PROFILES

We used a questionnaire with all respondents, looking at the family situations – nationality, age, number of children, religion etc encouraging respondents to make comments. With others we also held in depth interviews to gain a detailed account of their experiences. The questionnaire was also translated into Albanian to aid our interviewees but we encountered several problems during the in-depth interviews. Our inability initially to secure interpreters led to our dependence on the interviewees' ability to communicate in English. We also encountered problems with regard to having an interpreter present, due to the respondent's reluctance to share with someone they didn't know from their own country. We found that our own connection with the RC Church helped them to be open with us and to trust us.

3.3.1. COUNTRY OF ORIGIN AND WHETHER THEY CAME FROM A RURAL OR URBAN AREA

Firstly, we looked at their country of origin. Of the fifty families, forty-four were from Kosovo, five from Albania and one from Montenegro. Secondly, we looked at their background. Was it mainly rural or urban? We discovered that the majority of asylum seekers were from villages rather than cities (Table 3.1). Twenty-four of the respondents were from villages, while only five were from towns and seventeen from cities. Two informants who came to the UK from Kosovo grew up in Serbia originally but married Kosovans. Another stated that she was Yugoslavian but married to a

Kosovan. One had been studying Ecomonics at a Serbian University and had taken part in a big demonstration in 1981. She was asked to leave and because she also wanted to be free of the Serbian regime she went to Kosovo.

Table 3.1 Country of origin and whether they came from a rural or urban area

	City	Town	Village	Not disclosed	Total
Kosovo	12	5	23	4	44
Albania	4		1		5
Montenegro	1				1
Number of respondents	17	5	24	4	50

Source: Kosovan Families Survey 2003-04

3.3.2. SEX AND AGE OF RESPONDENTS

Although we were interested in the family, we only interviewed one member of each family who responded on the family's behalf. The majority of respondents were women (45) (Table 3.2). This was mainly due to two facts. Firstly most of the interviews took place at refugee centres where the women were receiving English lessons and had formed support groups for themselves and their children. The second reason appeared to be quite simply a reluctance on the part of the men to attend these classes and therefore it was more difficult to make contact with them.

Table 3.2 Sex and age of respondents

Years old	Male	Female
16 – 20		1
21 – 30		11
31 – 40	3	30
41 – 50	1	2
51 – 60	1	1
Number of respondents	5	45

Source: Kosovan Families Survey 2003-04

We asked the respondent's age (Table 3.2). The majority of thirty-three were in the age group 31-40, while eleven were aged 21-30. There were three aged 41-50 and only one aged 16-20. There were only two people over 50 at the time of the first interview.

3.3.3. MARITAL STATUS AND RELIGION

All the respondents had been married although two came to the UK single, one of whom came to join her boyfriend and married once she arrived in England (Table 3.3). Forty were still married and living with their partners, while circumstances had forced five couples to live apart, of whom two husbands had been deported. Five of the women's husbands had died during the conflict in Kosovo.

Table 3.3 Marital status and religion

	Married	Separated	Widowed	Total
Roman Catholic (R.C.)	11	3		14
Christian but not R.C.	1			1
Muslim	17	2	4	23
R.C. and Muslim	4		1	5
Greek Orthodox	1			1
Greek Orthodox and Muslim	1			1
Mormon	1			1
No religious affiliation	4			4
Number of respondents	40	5	5	50

Source: Kosovan Families Survey 2003-04

One young respondent told us that her mother and father went to England first in June 1998 and then her eleven year old brother went to England in September 1998. She had followed them with her husband in the August of 1999. She was eighteen years old and pregnant.

All the respondents apart from four couples, professed a religious faith, the majority twenty-three being Muslim. Sixteen were Christian, one Mormon and five were of mixed religious affiliation. In both Kosovo and Albania, Roman Catholics are minority groups. In Albania only 12% are Catholic. One family explained that because of that fact they had been unable to be baptized in Albania and had only succeeded in being baptized once they arrived in the UK in 2002. Another family, while not declaring their original faith affiliation, stated that they had converted to Christianity two years before. Yet another family said they were Muslim but sometimes went to church.

3.3.4. NUMBER, AGES AND SEX OF CHILDREN

We concentrated on families, the majority of whom have very young children. The average number of children in a family was two. Twenty-four families had two children, two families had no children, nine families had one child while fourteen families had three children. Only one family had four children.

The majority of the children (67) were under nine years old, while only thirty-six were over nine years old. Interestingly the families had fifty-eight boys and only forty-five girls (Table 3.4). Perhaps nature was compensating for the number of men killed during the crisis? Not all of the children were with their parents. One respondent told us that her fifteen year old son was missing in Kosovo and another told us that as she and her husband were separated, their son spent four days with her and three with his dad. Two respondents were pregnant. Both had baby boys who arrived after the initial interviews – one child in late June and the other in late July 2003. Not included in Table 3.4 are three new arrivals - a baby girl born in February 2004 and another two babies (a boy and a girl) born in August 2004.

Table 3.4 Number, ages and sex of children

Age in Years	0-2	3-5	6-8	9-11	12-14	15-17	18+	Total
Boys	6	13	15	10	4	6	4	58
Girls	10	10	13	2	5	3	2	45
Total number of children	16	23	28	12	9	9	6	103

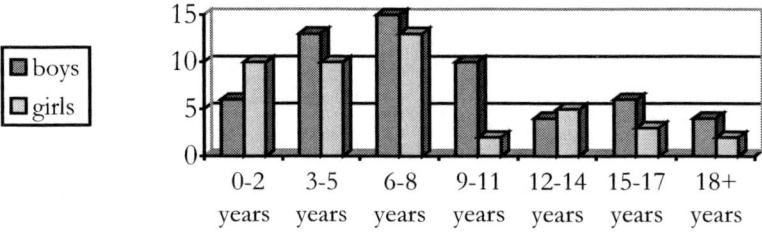

Source: Kosovan Families Survey 2003-04

3.3.5. EDUCATION RECEIVED IN HOME COUNTRY

The majority of the respondents said that they and their partners had received some education although they admitted that at times it had been sporadic due to the situation in the country (Table 3.5). The majority of respondents (42) had received at least eight years of education while eleven of those had proceeded to some form of higher education. Eight had received four years or less. Eight respondents were unable to say how long their partners had been in school. However the questionnaires showed that often the wife had received more education than her husband. Possibly the reason for this was an emphasis on the need for the husband to go out and earn a living as soon as he was old enough.

Table 3.5 Education received in home country

Number of Years of Education	2	3	4	8	9	10	11	12	14	16	17	18	19	Total
Respondents	1	1	6	11	2	2	1	15	1	4	3	2	1	50
Partners			2	13		4		15	2	3		1	2	42

Source: Kosovan Families Survey 2003-04

Naturally some of the older children had also received some education in their home countries but that also was sporadic and we did not attempt to quantify how much education the children had received.

3.3.6. OCCUPATION IN HOME COUNTRY

In Table 3.6 we compared the various working backgrounds the respondents and their partners came from. As we can see in Table 3.6 they come from a vast range of work experiences.

The majority of women (21) were housewives, with seven women directly working with children, either teaching or in childcare. The most popular occupation for men appeared to be working either in business or agriculture, while there was an architect, a plumber, a carpenter, a bricklayer and there were two electricians. One husband and wife were doctors while another man was a vet and another woman a nurse. Six people were engineers, four people had been working for the government in their home countries and there was one policeman. Four of the men were drivers. One woman was a hairdresser and one person worked in a shop, while another owned a shop, and two worked in banks. Nine of the women respondents did not specify what work, if any their husbands had done, while some admitted that while in Kosovo they had only been promised in marriage and didn't know what their husbands had actually done for a living.

In Kosovo and Albania they often have arranged marriages. It is traditional for the young peoples' parents to choose a husband or wife for them before they reach the age of sixteen. They are then promised in marriage although they might not actually marry for a few years. The young women are not allowed to mix socially with any young men unless with their parents and family present and they cannot go out alone even with their husbands to be. A young woman is allowed to meet the man chosen for her but only while chaperoned.

Table 3.6 Occupation in home country

Occupation	Respondent	Partner	Occupation	Respondent	Partner
Student	2	1	Doctor	1	1
Housewife	18	3	Nurse	1	
Plumber	1		Vet		1
Brick layer	1		Agriculture	2	6
Carpenter		1	Shepherd		3
Electrician		2	Mechanic		1
Architect		1	Driver		4
Teacher/ Child care	7		Shop owner /assistant	1	1
Policeman		1	Hairdresser	1	
Government worker	2	2	Business person	3	6
Engineer	3	3	Factory manager		1
Work in a bank	2		Unemployed	2	2
Accountant/ Economist	1		Not specified or n/a	2	9

Source: Kosovan Families Survey 2003-04

3.3.7. MEMBERS OF FAMILY RESPONDENT LEFT IN HOME COUNTRY AND THOSE WHO FLED ABROAD

Table 3.7 attempts to show how many of the Respondents' family members stayed in their home country and how many fled abroad.

Due to fear and poor communication within their home countries most of the respondents could say where their family members were only when they left their home country and they had no idea actually how many members were still at home, had fled abroad or had died. Those who managed to keep in touch were aware of the situation of only their parents or in-laws, having little idea of the position their brothers and sisters found themselves in. Therefore the table gives us a very unclear picture of the true situation. One respondent told us: 'My father died ten years ago. My husband was killed. I don't know where my in-laws are now.' Another said: 'None of our family are in Kosovo now. They all fled abroad.

Table 3.7 Members of family respondents left in home country and those who fled abroad

	Mother	Father	Mother-in-law	Father-in-law	Husband	Children	Your sisters	Your brothers	Partner's sisters	Partner's brothers
Still in home country	34	23	20	19	3	2	35	28	32	41
Fled abroad	4	4	2	3			18	12	7	11
Died	3	8	3	5	5					

Source: Kosovan Families Survey 2003-04

3.3.8. YEAR RESPONDENTS ARRIVED IN ENGLAND

All the families interviewed arrived during the period 1997 to 2003 (Table 3.8).

Table 3.8 Year respondents arrived in England

	1997	1998	1999	2000	2001	2002	2003
Jan-Mar		1	3	1			
Apr-Jun	1	3	6	3	1		1
Jul-Sept		3	9	1		1	
Oct-Dec		2	5	1		1	
Not stated		4	3				
Number of families	1	13	26	6	1	2	1

Source: Kosovan Families Survey 2003-04

As we can see the majority arrived immediately before the intervention of the United Nations in the Kosovan conflict or during the conflict or immediately after it, with thirteen arriving in the UK between March 1998 and December 1998 and twenty-six arriving during 1999, while only six arrived in 2000, one in 1997, one in 2001 and 2003 and two in 2002. Consequently as the majority of the families (45) had arrived in the

UK before October 2000 most of them were eligible for the Amnesty. Only five families had arrived too late to qualify.

CHAPTER FOUR

BECOMING ASYLUM SEEKERS

In this chapter we analyse the responses to the following questions: Why did the families decide to leave their own country? Did any of their family come to join them in England? Why did they choose the UK? Did they consider other countries? If so which other countries did they consider? Did they arrive legally? Had they passports? How did they travel to England? Which was their port of entry? When and where did they register? What were they given on registration? After registration where were they sent to or where did they go? How were they treated by the authorities (immigration officials)?

4.1. MOTIVATION TO LEAVE COUNTRY OF ORIGIN

The respondents were asked to give no more than five reasons for leaving their home country although some gave more than five and others less (Table 4.1). The majority (40) gave 'war' as the main motivation to leave their own country, twenty-four cited 'people being killed' while twenty-two people cited 'death threats' as another reason and twenty cited 'their own house burnt down'. Nineteen declared 'it was unsafe' and fourteen also declared 'women raped' as a reason for leaving. Many of the women admitted feeling unable to tell their husbands that they had been raped.

Table 4.1 Motivation to leave country of origin

Reasons given for leaving country of origin		Reasons given for leaving country of origin	
War	40	People assaulted	9
Religious persecution	11	Death threats	22
Political persecution	15	People arrested	8
People being killed	24	Women raped	14
Houses burnt down	18	Hope for a better life	3
Own house burnt down	20	Famine	2
It was unsafe	19	Poverty	2

Source: Kosovan Families Survey 2003-04

A third of the group cited 'political persecution' as a reason, while eleven cited 'religious persecution' as a reason for leaving. A small number (3) said they hoped for a better life. Some gave another reason to those listed – fear for their children's safety. Let us listen to some of the asylum seekers speaking about their experiences in Kosovo:

'All the houses were burnt. My uncle was killed. He left six children the oldest only thirteen. It was a very bad experience. I saw two young people who had their earrings pulled off and then their two hands put in the fire. It was horrible, frightening. I cannot forget their screaming, cannot forget what I saw. My family moved with an uncle to Macedonia. We heard guns. We were threatened with death.'

Another said: 'The situation was terrible. Houses burnt down and our cousins killed.' Another explained: 'I left my country because there was a war in which I lost my husband and my family. I wanted to save my own life and my son's.'

One of the Roman Catholic men told us:

'My Memory of Kosovo'
© Maljeza, aged 13

'We didn't want to leave Kosovo but when the bombs started falling we had to leave if we were to survive. If our family had stayed in Kosovo we would have needed to change our name or religion. Our family had always been Catholic but we were not allowed to practise our religion. I was attacked many times with weapons. I was shot through both legs, stabbed through my foot and in my side and also my head.'

Another lady with tears in her eyes declared: 'You wouldn't believe what I have seen happen... a child held in boiling water.'

© Laurana, aged 11

One lady told us:

'My father-in-law was killed and then I witnessed my mother-in-law being assaulted, having part of her foot cut off and then being raped before I was raped several times myself and left unconscious for three days.'

Laurana drew this picture of the graveyard where her Grandma is buried. Her memories of Kosovo were of death and loss.

One Muslim said:

> 'Every day and every night people were arrested. They came and killed people in the night. With our children we saw our house burnt down. My father was arrested. He was beaten and he died a few months later. He had been teaching for forty-two years. My mum died six months later. My mother-in-law and father-in-law were very sick. They are somewhere in Kosovo, aged seventy-five. My big brother was in prison for several years. When he came back he was very sick. After spending a day at the police station and finding their house burnt Mum said it wasn't safe to stay there. We took the car to Macedonia and stayed there for two weeks. Some friends found a lorry going to England.'

Another told us: 'I was beaten and lost my teeth and my husband was in prison twice.' A teenager translating for her mother told us: 'We had to leave our home. Her husband was killed during the war.' Another lady told us: 'My Husband's father was killed.'

Ilir Arnold drew a picture of his memories of Kosovo. The picture shows his home on fire, his dog being shot, many people being killed and many crying. He told Sister Anne:

> "When the soldiers came I was with my grandfather. The soldiers killed my dog and I was very upset. There were tanks everywhere and soldiers shooting."

An asylum seeker from Albania told us:

> 'My husband was killed two years before I left Albania in a blood feud. Consequently my whole family were in danger. I moved in with my boyfriend, which was not acceptable in our country. We were threatened and the situation became dangerous for both of us. When I realised I was pregnant, we both fled but I have no idea where he is now.'

'My Memories of Kosovo'
© Ilir Arnold Shega, aged 12

The only asylum-seeker we interviewed from Montenegro, told us:

> 'We had helped the Kosovan Albanians so the Serbs threatened us with death. I was arrested and released twice as there wasn't enough evidence.

However when I was summoned to the High Court for a third time I decided I must leave the country. My wife had been tortured in our country.'

4.2. FAMILY MEMBERS REUNITED IN ENGLAND

Only one respondent said her husband's brother had joined them in England. The majority (40) of the fifty respondents said that no family member had joined their family in England and they had not joined family members already in the UK.

However, seven of the respondents said that they had joined other members of their family in England. Two had come to join their husbands, another his wife. He had been in hiding when his wife and son escaped and only joined them in February 2002. One respondent had come to England in the hope of finding her teenage son who had fled with a group of teenagers after the death of his father when he, too, was threatened with death. Another respondent said that she had come to join her mother and father.

One family said that the other members of their family were scattered over many countries. Many of the families expressed sorrow that no family member had been able to join them but said that it was impossible now with the Government's new legislation. With great joy one of the Albanian respondents announced that her mother had just come to England. She had easily obtained a visa to visit her family for one month.

4.3. REASONS FOR CHOOSING THE UK

Thirty-six of the respondents said they had come to the UK with their families by chance. When they boarded a lorry in their home country, they had one and only aim: to get their families to safety, and as long as they left Kosovo they didn't mind where they were taken. Of those who said they had chosen the UK, six already had relatives in England, one of whom chose England in the hope of finding her husband while another came to join her boyfriend. Four also gave political reasons, while only one thought it would be easier to stay here. The overwhelming reason given for choosing the UK was for the freedom it offered. No one said they had chosen England for economic reasons. One lady declared that she used to dream of travelling to England because she had heard that it had a great name for democracy. Before she arrived she heard that England gave benefits etc and she thought it would be good to go to England. She had already learnt some English in Albania.

4.4. CONSIDERATION OF OTHER DESTINATIONS

The respondents were asked if they had considered going to other countries (Table 4.2). Fourteen had considered possible destinations, eight said the USA while two had considered Canada, one France and five had considered Germany. However the majority (36) of whom ten declared they would have gone anywhere, had given it no forethought before deciding that they must leave their own country whatever the cost.

Table 4.2 Consideration of other destinations

	Any where	Canada	France	Germany	Italy	U.S.A.	No
Number of families	10	2	2	5	1	8	26

Source: Kosovan Families Survey 2003-04

4.5. STATUS ON ENTRY AND TRANSPORT USED TO REACH THE UK

Forty-six of the families arrived illegally, that is without documentation while only four arrived legally with documentation. Since the families' arrival no one had been given a passport apart from one informant's son who was born here. There was no explanation for this. Other children born to asylum seekers in the UK had not been granted passports.

Gathering clear information about the asylum seekers' methods of transport proved fairly difficult to obtain (Table 4.3). While forty-three families were sure they had made at least part of their journey by one or more lorries because many of them had been unable to leave the lorry at any stage on their journey, they had no idea whether the lorry had gone by ferry to the UK or by Eurostar. Neither were they aware through which port they had entered the UK as they had disembarked from the lorry for the first time 'in country' and many were unaware of where they disembarked. At least fifty-three different lorries were used by the asylum seekers. Others were surer about their journey saying they had first travelled by a tiny boat (9) – a hazardous crossing from Albania to Italy and then got on a lorry, while others were aware of travelling by ferry (4) or train (11) or even by plane (4).

Table 4.3 Transport used to reach the UK

	Boat	Car	Van	Lorry	Ferry	Plane	Train
Number of respondents	9	4	1	43		3	7
Total journeys	9	4	1	53	4	4	11

Source: Kosovan Families Survey 2003-04

Let us listen as some of the asylum seekers describe their horrendous journeys from Kosovo:

> 'We travelled in a van for two days and then a lorry for five days without a toilet. There were five families with children.'

Another told us:

> 'There were many people in the lorry. We spent four days travelling, only able to get out when the driver was sleeping. I was very frightened. I had some food with me for my daughter.'

Another explained:

> 'When we got into the lorry we did not know where we were going. There was just our family plus one boy. The journey took seven days. When we got out of the lorry someone asked us – "Why did you come here?" I replied: "I don't know where I am." When we arrived we were put into prison for twelve hours and then sent to social services.'

Another said:

> 'The boat was a sixteen seat fishing boat from Albania. It took us to Italy. We lived for four days on the street in Italy and were then put on a lorry. We sat with carpets. They gave our six months old baby drugs to keep quiet. We were also given food and water. I was very frightened. When we arrived in Dover the police asked us to get out. I was terrified and pleaded, "Please don't take my baby." The police gave us a travel card to get to London.'

Another described in more detail what had happened:

> 'With my sister and her husband we took a train to Albania. With a lot of other people we got a tiny boat at midnight to cross over to Italy. I had never seen the sea before. I was very frightened and held my four years old son close to me. I hadn't realised how cold it would be and my son whimpered. The agent who had arranged the trip told me to shut him up or he would shoot him. I was frightened and kept whispering to my son to be quiet. We had no food and few clothes. On arriving in Italy we got on a lorry but on finding us in the back the drivers dumped us on the road miles from anywhere. I drew a picture of a train and a young lad told us how to get to a station. We were very hungry. An Italian lady asked why my son was crying and with signs I told her he was hungry. She produced from her bag two very hard biscuits, which my son sucked and eventually fell asleep. We got onto another lorry. It was full of bottles and we had to climb in between the crates

to hide. It was difficult carrying my son but I wouldn't be parted from him. I was afraid even to let my younger sister take him.'

A young mother told her story:

'We paid a lorry driver and saw nothing on the way. We had no idea where we were going but we were willing to go anywhere. The lorry took us from Albania. It took days. We didn't realise it was going to be such a long trip. We had no food with us. We had no idea how we got to England. We were not aware of travelling on a boat. We got out of the lorry at Waterloo market. The driver left us. We met an elderly couple who ran a homeless centre and invited us in for the night. We were given food, shelter and a shower. The couple instructed us to go to Croydon. We had no money but we were fortunate to meet a Kosovan man who gave us the money to travel to and from Croydon.'

Most of the journeys in essence were similar so we will relate only a few more: 'The journey was very difficult. We travelled by lorry for about four days via Macedonia.' Another lady told us: 'I spent seven days in a lorry. Paid several thousand pounds before we got into the lorry. My cousin helped to pay. We had food with us. The lorry took my family to Liverpool. When we got off the lorry someone saw me and phoned the police. My husband had to stay one night in a police station. We were interviewed separately in Manchester ten days after we arrived.'

A young woman explained how she had travelled with friends and it cost her $3000. The journey was about five days. She had no food with her and was very hungry. Another young family paid an agent to leave Kosovo and travelled by lorry. There was just their family on board. First they took a boat to Italy on which there were about thirty people. They were in the lorry for about three days. They arrived in Greenhithe, Tilbury, Kent. Some families went straight from Kosovo by lorry to England: 'Only our family was on the lorry. It took two and a half days.' Others had far more roundabout routes: 'We went by plane from Albania to Greece. Stayed there two days then flew to Spain and on to France. Took a train to England. We went by Eurostar from Paris to Waterloo. We had a visa as far as France but destroyed it. The trip cost us about $12,000.'

4.6. PORT OF ENTRY AND WHERE THE RESPONDENT FIRST SET FOOT IN THE UK

To the question: "Which was your port of entry?" twenty-four respondents had no idea, mainly because they had been inside a lorry and unaware how they had actually entered the UK (Table 4.4). Seventeen were aware they had entered the UK through

Dover, three through Folkestone, three through Portsmouth, one through Harwich, one through Tilbury and one through Heathrow.

Only twenty-two were actually clear where they had set foot in England. For many they were either too traumatized to remember or everything appeared so strange they didn't know where they were. Twenty-eight declared they had no idea where they had set foot in England while six remembered leaving the lorry at Dover and three in Portsmouth. Nine were aware they were somewhere in London, one in Harwich, one in Liverpool and one in Tilbury.

Table 4.4 Port of entry and where the respondent first set foot in the UK

	Dover	Folkestone	Harwich	Heathrow	No idea
Port of entry	17	3	1	1	24
Set foot in England	6		1	1	28
	Portsmouth	Tilbury	London	Liverpool	
Port of entry	3	1			
Set foot in England	3	1	9	1	

Source: Kosovan Families Survey 2003-04

4.7. APPLICATION FOR ASYLUM AND PLACE AND TIME OF REGISTRATION

When asked the question: 'Did you have to apply for asylum when you came to England?' of the fifty respondents, forty-eight needed to apply for asylum and only two hadn't needed to.

To the question: 'Did you know you would have to apply for asylum when you came to England?' only eleven of the respondents knew that they would have to apply for asylum when they reached England, while nineteen of the respondents had no idea that they would need to apply for asylum. Two respondents did not need to apply while twenty either did not understand the question or chose not to answer it.

As we can see in Table 4.4.1 three-quarters of the group (38) registered either immediately on arrival or the next day. Forty-four people had registered within three days while only six people took longer to register, with one person unable to remember when her family had registered. Twenty-seven respondents registered in Croydon and one in Liverpool, one in London and three in Waterloo that is thirty-two 'in country,' while twelve registered at 'the port' and five couldn't remember where they had registered. Only one did not need to register.

Considering the very difficult conditions the young families travelled under plus the fact that the families were under extreme stress and were unaware that they would have to register as asylum seekers, and could not speak any English, it is incredible that so many registered within two days. Let us hear what happened on arrival: 'When we arrived we were caught by the police and we were sent straight to hospital.'

Table 4.4.1 Place and time of registration

I registered ….	I registered in									
	Croydon	Dover	Greenhithe	Harwich	Liverpool	London	Portsmouth	Waterloo	No idea	Total
Immediately	6	5	1	1			3	3	2	21
Next day	13	2							2	17
After 2-3 days	4					1			1	6
After 4-5 days	2									2
After 6-7days					1					1
After 2 weeks	1									1
Don't know	1									1
No need to register										1
Number of respondents	27	7	1	1	1	1	3	3	5	50

Source: Kosovan Families Survey 2003-04

A lady told us: 'When we got off the lorry we walked and walked until we heard people speaking Albanian. They told us to go to Barking Social Services.'
Another said:

'When we arrived in England my daughter waved from the lorry and the police saw her and helped us. We were the only people on the lorry. The police gave us food, and a place to wash. My daughter was sent to hospital. She has had a leg problem for a very long time.'

Another lady told us:

'I travelled the whole way by a lorry. My husband had travelled the same way earlier. When we arrived the driver opened the lorry and looked surprised. He called the police. The police asked me where I wanted to go. I said I had come to find my husband who I believed was in London.'

4.8. REGISTRATION AND DESTINATION AFTER REGISTRATION

The respondents were asked what they were given when they registered (Table 4.4.2). All respondents (48) who required documents agreed that they were given IND (identity papers supplied by the UK Immigration and Nationality Directorate). Only twenty-two said that they had been given accommodation. Seventeen were given food and fourteen were given money. Some were unclear about what they had been given probably due to the fact that they were traumatized and exhausted when they arrived in the UK and some did not include the help they received from the Social Services department they had been sent to upon registration, later the same day. In fact the majority were given accommodation on the day they registered including some basic support.

Table 4.4.2 On registration I was given…..

	Identity	Food	Accommodation	Money	Not specified	N/A
Number of families	48	17	22	14	2	1

Source: Kosovan Families Survey 2003-04

One interviewee told us that on registration in Croydon (July 2000) they were given an interview, had their photographs taken and were then told to go to the Refugee Council in Brixton for accommodation and money. No one gave them any money for the fares to get to Brixton. The Refugee Council sent them to temporary accommodation in Kentish Town. Another interviewee with his wife and two young boys told us that they were initially given £284 to last them two weeks.

On registering, forty-two of the respondents were sent to London, one to Southend and another respondent to Aldershot (Table 4.4.3). Four respondents were staying with relatives. Another two were sent to an unspecified destination. However it wasn't always a simple procedure. One family told us they were initially sent to Brixton. From Brixton they were sent to High Street Kensington and then onto a hotel in Kilburn. One respondent told us: 'We were given IND. Later when our son was born we went to register him with Immigration but our papers were never returned so now we have no identity papers. Because we have no IND we have had great difficulty accessing benefits.' Social Services however acknowledged they were aware of the problem and eventually gave them benefits.

4.9. TREATMENT BY AUTHORITIES (POLICE, IMMIGRATION PERSONNEL)

The majority of families (36) claimed that they had been treated either very well or well by the authorities, police and immigration personnel (Table 4.4.3). Six said they had been treated okay while only two complained that they had been treated badly. A respondent who arrived initially in Portsmouth declared: 'We were treated well by authorities in Croydon but very badly in Portsmouth.' Another said with anguish: 'They didn't believe me.'

Describing her interview one Kosovan said:

'At the first meeting they took my finger-prints – people were very nice to me. There was an interpreter there. I was given some letters. However I wasn't told they must be returned within twenty-eight days or I would receive a negative. I waited one month and then went to solicitor but I wasn't given a negative.'

One respondent said sadly: 'Although some officials were polite, I didn't feel respected even by the Kosovan interpreters.' For most the experience was more positive: 'Social services were very respectful.'

Table 4.4.3 Destination after registration/treatment by authorities (police, immigration Officials)

Sent to	London	Southend	Aldershot	Other	Family	Total
Treated very well	24			2	1	27
Well	12				2	14
Okay	4	1	1			6
Badly	2					2
Very badly						
N/a					1	1
Number of respondents	42	1	1	2	4	50

Source: Kosovan Families Survey 2003-04

CHAPTER FIVE
INITIAL PROCESS OF INTEGRATION

In this chapter we analyse the following questions: What papers have the respondents received from the Home Office? Has the Christian community/their Faith group helped them to settle here? If so in what way did the Faith group help? How did other people in London treat them? Did they need English lessons? Was it easy to get English lessons immediately? How often did they attend lessons? How did they find English lessons? Was it easy to get their child/children places in school? What type of accommodation did they live in at the time of the interview? How had they found their present accommodation? How many rooms had their present accommodation for their single family's use – including kitchen and bathroom? How long had they been in that accommodation? If they were in a hotel at any time, how long had they been there? How many flats/ houses/ hotels had they lived in since they arrived in the UK? What benefits did they receive? Had they an immigration solicitor? How many immigration solicitors had they had? What had the solicitors' advice been like? How did they come by their immigration solicitor? Had they ever had a housing solicitor?

5.1. DOCUMENTS RECEIVED FROM THE HOME OFFICE/ IMMIGRATON STATUS

On registration forty-six families received identity documents (IND) that consisted of a single sheet of Home Office paper with the declaration that the family claimed to be …(with their name and nationality) and then the husband's name and age, his wife's and his children's. It included photographs. Four families already had documentation when they arrived in the UK and did not require IND.

At the time the respondents were interviewed in the spring of 2003 there were only three who had received Refugee Status, three had received Permanent Residence and three Exceptional Leave to Remain while there was some question about whether another respondent had Exceptional Leave to Remain or not. The judge had granted it on appeal but then the Home Office had refused. That respondent was eventually granted the Amnesty in February 2004. One respondent had her case closed and two respondents claimed that they had received other documents but the language barrier made it impossible for them to be more specific. One respondent had Discretional Leave to Remain. Of the group of fifty an astounding thirty-six had no status whatsoever and were in a state of limbo awaiting a decision from the Home Office. Two respondents' husbands had been deported while their wives and children were left behind.

When the respondents were re-interviewed in the spring of 2004, eleven were unavailable to be interviewed as they had been relocated or deported and consequently we were no longer able to contact them. Of the thirty-nine we were able to interview, only six had been granted the Amnesty introduced by the Government in October 2003 and only three other families had received the Amnesty questionnaire and were awaiting its outcome while another fifteen had not received the Amnesty questionnaire and were still awaiting a decision on their status from the Home Office. Another five respondents did not qualify for the Amnesty as they had arrived after October 2000 and were still awaiting a decision from the Home Office regarding their status. Two respondents still had Exceptional Leave to Remain and one Permanent Residence. One had Discretionary Leave, one had Humanitarian Protection while five had Refugee Status.

Table 5.1 Documents received from the Home Office/immigration status

Documentation from Home Office	Spring 2003	Spring 2004	Autumn 2004
Identity	46		
Refugee Status	3	5	2
Permanent Residence	3	1	
Granted Amnesty		6	19
No status - awaiting decision of Home Office (H.O.)	36	20	8
Exceptional Leave to Remain but awaiting decision of H.O.	4	2	2
Received Amnesty Questionnaire but awaiting decision of H.O.		3	2
Discretional Leave - awaiting decision of H.O.	1	1	1
Humanitarian protection – awaiting decision of H.O.		1	1
Other documents - awaiting decision of H.O.	2		
Case closed but appealing	1		1
Husband deported	2		
Lost contact		11	14
Total number of respondents	50	50	50

Source: Kosovan Families Survey 2003-04

By the Autumn of 2004 almost half that group (19) had been granted the Amnesty and two had received the questionnaire regarding the Amnesty but were still awaiting the outcome. In all fourteen families were still awaiting the decision of the Home

Office. Another family had had their case closed. The authors had lost contact with another three of the respondents, all of whom had been granted Refugee Status, bringing the total loss of contact to fourteen.

A lady told the authors about some of the problems her family had encountered regarding status since arriving in the UK:

'The authorities have tried to deport my husband twice. Each time he was detained. Three times he went to court. The first time was March 2000. He had to sign each week and they kept him at the police station. He was told to step through a door and then they told him they were detaining him. He was taken to Tinsley House near Gatwick Airport. I was afraid to go to see him in case I was also detained. A local Catholic charity helped. They had to push the solicitor to ask for bail. In the end the local priest got him out on bail. It was £2000 and put up by the church. My husband's solicitor had not done his work properly and my husband was detained again. Two weeks later he was taken to court again then freed for a few months. Last year he was detained again at Forest Gate Police station and taken again to Tinsley House. I received a letter from the Home Office saying I was to report on a Thursday and the whole family would be deported. A Downside monk managed to get my husband released on health grounds. The Home Office came to visit him and they phoned a local Roman Catholic sister who insisted they arrange for him to see a psychiatrist. The solicitor took it to the High Court and the case was thrown out. They were acting against human rights. Now I have to sign in every month at London Bridge. For eight months we had had to sign every week. My husband was healthy his first three years here but hasn't been well since then and especially during the last year. He suffered torture in his own country and had all his teeth pulled out.'

When the authors tried to interview the family again a year later in July 2004 the husband was so seriously ill that his wife, although wishing to be interviewed, was not able to do so. They had been granted the Amnesty earlier in the year but it had come too late and his health continued to deteriorate.

Another respondent stated: 'I have received a letter from the Home Office. I have to sign every month at London Bridge. I have heard nothing as yet about my status.' A young woman told us: 'My case was closed two weeks ago. At present I'm awaiting deportation. I am very scared to stay at home in case the police come for me so I stay outside as much as possible.'

And another:

> 'On arrival I learnt that I had to apply for asylum. I went to the solicitors on 30 April 2001. After my marriage I had to go again and take the form to the Home Office. I'm still awaiting (June 2003) a reply from the Home Office. I have to go to London Bridge every month to sign.'

A family had this distressing experience to share with the authors:

> 'This week the Home Office has granted us temporary leave but we have to go back in a week to collect an asylum seeker's card. As we never received any papers we have to restart our claim for asylum from the beginning.'

Many had similar experiences to relate:

> 'I received a refusal on 21 November 2002. Now I am applying independently from my husband. I have put in a separate appeal just for myself.'

Another lady told us:

> 'I received a negative from the Home Office. Then I went to court. The court said that they would write to the Home Office giving their support. I am still waiting.'

In June 2004 a respondent told Sister Anne:

> 'At present we have Exceptional Leave to Remain for two years but it runs out at the end of next month. I'm very anxious as we no longer have a solicitor. Our last solicitor couldn't take us any longer as he was only allowed to do five hours with legal aid (paid by State). I need a solicitor to help us appeal for an extension to our leave and we have a lot of paperwork to go through and present twenty-eight days before our Exceptional Leave runs out.'

Shortly after this conversation she received news that the Brentwood Roman Catholic Diocesan Refugee Support worker had found her a solicitor.

5.2. SUPPORT OFFERED BY FAITH COMMUNITIES

All respondents immediately took the question 'Has the Christian community/your faith group helped you to settle here?' to mean the Catholic Church, possibly because the majority of respondents were contacted through a link with the Roman Catholic Church. So perhaps it is not surprising that many, both Catholics and Muslims, said that they had received great support from the Church.

As one lady said: 'The Church helped us to place our son in a Catholic School and helped us with language lessons, food and when we were evicted from our home in 2000 found us suitable rented accommodation.'

Twenty-three people cited being offered 'friendship' while eighteen said that they had received 'spiritual support' from the Catholic Church. Many of the Roman Catholics had been unable to practise their religion in Kosovo and although they thought of themselves as Catholics and were a deeply religious people, they had received little Catholic instruction and many arrived in the UK without ever being baptized. They were delighted to find that they could practise here without retribution. Consequently the Roman Catholic Church found itself instructing many in their faith and administering the sacraments of Baptism, Confirmation and Holy Communion.

Fourteen said that the Church had helped them place their children in school. Only eight of the fifty respondents stated that they had not taken help from the Church or had no comment to make. Interestingly only one respondent said that she had received help from the Muslims: 'Muslims have helped and also the Catholic Church.' Perhaps that was because the authors interviewed only people who were in contact through Church organisations and hadn't interviewed anyone through a Muslim organisation. However the majority interviewed who declared they were Muslim appeared to have received no help from any Islamic organisation. One Muslim said: 'I have never been to a mosque here, so I don't know how to get in touch.' Another Muslim told us: 'We do not have any contact with any Muslim community in London,' while another said: 'I have no contact with Muslims. The Church helped me with clothes and anything else I needed.'

Table 5.2 Support offered by Christian community/Faith groups

	Spiritual support	Friendship	Work	Correspondence with authorities
Number of families	18	23	3	8
	Placing your child in school	Advice	Money	Food
Number of families	14	8	2	3
	Clothes/ furniture	Other	No help taken/no comment	No contact with Muslims
Number of families	2	7	8	8

Source: Kosovan Families Survey 2003-04

5.3. TREATMENT RECEIVED FROM OTHER PEOPLE IN LONDON

When asked how other people in London had treated them, when they first arrived almost eighty percent said they had either been 'welcomed as friends' (31) or were treated 'okay' (7). One said: 'I was lost. People felt sorry for me. I couldn't communicate.' Nine complained that they had been ignored as strangers, while one had actually felt unwelcome. A Catholic, she said: 'When looking for housing, I received religious discrimination and was asked: "Are you a Muslim?" before a landlord offered me housing.' Another respondent felt she wasn't trusted: 'I didn't feel trusted.' Only one stated that she had not been treated well: 'I had my window broken.' No one said they felt that they had been treated as terrorists or as scroungers.

5.4. NECESSITY OF ENGLISH LESSONS AND EASE OF ACCESS

With the exception of one respondent every other person needed English lessons. Nearly half the group (23) found it difficult to access English lessons. Those who were not attending classes at the time of the interview gave a variety of reasons. One lady in her early fifties stated: I feel I am too old to learn English.' A more common problem was illness or unspecified problems as one respondent said: 'I am very sick and unable to attend lessons.' Another said: 'No, I don't attend lessons. I want to sort out a few problems first.'

Many of the women expressed a desire to learn English but lack of available childcare came high on the list of difficulties. One man said: 'My wife went two days a week when we arrived here but since our baby arrived it hasn't been possible for her to attend. I feel unable to take lessons.' A lady stated: 'No, I'm not attending English lessons at present. It is difficult with a young child and pregnant.' Another said: 'It's not easy to attend lessons because I have to look after my child.' Another lady has a handicapped child aged four who needs her presence twenty-four hours a day. She was desperate to learn English and asked the interviewer if there was anyone who could teach her in her home.

In Table 5.3 we see that twenty-nine respondents were attending English lessons in the spring of 2003, nineteen attending at least three times a week. No one attended only once a week. Almost half (14) of the group of twenty-nine were taken by a friend to English lessons. One lady expressed the opinion of many when she said: 'The Form to apply for English lessons could not be completed by a non-English speaker.' Another lady on arriving with her daughter in the UK said: 'I was very sick for the first three years after I arrived here. My daughter encouraged me to get out and helped me to find English lessons.'

Table 5.3 Acquiring English classes and attendance at lessons

I was helped by:	Number of sessions a week					
	Twice	Three	Four	Five	N/a	Not attending
A friend	3	7	4			2
Child's school		1				
The Church	1					1
A relative		1	1	1		4
Advertisement			1	1		1
Social Services						1
Not declared	1	1	1			4
N/a					3	8
Total	5	10	7	2	3	21

Source: Kosovan Families Survey 2003-04

5.5. EASE OF ACCESS FOR CHILDREN TO LOCAL SCHOOLS

While twenty-six families had found it very easy or fairly easy to place their children in school and eight of the respondents' children were too young to require school when the family arrived in the UK, there were still fourteen families who found it difficult or very difficult. One respondent said: 'When our daughters started school, we had been in the country over five months.' A second respondent said that they were here three months before they could get the children into a school. One respondent stated: 'We had to wait three months. We tried schools in Ilford and Stratford.' Another respondent had had to wait six to seven months for a place. A respondent said: 'It was difficult to get our oldest son into school but since then everything has been fine.' In another family the mother said: 'It took about six months to get into a school, because of temporary accommodation. Eventually our son looked for schools on the internet and found a school himself - St. Bonaventures.'

Table 5.4 Ease of access for children to local schools

	Very easy	Fairly easy	Difficult	Very difficult	N/A	No comment
Number of respondents	12	14	12	2	8	2

Source: Kosovan Families Survey 2003-04

Some parents were more fortunate as one said: 'We had to wait a few days for a place in a Catholic school, meanwhile the children were placed in a local state school.' One Catholic family were dismayed to discover they had to prove they were Catholic before their child was given a place in a Catholic school. As the parent stated: 'It is very difficult when you have no documentation.'

5.6. ACCOMMODATION

5.6.1. INITIAL ACCOMMODATION IN UK

For many asylum seekers accommodation was a major problem on arrival in the UK. One family spent their first night in England sleeping in a park and then three days in a hotel before they were given accommodation. Another family told us that they had spent six months in a hotel in Dover. A family of four, although initially fortunate because they were invited to stay for three nights by a Kosovan family – who heard them talking on the street in Ilford to the children and recognised their language, were less fortunate once they approached the authorities. They had to spend their first eight months in the UK in one room in a hotel.

One respondent stated:

> 'For ten months I stayed with friends without money. I spent two years in Forest Gate and one year in Plaistow.' Another respondent told us: 'We spent two weeks in a hotel for homeless people in Liverpool and then social services gave us a flat. We stayed there for two years and then came to London to stay with a cousin who was sick. He has since been sent back to Kosovo.'

Another lady told the authors:

> 'We spent eight hours at a detention centre. They questioned my husband for seven hours and myself for two hours on my own. After that we received our IND and were allowed to go to London that afternoon at four o'clock. We stayed one night with friends.'

Yet another respondent said:

> 'When we first arrived in England we were placed in a one bedroom flat. There were five of us – my son, husband, my sister, brother-in-law, and I. There was just one bed. Three of us slept in the bed and two on the floor.'

Another respondent related her experience to Sr. Anne:

> 'We arrived in England one day in January at one o'clock in the morning. A friend had a brother in London who was meant to meet us. We waited at Brixton Station in south London but the man never came. We had no money. We went to the police station and talked using our hands but the

Police sent us away. No one helped us. We were crying. A sixteen year old boy took us to a house and gave us one room but no food. There was no heating. In the morning the landlady came and told us we must leave. She said, "Get out. It's my home!" We went back to the Home Office and were sent to Aldgate in East London. We phoned 999 and the police took us to overnight accommodation. There was one single bed with not even a sheet for the three of us and we stayed a week. We looked for church people who gave us food but wouldn't let us sleep in the church. For seven days in January we slept anywhere we could, at the station, in the underground, on a church bench. Each day we went to social services in Hackney. Eventually we were housed in Plaistow.'

The dispersal scheme set up by NASS to try to ease the stress suffered by local authorities in the London area by placing asylum seekers in other parts of the UK, caused great anxiety for the asylum seekers who naturally wanted to stay close to other people of the same ethnic group. One lady told us of her distress when NASS wanted to send her from London to accommodation in Glasgow:

'I was afraid to go. If I wanted to stay in London they said they would have to place us in another hotel with no benefits. My daughter had become sick in the hotel as she could not eat the food so my cousin helped to pay for me to supplement NASS and live in a house with him.'

5.6.2. INFORMATION REGARDING ACCOMMODATION

Moya Hamilton, a social worker in East London, spoke to the authors about accommodation in Newham. She said that traditionally the East End of London had always been an area where immigrants came to live. Newham was quite a cheap place for housing so many other boroughs (Westminster, Chelsea, Kensington, Haringey) placed people in Newham. The richer boroughs like Westminster placed all the families they had responsibility for in other boroughs such as Newham because it was cheaper to house them there. She went onto say: 'Newham is a very generous borough that welcomes people from other boroughs. That's why there is such a diverse mix of people here.' Ms Hamilton explained that fifteen to twenty years ago there was much more social housing in England but because it was sold off by the Conservative Government there was far less social housing available in 2003. People arriving in the country were usually placed in privately leased accommodation by the borough but in latter years more and more refugees and asylum seekers had had to find the accommodation themselves.

According to Elane Heffernan, a Refugee Resettlement Worker in East London:

> 'It was part of the Government policy to cap housing benefit at a level that was deemed to be a reasonable market rent. However, in reality the rents charged were far higher, and landlords tended not to push rents down to the reasonable market rent set by the rent officers, but upwards to the maximum they could gain from people desperate to remain in the area, so that asylum seeking and refugee families were forced to pay anything between £10 and £120 above the rent paid in benefits. Landlords were more likely to ask for and receive a higher proportion of the "top up" than could be obtained from UK citizens. The burden on asylum seeking families, who receive less actual income than other recipients of welfare benefits, caused families enormous problems. Government policy at the end of the twentieth century encouraged tenants to buy their council houses and therefore there has been less social housing each year, creating a real housing crisis in London' (Heffernan 2004).

5.6.3. PRESENT ACCOMMODATION

In Table 5.6 we can see that while a staggering thirty respondents had been in the present accommodation less than three years, nine of those had had to move house within the last six months. Only six respondents had been in the same home for five to six years. When we consider the remarks of the respondents regarding the state of their accommodation we must bear in mind that while some were basing their evaluation on their comparison of housing in Kosovo (which is considerably poorer than in the UK) and seeing the accommodation here as at least adequate if not good or very good, others were basing their judgement on the type of housing they would aspire to, with twelve stating that their accommodation was either fair or poor.

Elane Heffernan described the condition of housing in Newham. She told the authors that although most of the housing looked fine from the outside, 'inside it won't be fit to live in, with walls running with mould and windows not fitting properly. There is a real contrast between inside and outside.' She explained:

> 'When people went to complain about the state of their accommodation, often to local councils or NASS who have no staff in the borough, or asked for help they received little understanding as the advisers had not actually seen the housing and were unaware of the bad condition of the property. Even where properties were seen and the conditions were understood there was often no alternative accommodation on offer and little chance of being re-housed by the Homeless Persons Unit because if a large number of

properties are unfit for human habitation in the area, the standard at which action must be taken to re-house people is lower than in areas with good quality housing.'

Table 5.5 Length of time in and condition of present accommodation

Description of home	Less than 6 months	6 months to less than one year	1-2 years	3- 4 years	5-6 years
		Time in Present Home			
Excellent	1				
Very good	4	1	3	1	1
Good	2	4	4	3	3
Adequate			3	6	2
Fair	1		5		
Poor	1		1	4	

Source: Kosovan Families Survey 2003-04

When asked how they found their present accommodation twenty-seven respondents said that they found it either good (16), very good (10) or excellent (1). Eleven stated that it was adequate, six said it was fair and six described it as poor. Among those who thought their accommodation was good we heard the comment: 'Children like the garden. The house is in good condition.' Other respondents were far from content. The following comments were expressed among many: 'The bathroom is very poor. Water from the shower goes through to the kitchen.' Another stated: 'We have a very small kitchen with no window. It is difficult to cook as I have asthma.' And a third: 'It was empty with no furniture and needed cleaning.' Another respondent sadly told us: 'We are waiting for permanent accommodation. We spent four years in Tower Hamlets before we moved here. The move upset my son very much – he doesn't smile now.' Yet another: 'We live in emergency accommodation with another family who are from Iran.'

Although thirty-eight respondents appeared reasonably content with their accommodation, in reality accommodation has proved to be a major problem for the asylum seekers even after they have been granted Refugee Status or Indefinite Leave to Remain after the Amnesty. A respondent told us that their rent is £205 a week. They receive £140 in benefits. Their present landlord is evicting them because they wanted to return to Liverpool and because they told him that they had found alternative accommodation, he found new tenants, but their new accommodation in Liverpool has fallen through so they are now homeless. A third respondent told us that they have to move shortly as their landlord wants to sell the property. The asylum team will help them to find housing near the children's schools. Another respondent said: 'We have to share the bathroom, kitchen and living room. It is dirty. I'm afraid my baby son will catch something. He wants to touch everything.'

Figure 5.1 Length of time in and condition of present accommodation

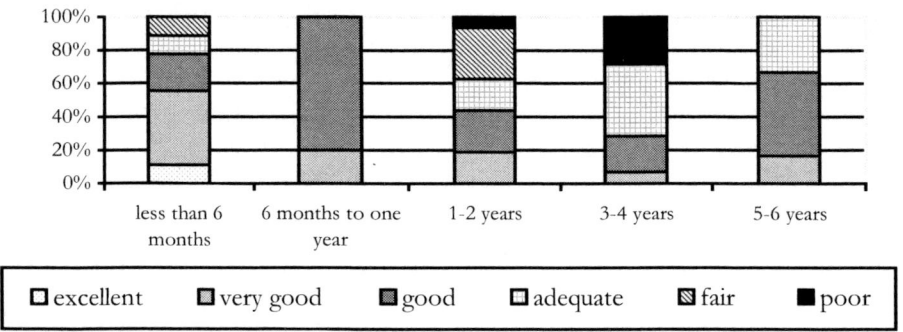

Source: Kosovan Families Survey 2003

While many have described their accommodation as good they have also been tolerant of many problems a family born here would not tolerate. For example: One couple with three children under six years old, were living during 2004 in a flat for a single person. Discovering that they had been without hot water for a month, Sr. Anne persuaded the landlady to take immediate action and within twelve hours she had installed a new boiler. A few months after moving into the flat the ceiling in their hallway collapsed on top of their two year old daughter who suffered cuts on her face plus a headache for days. The landlady, instead of looking into the cause of the collapse, asked the man in the upstairs flat to plaster over the ceiling and hide the damage. Whenever it rains, they have water flooding through the flat roof by their bathroom and they are infested with cockroaches and mice. An Environmental Health officer came to inspect and declared their home unfit to live in and a health and safety risk. In December 2004 they were told that they would be re-housed. At first nothing happened. Eventually the landlady agreed to make major repairs to the property. The family visited the Homeless Centre on 25 February 2005 with a letter of eviction from their landlady, saying that they had to vacate the house within three weeks. They had to wait to be placed in emergency accommodation until they could be re-housed. Over the following four months they were placed in three different temporary houses, the first one in the borough of Tower Hamlets, then in the borough of Barking and Dagenham where they managed to get their five year old son back into school. He had not been in school since they left Manor Park in the borough of Newham. In mid

June 2005 they were moved once again this time back into Newham. Once more the family had to try to find their son a school and their daughter aged three a nursery place. On making enquiries they were told that all the local schools were full and they would have to continue taking him to Dagenham until there was a vacancy.

5.6.4. NUMBER OF ROOMS FOR SOLE USE BY FAMILY

Each respondent was asked how many rooms (including the kitchen and bathroom) their present accommodation had for their family's sole use.

Table 5.5.1 Number in family compared to number of rooms in present accommodation

Number in family	1 room	2 rooms	3 rooms	4 rooms	5 rooms	6 rooms	7 rooms
2	1		2	2			
3		1		7	3		
4				3	9	6	1
5		2	1	1	7	3	1
6							1
Total	1	3	3	12	19	9	3

Source: Kosovan Families Survey 2003-04

There appeared to be little logic in the allocation of housing, with a family of four having seven rooms while another family of four had just four rooms. Two families of five had only two rooms each, while nine families of four had five rooms each and six families of four had six rooms each.

5.6.5. TYPE OF ACCOMMODATION

The majority (21) of the families interviewed were living in accommodation rented from housing associations.

Table 5.5.2 Type of accommodation and number of rooms for sole use by family

	1 room	2 rooms	3 rooms	4 rooms	5 rooms	6 /7 rooms
B & B		1		1		
Council			2	2	1	2
Private rented				6	8	4
Housing Association		1	1	3	11	5
Total number	1	2	1	12	20	11

Source: Kosovan Families Survey 2003-04

Eighteen families were living in privately rented accommodation; seven families were in either a council house or flat; two families were in a bed and breakfast hotel and one family was staying in emergency accommodation.

5.6.6. TIME SPENT LIVING IN HOTEL ACCOMMODATION

Many families spent time living in hotels or Bed and Breakfast (B&B). Some were actually placed in one hotel and then moved to another or even to a B&B. Two respondents were living in B&B's in the autumn of 2004. One had been in a B&B for four years and had lived in a hotel for a year before that. She hadn't lived anywhere else in the five years she had lived in England. In total thirty-five respondents were accommodated in hotels/B&B's and four of those spent time in more than one establishment. Only one respondent felt able to describe her hotel accommodation as excellent, while seven said their hotel accommodation had been good. The majority (15) described their hotel as poor. Seven had had to stay in a poor hotel for at least five weeks and eight had been in very poor hotels for six months to a year.

Table 5.5.3 Time spent living in hotel accommodation

Time	Excellent hotel	Good hotel	Poor hotel	Bed & Breakfast
Less than a week			1	2
1-2 weeks		1	5	4
3-4 weeks		2	1	1
5-10 weeks	1		4	4
6-8 months		2	2	
1 year		2	2	1
Over 1 year				1

Source: Kosovan Families Survey 2003-04

Thirteen respondents had stayed in B&B accommodation. The respondents were not asked to evaluate their B&B accommodation but Sr. Anne did visit a family of three - a husband and wife who were both ill and living with their sixteen year old son who was sitting his GCSE's. On being granted Refugee Status they had been told to leave their NASS accommodation and had been put into emergency accommodation for almost six weeks in one room in a B&B hotel in Ilford, Essex. It was dingy and dirty. Their room was a double room with a single bed also squeezed in. They hardly had room to turn around. There was a wardrobe and a chest of drawers. The bedding was stained and looked filthy. Breakfast was provided but they had to fend for themselves for all other meals. They had to eat out which was very expensive and difficult when they were also having problems obtaining benefits and having to rely on friends to lend them money. Another lady told us: 'I was sent to social services and I was given accommodation in a hotel for one year with my husband and son.'

Elane Heffernan told the authors that the bed and breakfast system could be psychologically damaging and that the temporary accommodation system, emergency accommodation or the choice of getting a deposit and then paying a top up could all be quite difficult for people to cope with.

5.6.7. NUMBER OF PROPERTIES LIVED IN SINCE ARRIVAL IN UK

When asked: 'How many flats/houses/hotels have you lived in since you arrived here?' some respondents did not include the first property they were placed in, the time they stayed with friends or in a hotel or B&B. Consequently the number in the chart below (Figure 5.2) is a little misleading.

For example a respondent who had stated on the questionnaire that her family had lived in three properties had actually lived in five properties and in 2004 they were about to move again as their present home had been declared a risk for health and safety. Twenty-three respondents said that they had lived in two properties; twenty-one in three properties; three respondents had lived in four properties and two respondents stated that they had lived in five properties.

Figure 5.2 Number of properties lived in since arrival in the UK

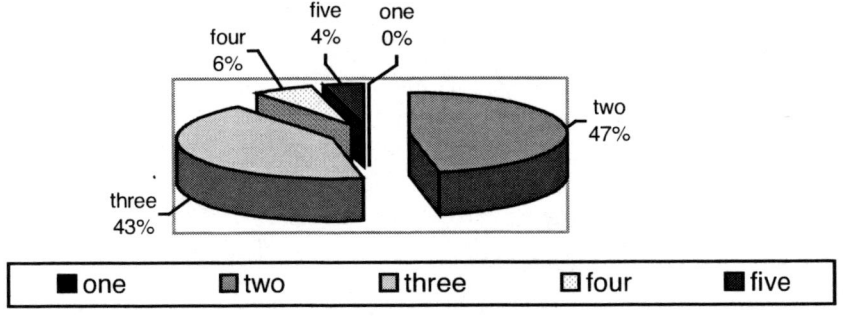

Source: Kosovan Families Survey 2003-04

5.6.8. ACCOMMODATION AFTER AMNESTY

Accommodation problems continued after status had been granted. Elane Heffernan explained that asylum seekers were tied into one of three or four different systems of support according to when they arrived in the UK. Therefore some peoples' houses were tied to a particular type of asylum support. After six years some people were still in NASS emergency accommodation, even though initially they had been placed there for only one week. As soon as they received the Amnesty they lost their house. Asylum seekers accommodated by social services asylum teams under interim provision, also often lost their accommodation on receiving status or the Amnesty. Each local authority had a different way of dealing with the people coming out of the Amnesty or into status. Newham tried to keep most families in the same houses and just switch them from one system to another as they were already paying top-up fees. Westminster would often simply leave people where they were and keep on paying the fees and let the people go onto the waiting list, while other boroughs required people with status to move out of their accommodation because it was expensive and social services had been paying the rent and getting the money back from central government. With status the families moved to a different system of support. The Housing Benefit system paid the rent instead of central Government. People were not always moved but it created some anxiety for the families. According to Ms Heffernan:

> 'The grant of permanent status can be experienced as stressful and disruptive because a person could be moving from a house, albeit not a good standard house, into a bed and breakfast hotel which is a step backwards for people in terms of their ability to resettle.'

Many families who lost their housing were eligible for housing but needed to be re housed though the Homeless Persons Unit that could require a move to another area. Often people preferred to stay in the area they had lived in for the last five or six years and wanted to apply to Newham for housing.

People did not understand the difference between getting Refugee Status or Amnesty. It was quite complicated. With Amnesty people could not just apply wherever they liked. If they were placed by NASS or by a local authority in an area not of their choice, then they could argue that they had a local connection in another area where their relations lived and they might be moved to that area. However if they came voluntarily to Newham, which a lot of the interim families did, they were not entitled to choose to live elsewhere.

Ms Heffernan said that a large number of people receiving the Amnesty thought it would be an end to their difficulties and that they would be allowed to participate fully and equally. She said:

> 'They got a shock when it did not happen. They had not realised that the level of racism was high and they were not the only people surviving on little money in poor housing. They had thought that as asylum seekers they were more excluded than other people so it came as a shock to them to find that

British people also did not get their full rent paid and that families could live in bed and breakfast for a time.'

The reality of housing in East London for everyone is not good until a person can get a council house or a decent job that allows him to get a morgage. As Ms Heffernan explained:

'It's getting worse for everybody and the unfortunate thing is that refugees and asylum seekers arrived in quite big numbers at exactly the same time as the housing crisis was impacting so on the surface many people thought that it was the fault of the asylum seekers whereas they were in fact moving in to the area because it has cheap housing of such a low standard that many citizens will not accept it.'

Ms Heffernan explained how the stress created psychological problems which made it harder for people to cope and deal with even quite minor problems. She told the authors that the asylum seekers' years as asylum seekers created a culture that lowered their confidence. As asylum seekers they were:

'never allowed to have a say, to discuss what was happening. They were told you go there and you do this and we do it for you. Four or five years later, how do you do it for yourself? It's a real problem. It's precisely destroying the kind of citizenship that the Government are saying is what they want to produce through the asylum system. It's a complete contradiction.'

5.7. BENEFITS

5.7.1. BENEFITS FOR FAMILIES WITH STATUS

According to Ms Heffernan the benefits were worked out on a very complicated system that meant the amount given is dependent not only on status, but family circumstances that could appear to be the same but be perceived differently. If a person received Refugee Status or the Amnesty he received the same benefits as any UK citizen but if he received Refugee Status in 2004 that person still had the right to back-dated benefits. If a person was granted the Amnesty that person was no longer entitled to back-dated benefits and that could be a considerable amount of money, as much as £7,000. Ms Heffernan explained: 'That would be enough to give a family the opportunity to settle and get on with their life.' It showed how little each asylum family had been paid during their time in the UK. Ms Heffernan said that she knew one lady with a child who received a back payment of £12,000. In spite of possible back payments, she said that to receive the Amnesty definitely had advantages to receiving other forms of status. With the letter granting Amnesty a person received their National Insurance Number and links between the Department of Work and Pensions (DWP) meant a seamless transfer to benefits. However with other forms of status such as ELR a person received no money at all until the new benefits had been sorted out which could take weeks if the person did not understand the letter or if something went wrong.

Nine of the families (Table 5.6) who had permission to stay in the UK shared with the authors the amount they received from mainstream benefits in 2004. Those deemed fit to work and actively seeking work or training in order to work were on Job Seekers Allowance while those who were unable to work were on Income Support. Due to their low incomes they were all entitled to free prescriptions plus free school meals for their children. Two of the families included in Table 5.7, even after receiving status were without benefits for a time. A couple with a little girl aged three, with Refugee Status, told us that they receive £88 a week Housing Benefit, £15.75 a week Child Benefit and £150 Income Support. Another respondent who also has Refugee Status, with two children under eleven, told us that they get £26.80 a week Child Benefit and £68.64 Working Tax Credit.

Table 5.6 Benefits for families with status

Family's Status	Number of children under 16	Support received	Amount a week	Housing Benefit a week	Child Benefit a week	Child Tax Credit
Amnesty	4	Job Seekers	£234.48	yes	£50	?
Exceptional leave	2	Job Seekers	£151	yes	yes	?
Amnesty	2	Job Seekers	£151	yes	yes	?
Humanitarian Protection	2	Income Support	£97	£110	£26	?
Discretionary Leave	2	Income Support	£97	£160	£16	?
Refugee	2	Job Seekers	£85	yes	£15	
Refugee	3	Income Support	£119	£90	£37.50	£93
Refugee	1	Income Support	£150	£88	£15.75	
Refugee	2	Working Tax Credit	£68.64	?	£26.80	

Source: Kosovan Families Survey 2003-04

5.7.2. BENEFITS FOR ASYLUM SEEKERS AWAITING DECISION OF HOME OFFICE

Thirteen families still awaiting status in 2004 talked about their financial support. They were mainly supported by NASS or Social Services as we can see in Table 5.6.1. All those families were receiving free prescriptions and free school meals for their children.

NASS and the various local authorities provide different amounts of support for families. A family with two children over 18, who were still awaiting a decision from the Home Office told us that they received £130 a week Job Seekers Allowance, Housing Benefit plus free prescriptions. A lady with two children under ten, stated: 'I receive support from NASS of over £150 a week. We also receive free accommodation, school meals and prescriptions.' Another respondent told us that although her child received free school meals she had not received any kind of financial support for the last year. Asylum seekers receive a fraction of mainstream benefits.

Table 5.6.1 Benefits for asylum seekers

Number of children under 16	Support from Social Services / NASS	Child Benefit (amount per week)	Have you ever been without benefits?
4	£120	£37.50	8 months for new baby
3	£127	£31	1 month
3	£147	yes	no
3	£147	£26.50	no
3	£148	yes	2 months and 3 months
3	£156	?	no
3	£170	?	no
3	£138	yes	3 months for new baby
2	£121	yes	no
2	£117	?	no
2	£97	?	no
2	£112	yes	6 months for new baby
1	£108	yes	no

Source: Kosovan Families Survey 2003-04

Some of the respondents elaborated for us a little on the state support they were receiving. Many families have also had problems receiving their benefits and have gone for weeks or even months without any money. One family told us that they were in Ilford for two weeks and then placed in rented accommodation in Manor Park. Shortly afterwards they were moved to another house and then after approximately one year they were evicted by their landlord because their Housing Benefit hadn't been paid for months due to the disorder and consequent backlog that had built up in the Main Benefits Office. They moved to a privately rented flat over a shop, with most of the rent being paid by the State in the form of Housing Benefit.

5.8. IMMIGRATION SOLICITORS

5.8.1. QUALITY OF ADVICE GIVEN BY IMMIGRATION SOLICITORS

The respondents were asked if they had an immigration solicitor and if so how many solicitors they had had and how they would rate the quality of their advice. They were all very vocal in their responses. Only one respondent, who entered the country legally, had not required an immigration solicitor. Table 5.7 shows us that one respondent had had a staggering ten solicitors! Half of the respondents (25) had had only one solicitor, with eighteen claiming that their solicitor was either good or very good. Four said that their solicitor was adequate and three actually declared that their solicitor was "useless." It appeared that they either did not know how to change to another solicitor or were afraid to do so in case it jeopardized their case. Although it perhaps sounds promising that so many had stayed with one solicitor it is extremely worrying that half of the group have actually had more than one solicitor. Fifteen respondents had had two solicitors, of whom eight had been declared useless, four poor and two only fair. Two respondents had received no verdict from their solicitors as they had recently changed solicitors and were unable to assess their abilities. Three solicitors were declared very good and six good, while five were judged to be adequate. Nine respondents had seen three or more solicitors. Four of those had seen three solicitors each, two of whom were judged very good, one adequate, one fair, three poor and five useless. Three respondents had taken their immigration cases to four solicitors each. One was declared very good, four good, three poor and four useless.

One man told us: 'We have had three solicitors and they have all been useless.' One lady who said that she had had four solicitors and they had all been good, explained that the reason she had had so many was because she had lived for one year in Birmingham. One respondent had actually seen five solicitors. Her present one she considered 'good' but two she declared were 'useless' and two were 'poor'. The respondent who had actually seen an incredible ten different immigration solicitors commented on only four of them declaring one to be 'adequate', two 'poor' and one 'useless'.

A few respondents shared with us why they felt that their solicitor was either poor or useless. One family had applied for asylum but after one year they were refused. They applied again and the authorities sent them to court. In January 2002 the judge gave them Exceptional Leave to Remain in England outside of immigration laws for a long time but the Home Office would not accept the judge's decision. They had asked to remain for five years but unfortunately the solicitor had made the wrong application, asking for permission for them to remain forever. Two months later they met the MP for Newham. He phoned the Home Office and they were told that they would not be sent back to Kosovo because their case was strong for Refugee Status. At the time of the interview they were waiting for an application form from the High Court for Human Rights. The family was granted Indefinite Leave to Remain in March 2004 under the Amnesty.

Table 5.7 Number of solicitors per respondent and quality of advice received

	Total number of respondents							
	1	25	15	4	3	1	1	
	Total number of solicitors per respondent							
Advice given by Immigration Solicitors	None	One	Two	Three	Four	Five	Ten	Total
Very good		6	3	2	1			12
Good		12	6		4	1		23
Adequate		4	5	1			1	11
Fair			2	1				3
Poor			4	3	3	2	2	14
Useless		3	8	5	4	2	1	23
No verdict			2				6	8
N/a	1							0
Total number of solicitors seen		25	30	12	12	5	10	94

Source: Kosovan Families Survey 2003-04

Other comments the authors heard about immigration solicitors included: 'The first immigration solicitor was hopeless and his advice was very poor.' And another: 'He was only interested in money,' while another said: 'Our first solicitor was useless. He showed no interest. I received a negative but he didn't tell me.' Another respondent, explaining their problems as a family, stated: 'We were sent a letter to attend the solicitors in November but the letter did not arrive until March so we had missed our appointment by four months.' One lady said: 'I had different problems with each solicitor I saw. I want to forget. Different people, different minds.' Another respondent told the authors that she had paid a solicitor to help. He had taken her money and then abandoned her. She said: 'The solicitor was useless. The solicitor asked for £350 for court but he gave me no receipt. He closed my documents without the court. We never saw the court. I was pregnant. We went to another solicitor who put our two documents together.'

Figure 5.3 Quality of advice given by solicitors

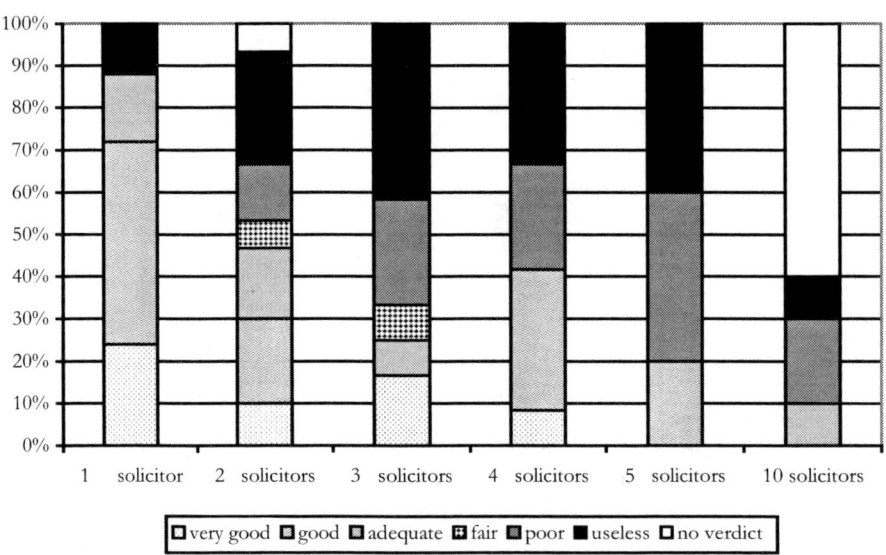

Source: Kosovan Families Survey 2003-04

The respondents had seen a total of ninety-four immigration solicitors between them of whom thirty-five were pronounced either 'good' or 'very good.' Fourteen were declared 'adequate' or 'fair', and thirty-seven were judged to be either 'useless' or 'poor'. We must remember that many of the respondents' partners actually had different solicitors to their wives because if they received a negative from the Home Office on appeal they were often advised to place separate claims for asylum. We made no attempt to evaluate the number of solicitors seen by the respondents' partners.

5.8.2. HOW RESPONDENTS OBTAINED THEIR SOLICITORS.

In Table 5.7.1 we see that eighteen of the respondents had found at least one of their solicitors through a friend and sixteen through a relative. That may seem surprising considering how few people came to join relatives in the UK and few had relatives who joined them. However, when we asked about relatives joining the respondents in the UK we had concentrated on immediate family who actually came to live with them or close to them. The Kosovans/Albanians have large extended families, and some of those have also found their way to England but live in other parts of London or the UK and have only a tenuous link with the respondents. It is members of these extended families whom the respondents were referring to. Seven people were advised on solicitors by neighbours, four by refugee charities or a church, four by Social Services, three through the Home Office and two through the Refugee Council, while two consulted an interpreter and three quite simply found a solicitor themselves by looking for a sign on the street. Some respondents did not explain how they found some of their solicitors so twelve cannot be accounted for.

Table 5.7.1 How respondents obtained their solicitors

Found a solicitor through	A relative	A refugee charity/ church	Social Services	Home Office	Refugee Council
Number of respondents	16	4	4	3	2
Found a solicitor through	A friend	An interpreter	Neighbour	Saw a sign	Not stated
Number of respondents	18	2	7	3	12

Source: Kosovan Families Survey 2003-04

The majority of the respondents (47) had had no housing solicitor. Only three had had a housing solicitor at some time since their arrival in the UK. The three who had housing solicitors had experienced more than usual problems with their landlords.

CHAPTER SIX
WELL-BEING AND INTEGRATION

In this chapter we analyse the following questions: How often did the respondents meet people from their own country? What contact did they have with their own country? Would they like to return home to live? What prevented them from returning home? How did their family live five years ago in their own country compared with how they lived now? Did they think that in the next year they would live better than today, or worse? What did they like about England? What didn't they like about England? What had been their greatest problem in the UK? How long was it before they found medical care? Had they or any of their family had any health problems since they came to the UK? Would they list their health problems? What were they most afraid of in life? Had they permission to stay in England indefinitely? Had they a National Insurance Number? Had their partner a National Insurance Number? Had they permission to work? Had they got a job at present? Had their partner a job? Was the job legal/illegal, full time/part time? What kind of job would they like? Were they in contact with any asylum seekers or refugee State/voluntary or Christian groups? What could they suggest regarding an immigration policy? What did they think the Church/Faith groups could do to help immigrants?

6.1. LINKS WITH HOME COUNTRY AND FUTURE INTENTIONS

6.1.1. CONTACT WITH PEOPLE FROM THE SAME ETHNIC GROUP IN THE UK

Two thirds of the respondents (29) said that they met with people from their own country if not every day at least a few times a week; thirteen met others less frequently and three had no contact at all. Of those who had no contact two had no contact by choice while a man, from Montenegro, said that his family were aware that there were other people here from Montenegro but had never met anyone apart from their interpreter who was a distant relative to them.

Table 6.1 shows how often the respondents meet with people from their own country. Only three people said that they had no contact. Thirty-three stated that they met people from their own country. Fifteen met every day while eighteen met a few times a week. Fourteen said that they met but less frequently with six meeting every week, five once a month, and three now and again. Many met through the NGO Support Centres and programmes referred to in Chapter Three. Many of the Kosovans and Albanians had joined groups where their children could receive tuition in their own culture, Albanian language and dancing which they gladly displayed for their new English friends at every opportunity.

Here we see a group of young Kosovan dancers performing during Refugee Week 2004 in Little Ilford School, Manor Park, East London.

© Anne Wells

Table 6.1 Contact with people from the same ethnic group in the UK

I meet people from my own country	Every day	A few times a week	Every week	Once a month	Now and again	No contact
Respondents	15	18	6	5	3	3

Source: Kosovan Families Survey 2003-04

6.1.2. CONTACT WITH OWN COUNTRY, DESIRE TO RETURN TO HOME COUNTRY AND REASONS GIVEN

When asked how much contact the respondents had with their own family in Kosovo (Table 6.1.1), thirty-five said that they had some contact, mainly by phone. Fifteen stated that they had no contact with their own country. One respondent said: 'My family never write. My mum didn't like my marriage. I left home without permission. I was twenty-three.' Another respondent, whose husband had been deported, explained the difficulties and distress experienced when the only contact was by phone. She told us that she had spoken to her mother recently but her mum didn't know where her husband was. She feared that he had had to go into hiding after returning to Kosovo but had no way of knowing if he was all right.

Table 6.1.1 Contact with own country

I have no contact with my own country	I have contact with my own country	I have contact		
		By Letter	By Phone	Through relatives and friends
15	35	5	31	3

Source: Kosovan Families Survey 2003-04

Only four people expressed any desire to return to their own country to live. One lady explained that she wanted to go home because she missed her family but she couldn't return because it was still unsafe in her area, Mitrovica. Forty-six people had no desire to return to Kosovo to live.

Table 6.1.2 Desire to return to home country and reasons given

Reasons I want to return home				
Miss family	Miss friends	Homesick	Prefer home culture	Prefer home climate
4	3	3	1	1

Source: Kosovan Families Survey 2003-04

6.1.3. REASONS RESPONDENTS CANNOT RETURN TO THEIR OWN COUNTRY TO LIVE

Most of the respondents indicated that they had reasons for not wishing or being able to return to their home country but few actually specified their reasons. Six stated that they could not return because they had been subjected to religious persecution, while four said that they had suffered from political persecution. Five said that had they faced death threats and one ethnic persecution in their home country. Four couldn't afford to return home, while five stated that they would find readjustment too difficult. Four said that they now have family commitments in the UK.

Among other comments we heard were: 'It is very difficult to live there.' Another gave the reason: 'My house was burnt down. I have a daughter over here and I am married. I am ashamed of my community and the horrible things that happened in Kosovo.' Another explained that a Muslim wife who separates from her husband, loses all rights to see her son if she lives in Kosovo while here she has equal rights. She said:

'I cannot return to Kosovo because of my son. If I lived in Kosovo I would have no rights over my son. I would never see my child. The father has all the rights. When parents separate both parents should see their child. I want my child to spend time with his dad as well as with me.'

Although not wishing to return another stated: 'We would like to be able to visit.' An Albanian respondent sadly stated: 'No, we wouldn't wish to return there to live. Many people sleep in Albania with a gun under their pillow. We never had one. There was a danger it might be used in anger.'

Table 6.2 Reasons respondents cannot return to their own country to live

I am prevented from returning home by	
Religious persecution	6
Political persecution	4
National/ethnic persecution	1
Death threats	5
Family commitments here	4
I could not afford to move home	4
Readjustment too difficult	5
Other reasons not specified/ No reason given	31

Source: Kosovan Families Survey 2003-04

6.2. COMPARISON OF RESPONDENTS' LIFE IN KOSOVO WITH UK

When asked: 'Do you think in the next year you and your family will live better than today or worse?' the majority (31) said that they hoped they'd live somewhat better and eleven stated: 'much better,' while eight remarked sadly that their standard of living would probably be 'the same' as now.

Table 6.3 Comparison of how respondents' families lived five years ago with now and asylum seekers' thoughts about their future living conditions

	Much better	Better	The same	Worse	Much worse
How did you and your family live five years ago in your own country?	12	7	6	12	13
	Much better	Better	Nothing will change	Worse	Much worse
Do you think that next year you and your family will live better or worse?	11	31	8		

Source: Kosovan Families Survey 2003-04

The respondents were asked: 'How did you and your family live five years ago in your own country, compared to how you live now?' Half the group (25) said that they had lived much worse or somewhat worse, while six said the same and nineteen said that they lived either much better or somewhat better. One person elaborated for us: 'We lived much worse. My father worked in metal production. You weren't given money like here to support your children. There were no social services to help support the family.'

6.3. ATTITUDES TOWARDS ENGLAND

When asked the question: 'What do you like about England?' three-quarters of the respondents (36) said that they liked the freedom in the country and three fifths said that they liked the language. Maybe surprisingly, considering the difficulties many experienced with immigration, almost half said that they liked the Law and nearly a quarter said they liked the culture. When asked: 'What don't you like about England?' almost half stated 'the climate' as not being favourable; five stated 'the Law' although one qualified the dislike as being in relation to 'Immigration Law' while at least twenty of the respondents found nothing to dislike about the country. Among the comments were the following: 'The Law is good but the administrator is not always so good' and 'This country is for lucky people.' Another said: 'We don't like being dependent on the benefits' system in this country. We would rather have the freedom to work and support ourselves.' Another person stated: 'There is no consistency about the Law.'

Table 6.4 Attitudes towards England

	What do you like about England?	What don't you like about England?
Freedom	36	
Law	23	6
Culture	17	1
Language	31	
Climate	5	24
Monarchy	3	
Respect for people	5	
Safety	6	

Source: Kosovan Families Survey 2003-04

6.4. GREATEST PROBLEM EXPERIENCED BY RESPONDENTS IN UK

Some respondents were unable to identify one problem as greater than another and identified more than one problem. The greatest problem identified by twenty-nine of the respondents was 'language', with twenty-five stating: 'dealings with Immigration/Home Office.' Eleven respondents also cited 'health' as one of the greatest problems. Nine expressed their difficulties with the fact that they were not allowed to work and eight stated 'housing' as one of their greatest problems. One widow who fled with her daughter to England, having lost her husband and her son, declared: 'Every thing was hard when we first arrived. We were just two women alone and we didn't know what would happen to us.'

Table 6.5 Greatest problem experienced by respondents in UK

	Language	Different customs	Health	Self esteem	Lack of occupation	Housing	Dealings with Immigration/ Home Office	Being away from home and alone
Number of families	29	1	11	2	9	8	25	4

Source: Kosovan Families Survey 2003-04

6.5. HEALTH

6.5.1. TIME IT TOOK RESPONDENTS TO ACCESS MEDICAL CARE

The majority of respondents (34) managed to register with a doctor within two months mainly because many were sick either immediately after their journey or became ill very soon after arriving in the UK. One respondent explained: 'I obtained a doctor very quickly because my daughter was sick while we were staying in a hotel.' Another told the authors: 'When we got off the lorry we were taken straight to hospital.'

Some found it much harder to acquire medical assistance. There appears to be a great shortage of good doctors with space on their lists for new patients while some of the doctors who are willing to take asylum seekers are not always the best doctors. One respondent said: 'We have had problems with our doctor and mis-diagnosis so we changed surgeries just before Christmas 2002. There is a shortage of doctors in the area.' A lady said: 'I have no doctor at present although my husband has. I couldn't get onto a list.' A young woman stated: 'It took three months to get a doctor even though I was pregnant.'

One man explained that he had medical cards only for his wife and baby. They had had to return their IND when the youngest child was born so that her photo could be added to the document but their IND was never returned to them. Without their IND no one would give them medical cards.

Table 6.6 Time it took respondents to access medical care

Time it took Respondents	One week	2-8 weeks	2-6 months	Longer than 6 months	N/A or not declared
to find a doctor	15	19	8	2	7
to find a dentist	10	12	14	3	9

Source: Kosovan Families Survey 2003-04

It took longer for most families to find a dentist mainly because they looked for a dentist only when they had problems with their teeth. If they hadn't had any problems then they hadn't attempted to register with a dentist. Consequently some of the younger children who had received no dental care for approximately three years after their arrival in the UK, experienced serious problems with their teeth and some of the children have required surgery to remove second teeth.

6.5.2. HEALTH PROBLEMS IN THE UK

A staggering forty-three respondents claimed that either they or their husband or both of them had suffered from health problems since they came to the UK (Table 6.7). One respondent told us: 'We both have health problems but it is difficult to describe them here.' Seven respondents stated that no-one in their family had suffered from health problems since they came here yet when asked if they had any of the symptoms in Table 6.7 many had suffered from one symptom or several since their arrival in the UK. One respondent said: 'None of my family have had any health problems since we came to the UK.' However she admitted on questioning that she had felt constantly tired although she was better now.

Generally the greatest health problems related to stress. Half of the respondents stated that they had had trouble sleeping since their arrival in the UK with seventeen of their partners also having problems sleeping and twelve of their children. Fifty-five of the family members were still experiencing insomnia with eleven family members complaining of nightmares or bad dreams. One lady told Sr. Anne that she would waken each night terrified after a nightmare in which a man came into her home to kill her. She had been raped in Kosovo and one of her family killed. Almost half of the respondents (24) suffered from depression and seventeen of their partners and nine children also suffered from depression. Six of the respondents have had psychiatric problems with three attending a psychiatrist at present and eight receiving counselling. A total of twenty-two family members suffered from panic attacks and while sixteen adults suffered from stress/anxiety, twenty-seven suffered from tension or feeling irritable. Forty-four adults suffered from migraines and seven from headaches all the time. Eighteen spoke of feeling constantly tired and fifteen declared that they had no interest in life. These figures are particularly striking and worrying when we remember that forty-five of the respondents were still relatively young – all under forty years old.

Let us hear what the respondents told the authors. One respondent said: 'I have very bad health – headache all the time, very depressed. I am attending a psychiatrist.' Another said: 'My husband has pain in his bones, arms, legs, whole body. I had had an operation in Kosovo for breast cancer. Now I am awaiting an appointment to see a specialist here. We are very stressed.' We heard from another lady: 'I have had a problem with asthma for four years since I came to England. My husband has a problem with his bottom. We are both very stressed.' Another respondent said that she went with her son to the Medical Foundation for Victims of Torture in Kentish Town. Her Husband had heart disease. A lady told us: 'I have to attend the hospital for psychiatric help.' Another lady said: 'One year ago my husband had a heart attack but it is under control with medicine. He is being treated with anti-depressants. The children are fine.'

Another respondent's daughter said:

> 'For the first three years, after we arrived in England my mother couldn't sleep properly. She would waken every few minutes with a start and was extremely anxious. She sleeps better now. She had very bad chest pains and was frequently very ill. She thought that she had heart problems but it was caused by anxiety.'

Not all the children of the respondents were well. In fact many were suffering as well as their parents and not just those who were born in Kosovo and underwent the horrors of the war followed by the traumatic journey to the UK. Many were seriously affected by the stress their parents were under.

In 2005 Sr. Anne met with a mother whose benefit had been stopped and who was about to become homeless. Her nine years old son was very distressed and deeply affected by the whole experience. He had come to the UK aged just five and within a few months was interpreting for his parents. His parents had become dependant on his support and knowledge of English and consequently his childhood was over and the family roles were reversed. Twenty-four children were having problems with their appetites, the majority eating very little which is most unusual for children under ten who normally eat well. Nine respondents said that they had a child who was suffering from depression, while seventeen children were extremely noisy. Thirteen children were pronounced overactive and four silent/withdrawn.

Table 6.7 Description of health problems

Are you or any of your family suffering from any of the following?	respondent	partner	1st child	2nd child	3rd child	total
Unable to sleep	25	17	11		1	55
Bad dreams/ nightmares	8	1	2			11
Lack of appetite/ excessive appetite	8	3	13	9	2	35
Feeling of tension/ irritable	16	11	1			28
Feeling constantly tired	14	4	3			21
Disinterest in life	7	8				15
Palpitations	7	3	1			11
Panic attacks	14	5	3			22
Headaches/ migraines	31	13	2			46
Headache all the time	4	3				7
Aches and pains/ abdominal pain	8	11	1			20
Heart problems	6	3				9
Kidney problems		1				1
Depression	24	14	7	2		47
Asthma	2	1				3
Psychiatric problems	6					6
Stress/anxiety	9	7				16
Very itchy rash	1	1	1	1	2	6
Child extremely noisy			7	8	2	17
Child over active			7	6		13
Child silent/withdrawn			2	2		4
Miscellaneous	2	5				7
Total number of symptoms	198	111	61	28	7	404

Source: Kosovan Families Survey 2003-04

One family Sr. Anne came to know shortly after they arrived in the UK had a three year old daughter. She was very friendly but Sister never heard her speak even in Albanian for at least a year after the family arrived. Her parents used to shout at one another, which puzzled Sister. Not understanding the language she thought that they were disagreeing with each other. One day an interpreter explained to her that they shouted because the family's hearing had been damaged by the bombs in Kosovo.

One respondent, whose oldest child was six years old when they left Kosovo stated: 'Our oldest child is silent and withdrawn. He was bullied in school.' Another told us: 'Our youngest child was thirteen years old when we came to England. He was so distressed by the whole situation that he was forever getting into trouble in school.'

One respondent told the authors:

> 'My son was very sick when we first arrived in England and needed psychiatric help. He suffered from all the symptoms in the list when we first came. The teacher in Liverpool was very supportive and helped a lot and he is happier now.'

Another lady said:

> 'My husband has not been well since he was beaten in the police station in Kosovo. He has serious nosebleeds and hurt his back. I am on medication for sleeping, pain in my hand and back. I go to the Medical Foundation every two weeks with my husband and every week with my children. Our oldest child receives twenty hours help a week in school. He has problems with hearing. Our youngest son was bitten by police dogs before we left Kosovo. He has difficulty sleeping and is depressed. The Medical Foundation helped him. At first he was very withdrawn but he is speaking about his experiences now.'

A mother told Sister: 'My oldest daughter suffers from bad dreams about her dad and mum dying.'

6.6. RESPONDENTS' GREATEST FEARS

In Table 6.8 we see that over half the respondents (27) were most afraid of 'forced repatriation.' One respondent stated: 'We are most afraid of repatriation.' and another said: 'Our greatest fear is forced repatriation.' Another remarked fearfully: 'I often can't sleep. I always think – the police might come tonight. I'm very afraid.' A male respondent told us: 'Each month when I register at the Police Station I'm afraid we will be sent back'. Another lady told us that she has to register at London Bridge once a month on a Saturday. Many people go there to register. Now that her eldest son is over eighteen he has to register each month himself. They are afraid to register together in case they are sent back so they go at different times.

The second greatest fear expressed was 'losing someone close.' Many had lost relatives in Kosovo so this is a natural fear. One respondent told the authors: 'I'm very afraid of losing someone close.' She lost two children before the war. Another lady told us that her husband had been killed and her teenage son was missing in Kosovo.

Ten respondents were afraid of the 'lack of stability' and ten were afraid of 'loneliness,' both understandable fears. All the respondents had lost their country and close family plus friends and since they arrived in England have been constantly moved from one accommodation to another and often from one area to another. The other fears expressed were more general and would probably be expressed by many of the population of the UK.

Table 6.8 Respondents' greatest fears

Greatest fears	Number of Respondents
Serious illness	9
Losing health, disability	7
Unsuccessful life	8
Unsuccessful marriage	2
Broken family	4
Losing someone close	15
Worsening of material situation	2
Worsening of housing situation	5
Poverty, misery , unemployment	8
Feeling loneliness	10
Lack of friends	4
Dull and boring life	3
Finding at the end of life it has been empty and wasted	4
Lack of success in carrying out plans concerning education or work	7
Abandoning certain ideals and plans that used to be important	4
Humiliation	4
Forced repatriation	27
Lack of stability	10
I'm not afraid of anything	0
Fear of being sent back when signing on at police station	1
Rape	1
Other fears	4

Source: Kosovan Families Survey 2003-04

6.7. PERMISSION TO STAY IN ENGLAND INDEFINITELY

Only six of those interviewed had permission to stay in the Spring of 2003. That number rose to seventeen a year later, the Spring of 2004. In the Spring of 2003 forty-four were awaiting the decision of the Home Office. By the Spring of 2004 we were only aware of twenty-two still awaiting the decision of the Home Office. However we were unable to gather information from eleven of those in the study group. The whereabouts of the eleven were unknown. It is possible that some had been deported. Among the comments we collected were: 'I have no permission to stay indefinitely but my husband has full Refugee Status with travel documents.' And:

> 'My partner has permission to stay from NASS but not from the HO. He is living somewhere else in London. He is scared because if he is found living with me, he would be arrested. It is unlawful. We have always lived separately but we are legally married.'

By the Autumn of 2004 just over half the group (28) of fifty had permission to stay. Of those, eighteen had been granted the Amnesty. Eleven were still awaiting the decision of the Home Office. We had lost contact with another three of the respondents but we already knew their status. The information regarding the status of the eleven we had lost contact with in the Spring of 2004 remains unknown.

Table 6.9 Permission to stay in England indefinitely

	Yes, permission to stay	Awaiting decision of Home Office	Information unavailable
Number of respondents in Spring 2003	6	44	
Number of respondents in Spring 2004	17	22	11
Number of respondents in Autumn 2004	28	11	11

Source: Kosovan Families Survey 2003-04

6.8. WORK

6.8.1. NATIONAL INSURANCE NUMBER HELD IN 2003/PERMISSION TO WORK AND TYPE OF JOB HELD

In Table 6.10 the majority of the respondents (27) and the same number of their partners had not been granted a National Insurance Number. Less than half the respondents (23) had been granted a National Insurance Number and eighteen of their partners, mainly for the purpose of obtaining benefits.

We can see that although nineteen of the respondents were allowed to work in 2003 only four were actually doing so. The same number of partners (19) had permission to work and a slightly higher number (8) were doing so. Only one respondent was willing to admit that her husband was working illegally. Of those allowed to work many were unable either to find work that wasn't illegal or had not enough English to succeed when interviewed. The others who were not working claimed it was due either to their own ill health or the need to assist their partners who were suffering from ill health. One lady told us that her husband had received permission to work first and was granted a National Insurance Number and now she also has a number. He was encouraged to work by the State and works part time but she cannot work while her youngest is still so young. Another said: 'My husband is allowed to work but is unable to due to ill health.' The majority of female respondents who were permitted to work explained that they could not because of very young children not yet at school.

Table 6.10 Permission to work and type of job held

	Permission to work	No permission to work	Legal Full time	Legal Part time	No work or n/a
Respondents	19	31	2	2	46
Partners	19	26	3	5	41

Source: Kosovan Families Survey 2003-04

6.8.2. PREFERRED JOB

It is possible to see from Table 6.11 that although almost half of the females (21) were housewives in their home country, only one wished to remain so in the UK. The most attractive occupation for women appeared to be childcare or teaching (8) while the most attractive occupation for men appeared to be as drivers (9), with builders (5) and businessmen (5) tying for second place. Four of the women expressed a desire to receive further education. The respondents who, we must remember, were mainly women, had held a number of different jobs in their home countries including a hairdresser, a nurse, two bank workers, three engineers, three business persons and seven ladies who had worked with children either as teachers or in child care.

The men also had had various occupations. At least nine had worked in agriculture, three of whom had been shepherds and six had worked in business; four had been drivers and three engineers; one husband and wife had been doctors and a man a vet. The vet had also worked for a time as a builder and at the time of the last interview had acquired legal work on a building site. Unfortunately it proved to be only temporary work. . One man who was very keen to get a job as a driver, had been receiving driving lessons. His wife commented: 'My husband received driving lessons. He has taken his test five times.'

Table 6.11 Preferred job

Occupation	Respondent		Partner	
	In home country	In the future	In home country	In the future
Dress making/hand crafts		3		
Plumber	1	1		1
Builder /Brick layer	1	1		5
Carpenter			1	
Electrician			2	1
Architect			1	1
Government worker	2	1	2	
Engineer	3	1	3	2
Social worker		2		1
Policeman			1	
Military				1
Teacher/child care	7	8		
Full time education/further education	2	5	1	
Work in a bank /Accountancy	3	2		
Secretary		1		
Factory manager			1	
Business person	3	2	6	5
Shop owner/shop assistant	1	4	1	1
Hairdresser	1			
Driver			4	9
Mechanic			1	1
Working in a hospital		1		
Nurse	1	1		
Doctor	1	2	1	1
Vet			1	
Agriculture /Shepherd	2	3	9	3
Any job		4		1
Housewife	18	1	3	2
Not specified or n/a	2	7	9	15

Source: Kosovan Families Survey 2003-04

6.9. CONTACT WITH ANY ASYLUM SEEKERS OR REFUGEE STATE/VOLUNTARY OR FAITH GROUPS

Although seven respondents stated that they were not in touch with any asylum seekers or refugee State/voluntary or Church groups, in fact all of the respondents were contacted through groups so at one time or another the respondents had been in contact even if they no longer considered themselves to be in touch with any groups.

The majority (43) stated that they were in touch with at least one group. Fifteen said that they were involved with Sure Start in Manor Park while another respondent said that she was being helped by Sure Start in Ilford. Twelve were involved with the Shpresa Programme in the Froud Centre, Manor Park - a support programme for Albanian women mentioned in chapter three. Eight were involved with RAMP in Harold Road and thirteen directly with Harmony House, a refugee support centre in Dagenham. Among the other support centres frequented were the Children's Society in Manor Park, visited by five people, while six visited the Didsbury Centre in East Ham, eight attended meetings at the Froud Centre on the Romford Road, while two went to the Medical Foundation in North London for support and two visited the Redbridge Refugee Forum.

Table 6.12 Which groups are you in contact with?

Children's society, Manor Park	5
Citizen advice	1
Didsbury Centre, East Ham	6
Froud Centre, Romford Road	8
Hand-in-Hand	1
Harmony House, Dagenham	13
Horizon project	1
Little Ilford , Manor Park	2
Medical Foundation	2
Newham Refugee Centre, Romford Road	1
MP Dagenham	1
RAMP Harold Road	8
Redbridge Refugee Forum	2
Shpresa programme – Froud centre	12
Sure Start, Manor Park/Ilford	16

Source: Kosovan Families Survey 2003-04

6.10. SUGGESTIONS REGARDING AN IMMIGRATION POLICY

The respondents were asked: ' If you are not already a British citizen would you like to apply to become one?' One respondent was already a British Citizen and all of the other forty-nine stated that they would like to become British Citizens. One respondent when asked, exclaimed: 'Yes, It would be a gift from God.'

In Table 6.13 we see that although some respondents gave two or more suggestions regarding the UK's immigration policy, over half (28) of the group thought that people should be allowed to work on reception of identity documents. Nearly everyone said that either there should be 'quicker processing of claims' or 'asylum-status should be granted within one year.' Almost a quarter (12) of the group supported the idea of short-term support centres for new arrivals, offering accommodation, interpretation, medical help and language courses. These were not seen as detention centres but as support centres where people would be helped but would be free to come and go as they pleased. Many of the asylum seekers had arrived traumatized and feeling totally lost. They had found themselves in a strange city not understanding anyone. They had been sent to register at one centre and then sent to another centre for accommodation and then often elsewhere all within a few days or weeks, and with no English they felt even more confused, lost and frightened. They thought that a single centre that could cover all immediate needs would be helpful.

Table 6.13 What would you suggest regarding an immigration policy?

I would suggest:	
On reception of identity given right to work	28
Quicker processing of claims	28
Asylum status granted within one year	28
Travel documents so when someone is working they can travel	1
On arrival – short term support centres – accommodation, interpretation, medical and language courses offered	12

Source: Kosovan Families Survey 2003-04

One teenager interpreting for her mother said angrily: 'They (the Home Office) should decide about status in one year not five years.' Another respondent told us: 'The real problem is status – not knowing if you can stay or not. If I had a document to stay I'd be happy with one room. I am willing to work. I don't want benefits.' One respondent thought that the UK did not act according to the Geneva Convention: 'Asylum seekers should be treated much better and according to the Geneva Convention.'

Another said:

> 'We are not happy with the lack of decision. We have plenty of documents, medical reports. The immigration authorities should give people a chance. The capital of Kosovo is safe now but not the countryside. It is fine if you have money but every village, factory is gone. We can't go back.'

6.11. SUGGESTIONS HOW THE FAITH COMMUNITIES COULD HELP IMMIGRANTS

Very few people commented on what the Christian communities or Faith groups should do to help asylum seekers although a few had comments to make: 'The Church should try to understand them and their problems. It should support them with spiritual advice to give back the faith and hope for life, and encourage them to do voluntary work. It should support them in their education by providing English classes.' ' The Church could give more help to immigrants by writing letters, support etc.'

However while some felt that the church could do more others were very impressed with the Church's involvement and declared that the Church was already helping them: 'Fr. John in Upton Park has been very helpful.' Another said: 'Harmony House and the Church have already helped.' A lady said: 'The Church has helped me when I have problems.' Another praised the staff at Harmony House: 'I'm very happy with the Church. Feel like I am at home in Harmony House. Sr. Margaret, Clare, everyone there are very good people.' And another: 'The Church is doing a great job for refugees.'

© Anne Wells

The photograph shows the father of a young family who had been persecuted for their faith in Kosovo. The youngest daughter shown here was born in London. The family received a great deal of help from the Church, and to their joy they were baptized shortly after their arrival in the UK.

While some respondents had looked to the Church for the Sacraments, other respondents simply asked for the members of the Church to pray and encourage asylum seekers: 'Would like the Church to encourage more - to say life is good.'

One explained a little more about the kind of support she would welcome: 'Put in a good word for the person, offer support, a shoulder to cry on and laugh on.' She added: 'It is difficult for asylum seeker adjusting to freedom after persecution, not being able to speak what's on your mind.' Another felt that the Home Office: 'should listen to the Church and respect people.'

CHAPTER SEVEN

SNAP SHOTS OF ASYLUM SEEKERS' LIVES IN THE UK

The following are true accounts of asylum seekers' lives. They are based on case histories which the authors compiled after holding in-depth interviews with the families and include some of Sister Anne's experiences working with a few of the asylum seekers' families on a day to day basis. Some names have been changed to respect confidentiality.

7.1. FAMILY 'A' - PREGNANT AND ALONE

When Sr. Anne first met Maria in late April 2003 she was very upset as her husband had been deported two weeks earlier. Maria came to the Sisters' house with her friend to interpret (Maria's first language is Albanian and her English is very poor). She explained how her husband had gone to sign on at the local police station as usual on Monday 7 April. However this time he was not allowed to return home. Instead he was taken to a Detention Centre at Heathrow and told that he would be returned to Kosovo on the following Thursday, 10 April. He was allowed to phone his wife and he told her to be ready with their two year old son to leave for Kosovo. Two days later he was told that he would not be travelling that week but the following one. He asked that his wife and child could travel with him and the immigration officials said that this would happen. To his surprise and shock he was wakened on Thursday the tenth at three am and taken to the airport. He asked where his wife and son were and he was told that they were already on the plane. They were not. He was flown straight back to the capital of Kosovo from where he phoned his wife and told her what had happened. She contacted her solicitor who insisted that he was still at Heathrow. Maria hadn't heard from him since.

Maria came to see Sr. Anne again in June 2003 requesting, through her interpreter, that Sister help her to obtain a push chair for her baby due to be born in late July. After several futile attempts to obtain a second-hand one through various charitable groups, Sister realized that they needed to buy a new one. Charities had waiting lists for many months and apparently most children were several months old before a pushchair for a newborn baby could be found. Having found the cheapest, Sisters Esther and Anne bought it and on the same day, 23 July, they went to deliver it to Maria. She was thrilled. Sr. Anne asked her when her baby was due and Maria explained using sign language that her baby was overdue by three days. She seemed anxious, indicating that she had some pain and the baby was in the breach position.

Sister asked her when she had to attend the hospital. She looked at her blankly, not understanding Sister's question. Eventually Maria showed Sister her appointment card and Sister saw that she was supposed to have attended the hospital that morning at eleven am. It was now eleven-thirty am so Sister phoned the hospital and apologized for the fact that Maria had missed her appointment and asked if Maria could have another as her baby was overdue and breach. The antenatal clinic told Sister to bring her immediately. They gathered together some food and a drink for the two years old son and Sr. Esther drove them all to the day clinic at the hospital.

So began a very long afternoon. First the staff checked Maria's notes and said that she wasn't due for another two weeks, although Maria still insisted the baby was due now (apparently the same thing had happened with her first child. Maria had claimed to be due and the hospital had said she wasn't; nevertheless the baby had come on time according to Maria's reckoning). Anyway the staff examined her and said she wasn't breach. The baby was just moving around but was correctly positioned for birth. They checked the baby's heart beat and said it was fine. They checked the mother's blood pressure and said that it, too, was normal. The next step was to check her urine after which a puzzled nurse declared that it had far too much protein in it and they would need to take a blood test. She asked if Maria had any other symptoms? It was only then that the nurse realized that Sr. Anne wasn't an interpreter. 'You don't speak, Albanian, do you?' she stated crossly as if Sister had been deceiving her. It was difficult – Sr. Anne couldn't explain to Maria what was happening. Sister could only assure her: 'Baby is fine, good, okay,' but Maria knew that something was wrong and Sister couldn't tell her what. Sister tried with: 'Your blood is not good but not bad.' The last thing Sr. Anne wanted was to worry her unduly. They would need to wait at the hospital for the results of the blood test so they all went for a sandwich. On returning to the ward they discovered that the blood sample was still awaiting collection by the porter so to speed things up Sister offered to take it to the laboratory. Meanwhile they placed Maria on a monitor for half an hour to check the baby's heart rate etc.

Another lengthy wait in a very hot ward and eventually, almost two hours later, the results arrived. Maria would need to be seen by the doctor. He, too, presumed that Sister spoke Albanian. Otherwise why would Sister be with her? He explained that he wanted to admit Maria that evening. It was then four pm. The baby was fine but he was worried that Maria's blood pressure would suddenly soar as a result of the high protein level in her blood and she would need admission as an emergency. The only way to remove the excess protein was to induce her baby and they would probably do that the next day. Maria phoned a Kosovan female friend, Luljeta who speaks some English and Sister explained what was happening. She would take Maria home to collect a few belongings and then return to the hospital. Luljeta agreed to meet Sister at Maria's house, collect Maria's son and look after him at her own home while Maria was in hospital. Sisters Esther and Anne would take Maria back to the hospital. The Sisters left Maria there at seven thirty pm explaining to the nurse that her English was poor but she could understand if the staff spoke slowly and used sign language.

The next morning Sister phoned the hospital at ten am to ask how Maria was. They told Sister that she was fine. Sr. Anne asked if they were going to induce the baby and they said they couldn't give information over the phone. Sister told them that she had been with Maria when the doctor said that they would probably induce her today and she needed to know because she had to inform the lady looking after Maria's other child. The nurse said: 'Probably later today. The doctor will see Maria at midday with an interpreter.' She added: 'You speak very good English,' to which Sister replied: 'Well, I am English!' They were still under the misconception that Sr. Anne was Albanian, for some reason or other! Sister phoned Maria's friend to put her in the picture and Luljeta said that she would take Maria's son to see his mum early that afternoon. It would take her over two hours by bus to get there. Sr. Anne said she would go later in the afternoon. They met at the hospital at four pm. They were about to induce Maria but said if nothing had started to happen in one hour nothing would happen and they would have to give Maria more medication at ten pm. Again if nothing happened, she would be given more at four am. Apparently it usually took three doses. There was no sign of the baby coming. Sister and Luljeta agreed that if the baby came during the day Sister would look after the children while Luljeta accompanied Maria. However Luljeta was concerned - she couldn't come to the hospital if it was during the night because of looking after her two children (six and three years old) as well as Maria's son, so Sister offered to be on call during the night. The hospital assured her that nothing was likely to happen. Eventually at seven pm they both left the hospital.

Sr. Anne went to bed at eleven pm sure that the baby would wait until at least seven am but with the phone beside her bed, just in case the hospital phoned. At one-forty am the phone woke Sister. Maria had been taken into the labour ward and was asking for her. Sr. Anne dressed, grabbed her bag, made a quick call to a taxi firm and within half an hour was at the hospital. The taxi driver insisted in finding out which entrance Sister should use to get into the maternity wing and left her in the cab. On returning much amused, the taxi driver told Sister: 'The ambulance driver wanted to know if you needed any help!'

Maria looked pleased to see Sister, although she was obviously in pain. The midwife immediately asked Sister: 'Do you speak Albanian?' To her negative reply the midwife said: 'Then we have a problem. I need to break her waters and I need to know whether she wants a pain killer but I can't do either without her consent.' Sr. Anne suggested phoning an interpreter but the midwife said that it wouldn't help as they couldn't get Maria to the phone. Sister said: 'Can't we use my mobile?' Although all mobiles have to be switched off in hospital the midwife agreed to waive the rule in the exceptional circumstances. Sister phoned Maria's friend twice during Maria's delivery and thought how bizarre it was, poor Maria wriggling and sweating in pain trying to listen to her friend on the other end of the phone asking her on behalf of the midwife if she wanted a pain killer. The baby arrived at three-twenty am – a beautiful little boy (four kilogram). There had been a moment of panic when the baby's cord was caught around his neck and the midwife had to cut it and asked Sr. Anne to summon assistance from another midwife, but all was well. After he had been wiped and dressed he was handed to his Mum who after a few moments handed him back and promptly fell asleep. Sister had the privilege of holding him for the next half hour or so. Maria's friend arrived and as she was staying Sister decided to go home and was back in her own bed asleep by five am.

The following morning Sr. Anne was at the hospital by eleven-thirty am and to her shock was refused admittance to the maternity ward, even though she had been with Maria during her delivery. Sister was told to come back at three-thirty pm. At that point Maria's friend appeared. She had been with Maria for nine hours and was exhausted. She told the midwife that she and Sister were working together to help Maria and that she needed Sister's help, as her English wasn't very good. The midwife still refused to let Sister in. Sr. Anne returned at four pm and stayed until seven pm. During that time the midwife appeared once and said that she would come back and speak to Sister but Sr. Anne never saw her again. Sister was told that Maria could probably go home the next day, after the paedetrician had seen the baby.

Later that night Sr. Anne phoned Luljeta and told her what was happening. The following day the hospital phoned at midday to say that Maria could go home. Once more Sr.

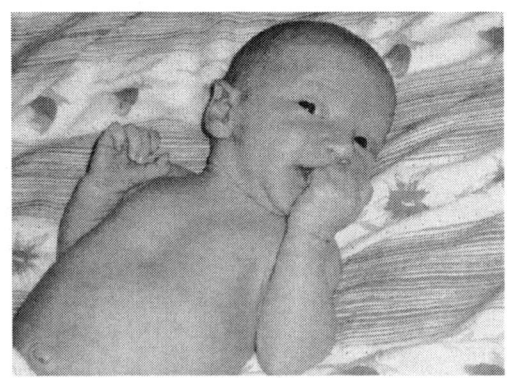

© Anne Wells

Anne phoned Luljeta and they agreed that she would go straight to Maria's home as Luljeta was bringing the three children with her and planned to stay with Maria for two weeks. Sisters Esther and Anne went to the hospital at two-thirty pm. Sr. Anne asked at the desk if Maria was ready to be discharged and if she needed anything. The hospital staff were very vague, telling Sister to ask Maria. Sr. Anne found Maria still in her nightclothes and the baby still unwashed. Eventually the staff explained that the mother of the baby was meant to bathe her own baby unless it was her first. Naturally Maria hadn't understood that. However a nurse needed to observe and the only bath in the maternity ward was in use. Maria got dressed and then went to wash her baby. Sr. Anne was asked to be the observer but she refused saying: 'I have never bathed a baby in my life.' She wasn't willing to take responsibility if anything happened. By three forty-five pm the baby was bathed and at last they were able to leave the hospital. Sr. Anne approached the nurses' desk once more and thanked them.

They had only been at Maria's flat for about five minutes when Sister's mobile rang: 'Why hadn't they collected Maria's file? She would need it for the midwife in the morning.' While Sr. Esther drove back to the hospital for it the midwife phoned Sister. The midwife apologized for the fact that the maternity staff had not called her and given Sr. Anne the file. She explained over the phone all that Maria needed to know so that Sister could explain to Luljeta for translation, when she arrived. Luljeta arrived laden with a huge case on the pushchair, shopping bags hanging from every handle and three young children in tow. She had gone to the supermarket on the way to Maria's.

The Sisters left them at five-thirty pm to sort themselves out. The following day Sr. Anne was out when Sr. Esther received a phone call from Luljeta looking for Sr. Anne. The midwife was concerned about one of the baby's legs and wanted him to be taken to casualty. Sr. Esther kindly drove them there and they waited a few hours until he was seen and could be brought home. Apparently it was nothing serious.

In December 2003 Sr. Anne learnt that in June, Maria had made an application to the Home Office for a general settlement claim on compassionate grounds outside of immigration rules. As that wasn't an asylum claim she ceased to qualify for support under the Asylum and Immigration Act of 1999 (Interim provision). She made a human rights claim under Article 3. In November 2003 she was informed that her support and accommodation were terminated, in spite of the fact that she had a baby of four months and a child of two years. Maria would receive a limited amount just for the children. Her immigration solicitor had asked her local council to continue her support. When Sr. Anne saw Maria she had just thirty pounds left to last her two weeks. Meanwhile, the local Sure Start Asylum Support Team were advising her and trying to get her a Community Care Solicitor. They managed to do so and her local council agreed to continue her support and accommodation.

In July 2005 Maria and her children were still awaiting the decision of the Home Office and had no status.

7.2. FAMILY 'B' - HOUSING FEARS

Family 'B' was a couple with three children under ten years old. In October 2003 the family were told that after a long wait, their two boys had been granted places in the local Catholic primary school in Manor Park. Unfortunately they also heard that the Council wished to re house them in Ilford in a couple of week's time. They approached the parish priest, Father Denis for support and Sr. Anne promised to go to the Council Office with the mother, Mira the following day. Mira told Sister that she was attending courses in English, Child Care, Computing and also Film making at one of the local schools. She had a bus pass but had to pay for the children so if they had to move they could not afford to send their children to the Catholic school as it would require four bus tickets every day.

Sr. Anne accompanied Mira to the Council Housing Offices in Ilford. A most helpful and friendly Council Officer explained that the reason the family had to move was the fact that the Council had been having problems with the landlord and had decided not to do business with him any more. The Council would gladly offer the family a flat in Manor Park if they could but at that time none was available. The Council Officer accompanied Mira and Sr. Anne to see a flat in Ilford. It was a first floor flat with no access to the garden, even to hang out the washing, without going through the kitchen of the downstairs flat. The flat was quite small and the kitchen in a bad state of repair while the bathroom was filthy. The landlady was informed that she would have to make several improvements before the Council would consider it safe for children to live on the premises. Mira was told that her family had to move out but the Council would try and postpone that deadline until the new flat was habitable. They were given a short extension to their lease. Two days after they were due to move, to their joy, they received a surprise phone call from the Council saying that they could stay in their present flat after all.

7.3. FAMILY 'C' – UPROOTED AT CHRISTMAS

In mid November 2004 Lena's family heard that they had been granted the Amnesty. Naturally they were very relieved and they set about transferring from NASS to mainstream benefits. They were living in Manor Park and their two oldest children were very happily settled in the local Catholic school and they had a toddler not yet in school.

At eight-thirty pm on 20 December 2004 Sr. Anne received a phone call from one of the Kosovans telling her that Lena and her family had to move out of

Manor Park the following day. Sisters Esther and Anne went immediately around to their house.

The family was in shock. There was an air of unreality as they sat beside their Christmas tree, their kitten tumbling at their feet and explained that having been granted the Amnesty they would be supported once again by the Borough of Kensington and Chelsea, that is the council that had originally housed them in Manor Park. The house they were in belonged to NASS and when they received the Amnesty they had been given twenty-eight days to transfer to mainstream benefits and move out of NASS accommodation.

Although distressed at having to leave their friends the father was quite positive about the fact that they had to move to the Borough of Hillingdon on the other side of London. He considered the flat in Hillingdon to be in a better area. It was temporary accommodation so they knew it might only be for a few weeks although it could be for over a year.

The mother's main concern was the fact that her children would have to change school yet again, just when they were so happy in the local Catholic school, St. Winefrides. The Sisters suggested that the father and eldest daughter, Fabiola should see the Catholic priest, Fr. Denis, to ask for his support in transferring the children to another Catholic school. When they first arrived in the UK they had had problems getting Fabiola into a Catholic school as they had no documents to prove that they were Catholics.

Fr. Denis wrote a letter to the parish priest in their new area asking him to admit them to the school. He also wrote a letter to the local authorities asking that the family would eventually be granted permanent accommodation in Manor Park and he offered to look after some of their property until they could transport it to their new home. Shortly before eleven pm the family said their goodbyes, promised to keep in touch and sadly returned home to pack.

The following day they moved. The flat was in a new building and they would be the first family moving in. The flat was on the fourth floor and had two bedrooms, a kitchen and a bathroom. They would have to share a living room with other families which was far from ideal so they opted for all five of them to sleep in the smaller bedroom and to use the larger bedroom as a living room.

Lena kept in touch with Sr. Anne. They managed to get the children into a local Catholic school but shortly before Easter 2005 were told that they had to move again, once more to temporary accommodation, this time in the borough of Tower Hamlets. It was a better flat but once again Lena had to walk the streets, children in tow, as she tried to find them another Catholic school. Eventually she managed to acquire a place in a Catholic school for their son, but they had no vacancy for Fabiola who had to attend another school. Life in July 2005 was still very uncertain for the family.

7.4. FAMILY 'D' - NIGHTMARES

The Roman Catholic mother, the widow of a Muslim, left Kosovo shortly after NATO's intervention in Kosovo, because of the effects of the war. Her house had been burnt down; she had been raped; her husband had been killed and her eldest son had received death threats. She told the authors:

> 'So many people died, so many houses burnt, my husband joined the fighting. After six months the commandant came to my house and said: "Sorry for your husband – a very strong man but he has died." Many of my family came to my house to say "sorry." This is tradition. My son was fourteen. Some people hit my son and told him: "You will die next". My son returned to our house and cried and cried. After two to three months some cousins arranged for my son to leave Kosovo and go to another country. I had no contact with anyone to know where my son was going and because of the war there was no telephone. After two to three days or more I heard that my son was with his cousin and had left on a lorry. I left my house and went to my husband's brother but he was an invalid and had six children so I couldn't stay. After six months, with help from my family, I paid $5000 to leave Kosovo.
>
> My youngest son, aged eleven and I came to Portsmouth. We were very hungry. We'd had nothing to eat or drink. We had an interview and we were taken to a hotel but I didn't understand what the manager of the hotel told me. He showed me the fridge and we ate a little bread and drank milk but I was afraid to eat anything else because I did not know what we were allowed to eat. The next morning we were taken for another interview. Immigration sent us by mini cab to a hotel in Aldershot. In the hotel there were many people drunk. We were upset. I phoned my husband's cousin. I didn't know where I was. He said: "Look outside, what can you see written?" I said "Aldershot". Later that evening he came and took me to their house. After we arrived in London we asked many people about the whereabouts of my son. Eventually someone told me that they knew of five boys who had arrived from Kosovo together. My son was one of those boys. He was living with a very good English family in Harwich. He had been living with five different families since he arrived here. After my eldest son joined me we went to Croydon after one month to register the fact that he was now living with me.'

When she first came she was placed in a very poor hotel for six months and she then spent a few weeks with friends. The authorities were dispersing asylum seekers and wanted to move her with her sons to Portsmouth. She appealed against the move as her sons were at last settled in school and she was concerned about the effect another move would have on them. Eventually she was moved to social housing and she has lived in several different properties with her two sons. When interviewed she described her present accommodation as fair. It was a flat with five rooms: kitchen, bathroom, living room and two bedrooms. When looking for housing she had suffered racial /religious discrimination. She had been asked: 'Are you a Muslim?' before being offered housing.

At first she was refused asylum status because her solicitor never told her that she needed to attend an interview so she missed her appointment and immigration declared that she had refused to attend that interview, but she hadn't refused. She went to court several times for two years or more. She made another appeal. Her first solicitor asked her to change and go to another solicitor. He could do no more for her. She had just five days to appeal. One relation said that he thought his solicitor, an English lady, could help her. She went to Twickenham to start another appeal. She said:

> 'I paid £400 and the solicitor said that she would be able to help me within six months. I went to court for the second time in August 2002. Afterwards the lady solicitor told me: "I am sorry but there is no hope." The person at the Home Office said that he hadn't my original documents. After a second appeal I was refused again and after ten days refused again. I went to see another solicitor. My friend lent me the money. I paid £500 for his services and he was two months late sending my appeal to the Courts so I lost my appeal. I still have no papers and have just changed solicitors once again. I can make just one more appeal. I have no documents.'

She still had no papers in November 2004 and had just changed solicitors once more. She could have just one more appeal but she had no documents.

Healthwise she was suffering from psychiatric problems and attending a psychiatrist once a week. She had a constant headache, found it very difficult to sleep, had no appetite and little interest in life. She was frequently woken by a nightmare in which someone had come to kill her. She worried constantly about her sons. The youngest (14) was afraid to sleep alone and slept in her double bed. She was afraid that the oldest would get into trouble with no father figure to keep him in check.

In the autumn of 2004 her brother died in Kosovo in an accident. She was devastated, not only because of the loss of her brother but because she couldn't offer any support to her elderly parents.

The family was granted the Amnesty in February 2005.

7.5. FAMILY 'E' - EMERGENCY ACCOMMODATION WITH HANDICAPPED CHILD

The Kosovan couple have three children under ten years old. The youngest is a little handicapped girl four years old. She arrived prematurely and suffered from a loss of oxygen to her brain during delivery. She now has epileptic fits, has problems swallowing, has very limited communication skills, cannot walk or hold herself up and needs twenty-four hour attention.

Sr. Anne met the mother in B&B accommodation in East London. The mother had been in the first floor flat for two months. When they were placed in the emergency accommodation they had been told that it would be for a maximum of two weeks. They had no heating and the fridge hadn't worked for a month. The landlord had refused to fix it as he said that the family should have moved out over a month ago. The flat was filthy and infested with cockroaches and flies. The mother told Sister through an interpreter that they had been moved out of their last accommodation because it was worse than their present accommodation. In the last house they had been so badly infested with mice that the mice were running around the skirting boards during the day and observed by the inspector from Environmental Health who insisted that the family must move out immediately. It was a health hazard. The family were moved into their present emergency accommodation by the HPU (Homeless Persons Unit) but that week in July 2004 the HPU had suddenly decided the family were not their concern and that they must move out immediately. A Benefits Housing Adviser for asylum seekers was trying to re-establish their right to be housed by the HPU. While they were in the flat the little girl was unable to have the equipment supplied by the hospital as there was not enough space in the flat for the special chair, and the wheel chair was deemed unsafe for use in a first floor flat. Sr. Anne went with the interpreter to try and obtain a fridge. The flat's rent was paid for by the HPU as furnished with a fridge but the landlord refused to replace the fridge until the HPU had established that the family had the right to continue to reside there.

Eleven months later the family were still in the same bed and breakfast accommodation and still had received no decision on their asylum application (June 2005).

7.6. FAMILY 'F' - DETAINED BY A SOLICITOR'S MISTAKE

When Mark and his wife Lindita decided to leave Kosovo with their two daughters under ten years old, they went first to Albania and stayed there for two days. They had arranged to take a boat to Italy. It was only a small inflatable boat meant for a few people but about forty-five people went on this boat. The journey by sea took four hours in the dark. The night before two boats had collided in the dark – one travelling from Albania, the second from Italy. All forty-five asylum seekers were drowned. Knowing that made the journey even more frightening. It took the family three attempts before they got safely to Italy.

From Italy they took a lorry through France. It was meant to take them to London but it took them to Spain. They were on the lorry for two days and nights with nothing to eat. In Spain they were asked what they wanted to do and they said that they wanted to go to England. They were taken straight to Paris. In Paris they were put, at night, on to a big lorry. They travelled by this lorry to Dover. They started the journey with 25,000 marks and by the time they reached Dover, they had only 5,000 marks (about £1900) left of their money.

Once in Dover they got out of the lorry and they registered immediately and were given IND and told they were free. People were kind to them. They went to London.

They needed English lessons but it wasn't easy to access English lessons or even to know how to find a school, a solicitor or how to travel on the tube but they managed with help from a family member who came over from America to help them settle in. She stayed with them for six months. In 2000 the children started school in Manor Park. They had been in the country for over five months.

The family applied for asylum but after one year they received a refusal. They applied again and the authorities sent them to court. In January 2002 the judge gave them Exceptional Leave to Remain in England outside of immigration laws but the Home Office would not accept the judge's decision. They had asked to remain for five years but unfortunately the Solicitor had made the wrong application. The solicitor had asked for permission for them to remain forever.

Every week Mark had to go and sign on at the local police station in Forest Gate. One day in December 2002 he went to sign and was detained and told that he would be sent back to Kosovo. When he didn't return home Lindita contacted the local refugee support worker, attached to the children's school (Funding for this post ceased just before Christmas 2002). The support worker contacted Sr. Anne and asked her if she could stay with the three children (a third daughter had been born in 2000) while she went with Lindita to the police station. Lindita didn't want to take the children with her in case they were all detained.

On arriving at the police station she wasn't allowed to see her husband, nor was his solicitor. Apparently Mark had misunderstood a question regarding his solicitor (there was no interpreter present) and had said he had changed solicitors. Eventually after three attempts the solicitor was allowed to see him. It appeared that his papers had been lost. That evening at eight o'clock his twelve year old daughter received a phone call from the police station. She was expected, over the phone to give details of her father's medication for his heart problem! No-one had asked if there was an adult with the three girls all under twelve. An hour later Lindita returned home. She hadn't been allowed to see her husband at all and was told to return the next morning at eight o'clock. She went early but still had not been allowed to see him at two pm. She managed to get a doctor's note regarding his health and the solicitor eventually managed to get copies of his papers from Dover. He was released at four pm having been detained through a misunderstanding for thirty-six hours and the whole family having been put through incredible unnecessary stress. Two months later

they met the MP for Newham, Stephen Timms. He phoned the Home Office on their behalf and they were told that they would not be sent back to Kosovo because they had a strong case for Refugee Status. They had to wait for an application form from the High Court for Human Rights but they were given a paper telling them not to worry that they wouldn't be sent back because the husband had a medical record of the injuries he had received in Kosovo.

After five years of worry and stress over their status the family were granted Indefinite Leave to Remain under the Amnesty in February 2004.

© Anne Wells

7.7. FAMILY 'G' MAIN CASE STUDY

7.7.1. DESTINATION SAFETY

Neta, the respondent interviewed was married and had two children Kristian aged five and Brixhilda aged two, when she and her husband made the decision to flee from the religious and political persecution of Kosovo and seek safety in another country. They came from a village in Kosovo where the husband was a shepherd and builder. Neta was a housewife in her thirties and like the majority of Kosovan wives had no other occupation.

One day in January 1999, having gone into hiding in the hills several times fearing for their children's safety, they decided that they had no option but to leave Kosovo. They boarded a lorry to a destination unknown but promising safety and travelled overland for two days. They were unprepared for the conditions of the journey. There were thirty people travelling in their lorry and it was very uncomfortable, extremely hot and they had brought only a little bread to eat. The driver was carrying them illegally and because he was afraid they would be spotted by the police they were not allowed to look out or to get out. They were in the lorry for two nights. Eventually they arrived in Dover where the police discovered them and gave them food. The police took them to Croydon where they spent one night at the police station. They applied for asylum, were registered and given identity papers and then at three am they were sent back to Dover where they were given a room in a hostel, some chips and a bottle of milk but no money. They spent two days there before they were sent to a Social Services Centre in East London for support and accommodation.

For their first two weeks in the UK the family lived in a bed and breakfast hotel in Southend and were then sent to Ilford, where they stayed in another hotel for two to three weeks until they were placed in a private rented house in Manor Park. A few months later they were moved to another house elsewhere in Manor Park. Their new home was far from ideal. It was infested with mice. The bathroom was damp and there was a problem with drainage. The fridge wasn't working properly and there was no washing machine.

7.7.2. COMMENCEMENT OF INTEGRATION

In April 1999 feeling a little more secure in their new home the couple, both Catholics, approached the local Roman Catholic (RC) church with their two children and meeting the priest, Father Denis, they said the only word they knew in English 'school' indicating the oldest child. Fr. Denis arranged for the child to be admitted to the local RC Primary School the following Monday. Sr. Anne met Neta that morning in the school entrance and using sign language discovered where she lived. Neta didn't even understand the word 'Hello'.

That week Sr. Anne accompanied the couple to the local Adult Education Centre so that they could receive English lessons. They were asked to come back on a specific enrolment day and so later that week returned. On arrival they were handed two application forms for the 'Beginners Course' in English to fill in - name, address, date of birth, education received and requesting them to write a passage in English stating why they wished to attend this course and their previous experience of English!' The couple looked at the forms in total bewilderment and so Sr. Anne had no alternative but to take the forms to fill in herself. With great difficulty, as they had no common language other than sign language, she managed to establish when they were born and that although Neta had received some primary education and could read and write in Albanian, her husband had never been to school and could not read or write. Suddenly the lady who had given them the forms noticed that the applicants were not completing the forms themselves and became quite irate, insisting that Sr. Anne let them complete the forms themselves. Sr. Anne's explanation that they were hoping to follow the course because they had 'no English' apparently was of no significance to the registrar and had no bearing on the matter. So they handed in two almost blank sheets of paper and the registrar told them that there was a three months waiting list.

For the next few months Sr. Anne went almost daily to their house and slowly collected a small group of Kosovan women to whom she gave English lessons. There were no Albanian books, no dictionaries available in the Public Libraries and even the Albanian Embassy was of no help (Now the situation has improved and there are many centres offering free English lessons and there are even some Albanian books available but in the year 1999 the situation was very different).

One day Sr. Anne managed to meet Neta with an interpreter present. She discovered that shortly after they had arrived in England their daughter had spent a week in hospital but no one had been able to find an interpreter to tell her parents what was wrong. She recovered but her mother never discovered what was wrong with her child. At that time it was almost impossible to find anyone who could speak both Albanian and English. In January 2000 their daughter was given a nursery place in one of the local schools.

Another baby was born in March 2000 and they obtained baby clothes, a cot, pram etc from various local charities. Sr. Anne helped them apply for a grant for a washing machine, but the grant was refused. Struggling with the washing, in April 2000 they applied for a loan to purchase a washing machine but it took several months to be granted.

7.7.3. HOUSING PROBLEMS

When the baby was five weeks old, their landlord called to see them and declared that he was going to evict them in mid April 2000 as their housing benefit hadn't been paid since November 1999. They were naturally very distressed as they were not to blame for the lack of payment. The family had applied on time for Housing Benefit but the Housing Benefit system was in total chaos and was still processing their claim. The family's solicitor was contacted through the assistance of the Children's Society and the landlord was notified. He was informed that no eviction order was binding unless put in writing and the family given at least one month's notice against which they could appeal. However the landlord apparently ignored the Solicitor's letter and decided to try to get them out by other means. One day when the family returned from taking the baby to the doctor, they discovered that a 'To Let' sign had been put up outside their home. They had still received no written letter of eviction. Sr. Anne decided that they must try and sort out the Housing Benefit so she went with the husband to the local Housing Office. They waited for two hours and were then told the computer was malfunctioning. Two hours later they were seen and the family were told to go to see a Housing Adviser in East Ham. The Housing Adviser sent a letter to their landlord explaining why he couldn't evict the family and the 'To Let' sign was removed.

In early June 2000 the family began to have serious problems with their toilet in the bathroom behind their kitchen. The whole bathroom floor was awash with sewage. It was suspected that they had a blocked drain. The landlord refused to come and attend to the matter as their Housing Benefit still hadn't been paid. Suffering from ill health the family were advised by their doctor to get written confirmation from the Council that their house was unfit to live in. On phoning the Environmental Health, the officials there said that they could do nothing about the drains but would come and check on the damp. Eventually Thames Water came to see the drains and announced they were fine but the toilet pan was cracked. The landlord still refused to do anything. Eventually one of the parishioners kindly paid for a plumber to install a new toilet and Sr. Anne's community bought the toilet for them. As if life was not hard enough the toilet had no sooner been fixed when the family's gas supply failed, therefore for three days they had no hot water and no hot meals. The landlord still refused their appeals for help.

As winter approached they began to suffer more serious racial harassment. One day while the husband was alone in the house someone came and put a padlock on his front door effectively locking him in. He had to call the police to let him out. Another evening that winter a car pulled up and two youths threw bricks through the living room window and the children's bedroom window, making huge holes in the glass and narrowly missing the children. The landlord refused to mend the windows. The children were too afraid to continue sleeping in the room and they could no longer use the living room because of the cold. The windows were never mended. Eventually in March 2001 a year after the landlord had first threatened the family with eviction, the family were evicted because their Housing Benefit still hadn't been paid due to the disorder and consequent backlog that had built up in the Benefits Office.

The bailiffs came at nine am one Monday morning. Sr. Anne went with the family and an interpreter to the Homeless Persons Unit in Plaistow. Neta's greatest fear was that she would be separated from her children and despite Sister's efforts to assure her through the interpreter that her fears would not be realised she continued to become more and more upset. The family were told that they would be placed in a bed and breakfast in Southend. When they expressed their concern and distress about having to go so far and asked about the children's school they were told that they could stay at school in Manor Park and travel by train. When Sister said that it was hardly practical to bring three young children that distance by train every day, the interviewer to her surprise stated: 'But the children are teenagers.' Sister pointed out that the three children in question were before her and all under six years. Apart from their age it would also be very expensive and Sr. Anne asked: 'Who will pay?' They were told: 'Well, they get child benefit, don't they?' The interviewer seemed to have no idea of the situation of the family before her. The only other option the family had was to stay with friends and come back the next day. Apparently, the situation varies from day to day. Each morning one of the advisers phones a number of assigned hotels/hostels in the London/Essex area and is informed how many available rooms they have for single people and families. That morning there was no accommodation available for a family of five in the London area. The family left the unit feeling very despondent and praying for a miracle.

While the older children went back into school for lunch, Sr. Anne took the rest of the family to Fr. Denis and he gave them lunch. Their miracle occurred shortly afterwards. He received a phone call. A parishioner had a flat that the family could have and he was willing to wait for however long was necessary for the payment of Housing Benefit. To their joy, they were able to move in that afternoon. The landlord, a generous benefactor, even gave them money for food and for over two years they lived very happily in his flat. However during that time they had endless problems with benefits, going for many months without any money coming in at all. This was taking up a huge amount of Sister's time. Fortunately, the local Methodist Children's Society came to her aid, assigning a Key-Worker to their case. The lady, a volunteer, would visit the family once a week and assist with chasing up benefits, reading and replying to official and unofficial mail and generally supporting them in whatever needs they had. She also kept in close contact with Sister, keeping her up to date with their situation and asking for assistance when necessary.

In June 2003 they acquired another housing problem as their landlord died and his son gave them verbal notice of eviction because he wanted to sell the property. Their lease expired in mid August 2003 and they were supposed to have vacated the premises by the end of August. The landlord, realizing their situation, didn't however press for them to leave immediately. In September the husband was working, helping to refurbish a house just two doors away in the hope that they could rent it, but unfortunately that hope never materialized. Meanwhile the husband was working part-time in Leyton but his 'working tax credit' had not been transferred from his last place of work and he was owed £57 a week since April 2003. The Key-Worker had applied for him but it took until February 2004 - even with his official consent for her to negotiate on his behalf, for the money, amounting to £900, to be repaid!

Apart from housing problems the family also had problems with their doctor and mis-diagnosis. At one stage the doctor insisted that they all had chicken pox even though the spots had lasted over a month. In desperation Sr. Anne asked a parishioner who is a nurse to look at them. She diagnosed scabies and advised Sister to take them all to casualty. The hospital confirmed the diagnosis. Later that year, just before Christmas 2002, they tried to change surgeries but there was a shortage of doctors in the area. Eventually the local chemist informed them that a local doctor was taking on new patients and gave the family a letter. It took them until early 2004 to find another doctor able to accept them.

During this time Neta was attending English Lessons three times a week at the Froud Center and Little Ilford School and also cookery lessons where she was able to meet other asylum seekers from many other nationalities and learn to cook English dishes. She also attended a childcare course. Her husband, unable to read or write in Albanian, found the idea of lessons too daunting to even begin classes and continued with his part-time work.

In early October 2003 the husband was off work for two weeks with very high blood pressure. Many years ago in Kosovo he had cut his foot with the result that he can no longer move his big toe. Whenever he walks his lower leg goes numb. He was getting a very bad pain at the back of his head and the doctor said that it was connected to his leg. That month he underwent tests for his heart. They proved negative but he discovered that he had asthma.

The Key-Worker and Sister continued to try to find them new accommodation. At Sure Start one Tuesday, Neta told her that one of her Kosovan friends had told her that the ground floor flat in their house was vacant and suggested she should apply to the landlord. That afternoon they all went to see the flat. It was not ideal. The workmen had gone but had left it unfinished and there was no flooring. The kitchen needed some work done and a new cooker. The second bedroom was really an extension of the living room and would need a curtain to separate the two rooms but it would do. The following day Sister went with the Key-Worker, Neta and her husband to meet with the landlady. The landlady was a little vague about the time scale but it looked promising and Neta was thrilled. The Key-Worker agreed to do all the negotiations and paperwork and to contact the Housing benefit etc. The fact that the family had no status and officially had received a negative from the Home Office, complicated matters and they realized that it would help if proceedings regarding the house were delayed until after their appeal. Neta was so anxious to move in and acquire the flat that she spent a whole day in October cleaning it and the landlady, obviously realizing she was onto a good thing, asked Neta to clean the battered old cooker. Their Key-Worker was concerned that the landlady was unreliable and using her as free labour before any papers had been signed, and advised them not to take the new flat. Another asylum-seeker's family moved into the flat just after Christmas and had considerable problems with part of the ceiling falling down. Eventually they were moved by social services.

By November Neta and her family were still desperately looking for accommodation that they could afford in the local area. Although they received Housing Benefit the amount is calculated in relation to each accommodation and the tenant has to pay the rest (as explained in chapter five).

7.7.4. REDUNDANCY

To make matters worse in mid December 2003 the husband was made redundant. By the beginning of February the family's own landlord was still silent on the subject of their vacating his flat so no decision had been made. They had heard nothing about the court hearing. They presumed that the Amnesty had put all appeals into abeyance although according to the Amnesty regulations their family did not qualify for the Amnesty as they had at one stage had Exceptional Leave to Remain in the UK. At the end of March they heard that it was possible to apply for a questionnaire regarding the Amnesty and phoned the Home Office to check firstly that their papers had been transferred from the Courts to the Home Office and to ask for an Amnesty questionnaire.

In mid April Sr. Anne attended a two hour meeting with the family, an interpreter and a Benefits Adviser for asylum seekers from the borough of Newham. The family were very concerned because the husband hadn't been working since mid December and their working tax credit had continued. Therefore they would have to pay back the money that they were not entitled to receive out of the £900 back pay. At that time they were receiving only Housing Benefit (which they are not entitled to) and Child Benefit of £37 a week. The Benefits Adviser explained that according to the Law they were not entitled to receive benefits. Just like anyone entering the UK from the new EU member states, they were expected to work if they came to the UK but were not entitled to receive benefits. They could receive support from Social Services but only if they were destitute and when they last applied to Social Services in February they had just received the back payment of Working Tax Credit and were still receiving that along with Child Benefit, Child Tax Credit and Housing Benefit and so were not destitute. The Benefits Adviser realized that they should not be receiving Housing Benefit and said that she would inform the Benefit Office. This action in effect would make the family destitute and therefore entitled to support from Social Services. She emailed a letter for Sister to take to Social Services the following day when she went with Neta to apply for support from Social Services. The husband had been trying for a job but so far had had no luck. Whenever he showed that he could legally work, the agencies said that they had no vacant places but could give him a job, below the minimum wage. In other words they would employ him illegally for very little pay. No doubt they thought that he would be so desperate he would take it. The Benefit's Adviser told Sr. Anne that thousands of people were in that family's position. Once a person received status they would be able to apply for main stream benefits again and the husband would be able to apply for work.

The Adviser asked whether the family were on the Council waiting list. They weren't. Neither the Key-Worker nor Sister had realized that when their ELR had ended in Sept 2000 they were still technically considered as having ELR until they actually received their refusal in September 2003. Consequently they could have applied to be on the Council Housing waiting list. When they were evicted they would have been placed in temporary accommodation and by now would be in a council house. This had never been explained to the family or their support workers. Even the Housing Adviser in East Ham who saw them in April 2000 had never mentioned that they should be on the waiting list for a council property. He had just advised them to attend the Homeless Unit in Plaistow once they were evicted.

The Adviser said that she would contact the family's solicitor on Monday to confirm their status and also contact NASS to see if they were still considered to be asylum seekers and therefore could be supported by NASS rather than Social Services. If that was the case they would receive better support. Sister accompanied the family the following Friday to the Local Service Centre to notify Social Services that they had a change of status. Their ELR had been refused and their Housing Benefit had been suspended. They were told to return on the following Monday.

On the Monday after all their documents had been scrutinized and photocopied the family were told that their application for support from Social Services had been referred and they would hear news within the next two days from the CAIT team at Social Services. By this time the family were desperate. When their papers initially expired in April they were without money for four weeks and depended totally on charity and borrowing from friends. By that time they were receiving Child Benefit and Child Tax Credit amounting to approximately £130 a week for the five of them. They had to pay for food, clothes, electricity and gas out of this meagre sum of money. They weren't even entitled to free school meals because they had no documentation to prove that they were on a low income. However the school kindly agreed to let the children have free school meals.

Three days later, as the family had heard nothing Sister contacted a CAIT team member whom the Benefits Adviser had recommended and was told that no one had the right to inform a client that they would be contacted within two days. She couldn't talk to Sister as she was supervising a student but she passed Sister over to another member of her team who asked endless questions and then passed her onto another team member who promised to phone her back later. By three pm Sister had heard nothing so she phoned the lady back and she said that she realized it was urgent and had passed on the message for the attention of the first lady Sister had spoken to, (the lady too busy to talk.) Sr. Anne felt as if she was going around in circles and getting nowhere. However the lady she was speaking to told her that she knew the other lady had seen the message and was sure that she would phone back. She didn't phone back. Sr. Anne tried contacting the Benefits Adviser but although she answered the phone she informed Sister that she couldn't talk to her as she was on strike and she advised her to phone back the next day.

The following day Sister phoned CAIT and spoke to another member of their team who was most helpful and said she would investigate what was happening. She phoned Sister back within twenty minutes and told her that their duty manager would phone her on Monday. If he didn't phone she should phone him. Four pm came and Sister had received no phone call so as instructed, she tried to contact the duty manager who apparently was not answering his phone. Three days later she phoned CAIT once again and was told that the duty manager had the situation in hand and was trying to find a caseworker for the family. They would be interviewed in Albanian and it would probably take seven days to assess all their needs. Sister was asked if the couple could read and write.

Two days later they were told that they had an interview booked with a member of CAIT team for the following week. The parents and children attended the hour-long interview with a Social worker from the CAIT team to see how the Team could best support the family. There was an interpreter present supplied by the family, and Sr. Anne.

The following day Sister received a phone call from the social worker who had interviewed the family, seeking more information. As the family was no longer an asylum issue they would not be catered for by the asylum team and could need long-term support, therefore the CAIT team needed to know why the family had been refused an extension of their ELR. Sr. Anne needed to establish the reason and phone the social worker back. The following day she informed the social worker that the Home Office had stated in a letter to the husband:

' You have applied for further leave to remain in the UK on an exceptional basis but the Secretary of State is not satisfied that variation of leave to remain is being sought for a purpose covered by the Immigration rules. The Secretary of State therefore refuses your application.'

The Social Worker informed Sister that the family were not the responsibility of the CAIT team and would be referred to the Non Habitual Resident Team (NHRT) and hopefully they would hear something soon.

Six days later the social worker on the CAIT team told Sister that she had been advised to close the case and two days after that they heard that the NHRT had accepted the family's files. It took another week before the family heard anything from NHRT. A social worker went to see them and gave them a piece of paper telling them that they had to move house and were to collect the keys to their new house the following morning. The Key-Worker and Sister met with the family that morning. It was now towards the end of May, almost six weeks since the family were deemed to be destitute. The Key-Worker and Sister were puzzled that the family had to move for although their landlord wanted them to move he hadn't actually given them eviction papers. A member of the NHRT told Sister when she phoned that the family needed to move because their present rent was £548 a week and the social services were not willing to pay so much. Sister expressed surprise and said they were actually paying only £170 a week. The lady promised to phone Sister back once she had located the file. The Key-Worker phoned their present landlord who confirmed that they were paying £170 a week a week but expressed relief that the family was about to be re-housed as he wished to sell the property. The Key-Worker also phoned the solicitor who told her that the exclusion clause in the Amnesty stating that 'if the family had ever been granted Exceptional Leave to Remain they did not qualify for the Amnesty,' had been removed and the family now qualified for the Amnesty. However they might have to wait another year to hear the news. Later that afternoon the interpreter and Neta went with Sister to collect the keys to the new property and to see it. A rent of £975 a month would be paid by Social Services plus water rates and Council Tax.

7.7.5. A NEW HOME – MORE HOUSING PROBLEMS

The family moved that evening into their new home. It was a good size property with a tiny garden but there were a number of problems that the landlord needed to fix. Among the more serious problems was the fact that two electrical points were hanging off the wall with wires exposed. In addition the kitchen door had five panes of glass missing so that anyone could get in, also the downstairs toilet was not fixed to the floor.

The following day Kristian had to go into hospital as a day patient to have several teeth removed under a general anaesthetic. None of the family had been to a dentist since they arrived in the UK. The next evening Sr. Anne received a phone call from Neta. She was concerned because the landlord had come to the house and removed one of the two tables and four of the chairs leaving them with three chairs, two of which were broken. No one had explained to the family how to work the gas key-meter so they had no gas or electricity. The next day Sister phoned the family's Letting Agency asking for someone to explain to the family how the key-meter worked for the gas and electricity and to give them time to arrange for an interpreter to be present.

Another job Neta asked Sister to do at this time was to phone Social Services to ask if the family could have a letter saying that they were entitled to free school meals. Neta was concerned that the school was still paying for the children's meals. However Sister was told that they probably were not entitled. The request would be passed on.

The following Saturday just five days after the family had moved in to their new home Neta visited Sr. Anne to show Sister the corpses of several bugs she had found in their home. She told Sister that they came out at night and were all over the floor and walls and in their clothes. Sister phoned the landlord. He already knew about the infestation but said he hadn't had time to do anything about it and couldn't until after the bank holiday. Sister expressed her concern because of the children in the house.

Two days later she visited the family and showed the workmen next door (who had worked on both houses) the condensation between the double glazing in the main bedroom and the badly fitting front door. They said that they would come and correct it. The family also told Sister that there was a hole in the garden that their youngest child aged four had fallen into. It turned out to be quite a deep drain with no cover and it had been overgrown with vegetation. They also had no fence on either side of their property. The other problems had still not been fixed. Sister phoned the Benefits Adviser for advice and support and she promised to contact the landlord.

Two weeks after moving in, the family was still having problems as nothing had been repaired. Sr. Anne went with the mother to the Local Service Centre (LSC) as the mother had received two letters about Housing Benefit and Council Tax. The LSC said that the family had only cancelled the Housing Benefit when they moved house on 24 May. They had no evidence that the benefits adviser had cancelled it in mid April. Sister wrote a letter of complaint to the LSC regarding the distress caused by the confusion regarding Housing Benefit and Council Tax. Sister eventually received a letter back saying that they didn't understand what she was complaining about.

Sr. Anne visited the LSC with Neta. They could find no proof that the Housing Benefit had been cancelled in mid-April. Eventually they established that the family could not claim for school meals even though they were on the lowest level of income deemed acceptable. A Benefits expert came along to advise and he confirmed that the Housing Benefit had been paid up to the 24 May 2004 and that was correct.

While Sr. Anne and Neta were at the LSC, Neta showed Sister the tenancy agreement that the Letting Agent had given her. It was the wrong Agreement, an agreement for another property. She showed it to the LSC adviser who was horrified and said that it was a serious breach of confidentiality and advised Sister to write a letter of complaint.

Sr. Anne phoned the Letting Agent to complain that the family had received the wrong tenancy agreement and that it was a breach of confidentiality. She was shocked when the agent declared that it was 'only an error' and he couldn't see why she was upset about it. Sister also expressed her concern regarding the electrical problem that the landlord still hadn't fixed. She said that there was a danger the four year old would be electrocuted and she was assured that the previous day the Agent had spoken to the landlord and he had agreed to have it fixed within twenty-four hours. If he didn't the Agent would bring the matter to Social Services. Later that day Sister wrote a letter of complaint to the Letting Manager and returned the tenancy agreement asking him to replace it with the correct document.

Two weeks later Sister heard that Environmental Health had come to treat the infestation and stated that the problem was cockroaches. A month after moving in the family still had not received their correct tenancy agreement. However the electricity cable had been secured and the fence was slowly being erected and the back garden was being paved.

That week Sister arranged for the mother to pay, in instalments, the gas bill for her last house. Sister also informed the Letting Agent that although the family had gas they no longer had hot water. The agent promised to send someone around to check the boiler later that day but no one came.

Three days later the family were still without hot water. Sister phoned the Letting Agent at eleven am and he said that he would send someone around. At four pm the family phoned to say that no one had come. Sister phoned the Letting Agent who was most unpleasant, declaring that the family was awkward and indirectly accusing them of breaking the boiler because they didn't want to stay in the property.

He accused Sister of placing unsuitable tenants with his Agency to which Sr. Anne responded: 'One minute - I have nothing to do with placing them as your tenants. I do not work for Social Services.' He then had a long tale about Sister demanding that the landlord put down paving stones in the garden when he wanted to put down grass at one end. Sr. Anne said that she had only spoken to the landlord once about the insect infestation and had no idea what he was talking about. But he must remember the family spoke limited English and perhaps they hadn't understood what the landlord intended to do with the garden. She said that they were very happy with the house but were unhappy that they had no hot water. He said that someone would go around that day to look at the boiler. It was fixed.

A couple of weeks later they began to experience problems with one of their electric lights which continually switched on and off. The landlord came round to fix it and pushed some paper into the socket to keep the light off – the result being that the paper caught fire and they could have had a serious fire. The landlord promised to send someone else to take a look at it.

Later the same evening the Key-Worker phoned Sister to tell her that the family's Child Tax Credit needed to be reapplied for and she had discovered that they were no longer entitled to claim. This however proved to be incorrect information. They were eventually awarded Child Tax Credit until July 2005.

7.7.6. PROBLEMS WITH STATUS

In September 1999 the family had been granted Exceptional Leave to Remain in the UK for one year and in October 1999 the husband was given a National Insurance Number and given permission to work although at the time he hardly spoke any English and had no hope of finding work. While seeking employment he was given Job Seekers' Allowance.

In September 2000 they received notification from the Home Office that their case was under review and were requested not to contact the Home Office regarding their case as it would hold up proceedings. Elane Heffernan told the authors that people, like Neta's family who 'get Exceptional Leave before the Amnesty came into being found themselves in a "never, never land" because their Exceptional Leave had run out. It would not be renewed so they found themselves with no status in a "kind of limbo" which was very stressful'.

In April 2003 having heard nothing from the Home Office since September 2000 they were suddenly summoned for an interview. After that interview in June 2003 they were told that their application for asylum had been refused.

Ms Heffernan explained that Neta's family's problem with status arose because they didn't get their Exceptional Leave papers until very late after it had been granted. It was necessary to apply for an extension to ELR before the time already granted ended. Once a person applied for an extension the Exceptional Leave continued until the Home Office made a decision, but as the family did not apply in time they lost their Exceptional Leave to Remain. They had the right to reside in the country legally but as regards benefits status they were considered as people from abroad and therefore would be supported not by NASS but by Social Services under Section 17 on Real Crisis Payments. Ms. Heffernan said that it was a very complicated system whereby 'two families who appear to be the same can't comprehend why they are not treated equally.'

In the Autumn their solicitor arranged for them to appeal against the negative decision on the grounds they were now fully settled and integrated into the local community. When the husband attended the interview, to his interpreter's dismay he once again pleaded on the grounds that it was unsafe to return to Kosovo, bringing up fresh evidence about their time in Kosovo, rather than appealing on the grounds advised by the Solicitor. The interpreter realised that the husband had a learning disability and after the interview arranged for him to see his doctor. They hoped to be allowed to re-appeal on the grounds of his learning disability and they hoped that his wife would be allowed to speak on his and their family's behalf. Their solicitor put in another appeal for them, including a petition signed by over one hundred people in the locality, saying that they were well thought of and respected members of the local community, adding: 'We strongly recommend that this family, who have proved themselves to be excellent citizens and are so happily settled here, be granted permission to remain in England.'

© Anne Wells

In September 2004 the family were still waiting for a hearing date and had heard nothing. It had been expected before Christmas 2003 and yet by then it was almost Christmas 2004!

7.7.7. AMNESTY GRANTED

Eventually, shortly after the family were interviewed in early October 2004, the family phoned Sr. Anne to inform her that they had received the Amnesty questionnaire. A few weeks later, to their great joy and relief, they were informed that they had been granted the Amnesty and were entitled to remain indefinitely in the UK.

They immediately set about transferring from Social Services to Mainstream Benefits with the help of the Shpresa team at the Froud Centre. As the husband has a learning disability, they decided that it would be wiser for him to remain at home and care for the children while his wife applied for full-time English lessons, leading onto full time training and work. In the spring of 2005 Neta began full-time education and received Job Seekers Allowance.

Six years after they had fled Kosovo, the family was able at last to truly rebuild their lives. No longer did they live in limbo, under the constant fear of forced repatriation and the knowledge that for their basic needs they were totally reliant on the State which could demand their deportation at any time. They were free to settle and fully integrate and take an active part in UK society.

CHAPTER EIGHT

CHALLENGES FOR THE CHRISTIAN COMMUNITIES

In this chapter we will consider the challenges that face the Christian communities in the UK to help genuine asylum seekers to settle and integrate as fully as possible. Firstly we will consider the ways in which the RC Church and in particular the Church within the Deanery of Newham, have been facing this challenge. We interviewed two Roman Catholic priests and two Roman Catholic sisters who responded on behalf of their parishes – St. Stephen's and St. Nicholas', Manor Park; St. Michaels', East Ham: St. Margaret's, Canning Town and St. John's and St. Mark's, Silvertown and Beckton. Secondly we interviewed another Roman Catholic sister who responded on behalf of her parish - St. Antony's, Forest Gate and RAMP – the NGO she works with. We asked questions about each parish's ethnic composition, the percentage of recent arrivals (those who arrived within the last five – six years): whether the recent arrivals were refugees or asylum seekers and the percentage that were families; the type of help requested; how much of their ministry involved children. Lastly we invited them to share some of their own personal experiences and reflections on what the Christian communities can do to help refugees and asylum seekers to integrate.

8.1. ROMAN CATHOLIC DEANERY OF NEWHAM

In 2005 there were eight parishes in the Roman Catholic Deanery of Newham, with approximately 7,000 practising Catholics. The deanery was one of the most ethnically diverse in London with seventy to eighty countries represented. Some parishes had a greater diversity than others while others had one larger ethnic group than the rest. For example East Ham had a large Kerala population, while Manor Park had a greater Sri Lankan population and Forest Gate had more Tamils.

8.1.1. ST. STEPHEN'S AND ST. NICHOLAS' CHURCH, MANOR PARK

In 2002 Father Denis Hall asked his parishioners in Manor Park where they were from and discovered that about sixty countries were represented. Many more arrived in the following three years. He told the authors that 'many new parishioners arrive every week.'

When Fr. Denis was interviewed in February 2005 he reckoned that there were probably about seventy countries represented in the parish. He said that the 'going and coming was very fluid' and he was unable to put a figure on how many were asylum seekers or refugees as they rarely told him. However he had approximately one person every fortnight asking for help with documents. In the last year there had been many more Nigerians and Eastern Europeans arriving.

The predominant arrivals were from Africa (Uganda, Nigeria, Ghana, the Congo) and many others from Eastern and South Eastern Europe (Kosovo and Albania). The parish had very few new parishioners from South America although there were some from Ecuador. He explained that on arrival the refugees usually tended to look for others from their own ethnic group and once found, stuck together. Many of the South Americans had congregated in other parishes.

The majority of new arrivals were families (approximately 80%) although it was not always possible for all members of a family to arrive together. Often one or both parents arrived first to be joined at a later stage by their children. Frequently the parents had been in the parish some months when their children arrived, and went to Fr. Denis looking for help to find a Catholic school for the children.

The majority of people who came looking for help were Catholics but they sometimes came to ask for help for their Muslim and Hindu friends. Various forms of help were requested. The most frequent request was help to find work. Many Africans and East Europeans thought that the Church would help them find work. Fr. Denis usually directed them to work either in childcare or cleaning. The question of whether they were legally entitled to work never arose.

Another constant request for help was to place a child or children in the Catholic school. Many of the African families' children who came to the parish from war zones had been unable to receive the sacraments. Once the children were settled into a school the parents came to the parish requesting Baptism and First Communion for their older children. Every year there were as many as ten to fifteen children aged 10-16 years old, in that category.

Many of the families came to Father hoping that the Church could solve their problems whether they were moral, spiritual or psychological. Others had more practical problems. Many immigrants had dubious housing which was often unsuitable for their needs so they came to the Church for help to acquire more suitable accommodation. Sometimes they asked for food or clothes or furniture. They were usually very specific about the type of support they needed and Father had had requests for a microwave and a washing machine. Very few people actually asked for money and many did not want even to be lent money when it was offered.

Fr. Denis was frequently asked for help regarding documents and therefore had a lot of contact with officials. He pleaded with officials, sent faxes and letters while encouraging and supporting the immigrant families. He said that he persisted in asking for help for those in need.

Fr. Denis shared some of his personal experience with the authors. One family came to him in great distress in April 2004. They had been granted the Amnesty a month previously and had to move out of their NASS accommodation into temporary B&B accommodation. The son was about to sit his GCSE's, the father was physically ill and the mother was suffering from depression. They had gone to Fr. Denis for help and support. He helped them to move out and stored their possessions for them. The mother was still very depressed in February 2005 but at last they were settled in a proper house.

Fr. Denis told the authors that the majority of the Catholics who came from overseas had suffered for their faith. They valued the freedom to worship in the UK and had a deep sense of community which was helped by seeing other members of their own community present in church. Many were looking for spiritual help. Others wanted any help they could get from the church, even though they didn't have strong ties with the church in their own country while some had strong faith and wanted to get established with psychological and social help

One of the authors is a member of the Sisters of the Sacred Heart of Mary who have a small community in the parish. They also support the asylum seekers, advising, filling in forms, collecting and distributing clothes. They take some of the donated clothes to the Didsbury Centre in East Ham which has a clothes store for refugees.

Sometimes a family without benefits was put in touch with the sisters by one of the NGO's and then the sisters organized a food collection within the parish for a few weeks until the family were able to support themselves. The parishioners were always extremely generous.

8.1.2. ST. MICHAEL'S CHURCH, EAST HAM

Sr. Monica Butler lives in the Roman Catholic parish of East Ham. She told the authors that she was not sure how many nationalities were actually in the parish but there were many Filipinos, Irish and Africans as well as Indians from Kerala. Although there were many refugees and asylum seekers in East Ham, it was not so obvious in the parish structure and there was no one in the parish working specifically with asylum seekers and refugees. The predominant arrivals were from Nigeria, Kosovo and Uganda.

In Sr. Monica's experience the people coming looking for help were mainly single Ugandan young men and some Kosovan families. One of the Kosovan families was Muslim but all her other contacts were Catholic. The main request for assistance was help with documents, to understand, appeal, deal with benefits. They also needed psychological help. She had had no requests for help to acquire furniture, clothes or help with accommodation but she helped with those issues as well.

The two Kosovan families she had befriended had both received the Amnesty. She told the authors:

> 'They had no real problems with the transition to mainstream benefits apart from natural difficulties. The hand over was rather abrupt. There was nothing in place to help them. NASS just said they were no longer their responsibility and they were left to fend for themselves. There was no introduction to the new system. If they hadn't English friends I don't know how they would have managed. We helped them through the system.'

One of the two families received the Amnesty in the Spring of 2004. In the following year they were moved three times into different areas and in the Spring of 2005 were still in temporary accommodation. First they had been moved to Romford. That flat was dirty and it had rats so they were moved to West Ham where the flat was upstairs and the mother who had bad legs was unable to cope with the pushchair and so many stairs so they were moved to East Ham. In February 2005 they were living in a fifth floor flat. There was a lift but it was difficult with four children. As the mother was aware of the children's need for stability, the children remained in the same school throughout all their moves but travelling was difficult, costly and time consuming.

A great deal of Sr. Monica's work with that young family had involved schools. The Roman Catholic family had been anxious to get the children into a Roman Catholic school. Sr. Monica negotiated with the school authorities and the parish priest. As Sister told the authors: 'It was important for them to have someone who understood how the system worked and where to go. They needed someone to be a voice for them.' She had met with the headmaster and made sure that he understood the children's background.

Sister related a story from her experience of what had happened to some Kosovan friends of hers. One morning while the mother was out at the doctors with her children, the police arrived at the house in a minibus. They had a battering ram with them. Unable to get any answer from the occupants or their neighbours they made an official raid and broke down the door. They went through all the family's documents and were just leaving as the mother returned. It was very distressing for the family. The police acknowledged their mistake explaining that the previous occupants had been on the wrong side of the law and they were unaware that the house had had a change of occupants. When Sr. Monica expressed her concern about the door, they promised that someone would come and fix it later that day. No one came. The family contacted their landlord but as he was very poor he could not afford to fix it. Sister eventually managed to get a response from Scotland Yard and the police authorized a new door.

Another Kosovan family Sr. Monica was in contact with were broken into just before Christmas 2004. They called Sister for help and she rang the police and conducted the interviews for them.

With Sr. Monica's support three Kosovan families have been able to invite their elderly parents over to visit them in the UK. Sr. Monica told Sr. Anne that one elderly mother was desperate to visit her daughter in England. She herself was living in a hut with her husband up a mountain. She went to the UK embassy in Albania and requested a travel document to visit her daughter in the UK. Expecting a refusal, she had pleaded: 'Just let me see my daughter for one hour.' The official had said that he would send her for six months and she burst into tears thinking he was refusing. It was only when she got outside and a relative saw the paper that she realised she really could go to England for six months and then her tears of sorrow turned into tears of joy.

Sr. Monica told the authors that Stephen Timms, the local MP for Newham, had been very good and helpful. He was always ready to help asylum seekers in any way he could. She told the story of how he had gone incognito to the Serbian Embassy in London with a family to apply for a travel document. The family could apply for a travel document to visit elderly relatives but had to go to the Serbian Embassy (as Kosovo is a Province of Serbia). Along with many other Kosovans they had tried to obtain travel documents from that embassy but had been refused. The embassy had not even given them a letter of refusal so they could not apply to the UK for help. In desperation they had asked the local MP for help. Afterwards he declared that the embassy had 'fobbed' him off with a meaningless letter and would not give him a letter of refusal.

Sometimes Sister takes one of the Kosovan families she has befriended to somewhere beautiful and peaceful because she has found that it helps them.

Sr. Monica told the authors about a Ugandan married man who came to the UK seeking asylum about three years ago. His wife and four children were still in Africa. He had been in prison in Uganda and managed to escape five times. He was tortured and went into hiding. Eventually he was smuggled into Kampala and managed to leave the country. His application for asylum in the UK was withdrawn and therefore he was no longer entitled to benefits. A charity was giving him thirty pounds a month for food and he gave that money to a refugee family who had kindly allowed him to sleep on their sofa.

8.1.3. ST. MARGARET'S CHURCH, CANNING TOWN

Sr. Joyce Bell kindly agreed to assist the authors in their research in the parish of St. Margaret, Canning Town. She told Sr. Anne that there were many nationalities in Canning Town including Chinese, Japanese, Caribbean, Sri Lankan, South American and African, particularly from Ghana, Ethiopia and Kenya,

Sr. Joyce shared some of her personal experience of working with asylum seekers in Canning Town. She told Sr. Anne that she was in touch with two families, both from Sri Lanka. The first family was Singalese and had five children. The oldest was thirteen when they came to the UK in 2001. Sr. Joyce told Sr. Anne what had happened to the family in Sri Lanka. One day the family had been entertaining some Tamils in their home. Shortly after the Tamils left the local Singalese officials began to round up the Tamils and accused the family of sheltering Tamil Tigers. The father was threatened and had to leave Sri Lanka. After his brother-in-law disappeared his family also fled. Sr. Joyce met them when they came to the parish looking for a Religious Service. At the time the children were helped by an asylum education support team (disbanded by the Government in 2002) and the younger children were placed in school almost immediately by the authorities. However the family had difficulty placing the eldest girl in school and even with Sr. Joyce's help it took three months to get her a place. The family's case came up in court several times. When their case came up in 2002 and was accepted by the adjudicator there wasn't a Home Office official present so they had to appeal again. They made another appeal in 2003 and another in December 2004 but that one was postponed due to the husband's poor health. He was very depressed. They were to appeal again in early February 2005.

When they arrived in the parish the husband and wife could speak very little English but their children had been at an international school in Sri Lanka and could speak English fluently. The Franciscan Friars in Canning Town and the Sisters befriended them and they were encouraged to join in various activities in the parish. The children received the sacraments and the family began to settle. Then in July 2004 they were suddenly told they had to move to Sunderland. Sr. Joyce contacted the Sisters of the Poor in Sunderland and they agreed to help support the family and help with clothes. The Franciscans from Canning Town helped the children to get into good Catholic schools in Sunderland. However in August 2004 the family received shocking news. The authorities told them that the contract for their house had terminated and they would have to move to Glasgow. One of the religious sisters in Sunderland made a big fuss. She contacted the MP and the Home Office and complained that it was wrong to move the children yet again. Her intervention meant they were allowed to stay in Sunderland but they still had to move out of their present home. They were put into B&B accommodation. After a couple of days they phoned

Sr. Joyce and asked if they were allowed to eat in the hotel because eating out was terribly expensive. Sister phoned the hotel management. Even they did not know if the family were entitled to eat in the hotel and had to make enquiries. Eventually the family was told that they could have breakfast in the hotel and a short time later they were told they could also have supper in the hotel. A few days later they were moved. In total they were moved four times to houses in different locations because the housing authorities couldn't find suitable accommodation for them. Eventually the authorities found a house big enough for the seven of them where they could stay on a more permanent basis.

For the appeal in February they had to travel from Sunderland to London. Travel is very expensive so Sr. Joyce tried to get them free travel. In order to get the documents they needed a letter from the father's doctor saying that the husband was under treatment for depression. Sister was unable to obtain the letter as apparently the solicitor had to write to the doctor for the letter but the doctor never wrote back. In the end one of the sisters in Sunderland contacted the doctor and offered to pay for the letter and the document was produced.

The Franciscans have been up to Sunderland to visit the family and Sr. Joyce called to see them at Christmas 2004 when she was visiting her family up north. The oldest girl was feeling very lonely and strange because all the other children in the area were white. Her parents were finding it difficult to make friends because there was a certain amount of bias against asylum seekers in the area.

The second family Sr. Joyce knew were also Singalese. At first the father came by himself to the UK. He was a businessman with a good job in Sri Lanka. One day a new man came to work in his office. He trained the man unaware that he was a spy for the Tamil Tigers. The Singalese authorities blamed him for employing the spy and he had to leave. Initially he left his wife and two children behind and fled. His case was taken up in the UK and he was granted asylum. His wife and children have since joined him.

8.1.4. ST. JOHN'S AND ST. MARK'S CHURCH, BECKTON

In January 2005 the parish of Beckton had two churches - St. John's with approximately seventeen different nationalities and St. Mark's with forty-three different nationalities. Approximately thirty new families came into the parish every year. When interviewed in 2005 Fr. Ray Collier SSC, the parish priest, was aware of twenty families in the parish who were refugees or asylum seekers. He said that six families had come into the parish in the last two years. The new arrivals were mainly from the Congo, Sudan and Kosovo and had all benefited from the Amnesty. There were also parishioners from Ghana and Angola. Sixty percent of the refugees/asylum seekers in the parish were families.

Fr. Ray told Sr. Anne that they had had requests for help from Muslims and Christians of other traditions as well as from Roman Catholics. The Muslims said they came because they could not get help anywhere else. He had never asked them if they had asked other Muslims for help. At that time there were eighteen different Muslim sects in Newham so it was possible that they were afraid in case they approached a different sect to themselves.

Fr. Ray channelled all help through the Harold Road Centre (RAMP). If parishioners gave him food or clothes he automatically took it to RAMP. When people asked him for help he sent them to RAMP. He had had requests for food from people with no benefits, people needing help to complete immigration documents and also people asking for psychological help. Once he had a lady suffering from bad dreams who asked him if he could help her. He had had no requests for spiritual help and very few people had asked for help to get their children into a Catholic school but then many of the people who came were not Catholic and the parish had no Catholic school.

Asked about his personal experience in supporting refugees, Fr. Ray told Sr. Anne that he mainly accompanied families, wrote to the MP on their behalf, went with families/individuals to Croydon for interviews and once he had gone with a family to the Medical Foundation for Victims of Torture. At the family's request he had arranged for a psychological assessment for their children. Happily the family recovered from their experiences.

One Malaysian family he accompanied was granted residence in the UK in September 2004. In the following month the wife discovered that her mother was seriously ill. Fr. Ray helped the whole family to go back to Malaysia to see the mother. Shortly afterwards the father became gravely ill and once again Fr. Ray helped the family with letters of support to return to Malaysia. It was particularly important as the father and his daughter had fallen out. The father and daughter were reconciled.

Another family with three children had been facing imminent deportation. When the police arrived at their home the wife locked herself in the toilet and threatened she would commit suicide. Fr. Ray phoned the Home Office and warned them that if they pushed this family the wife would commit suicide. The Home Office ignored Fr. Ray's warning and declared that the deportation was to proceed. The wife overdosed and the paramedics had to be called. The medics came and were excellent. The family were eventually granted permission to stay.

Father told Sr. Anne about a man from Nigeria who was married to an English-born Nigerian. The Home Office would not recognise his marriage, declaring it to be 'a marriage of convenience', even though the couple had two children. Each Saturday he had to sign on at the Police station. One bank holiday Saturday when he went to sign on he saw the deportation van in the police yard. He realised that he was about to be deported and using a bicycle chain locked the police gate. The police did not realise what had happened and when they went to open the gates the hydraulics broke and they had to call the fire brigade. The man was placed in a detention centre near Portsmouth but he could not be deported until the case for criminal damage had gone to court. Fr. Ray went with him as a witness and the Nigerian chose to defend himself. It was stated that the fire brigade had charged ninety pounds to cut the chain but Fr Ray was able to prove that on a similar occasion the fire brigade had charged only seven pounds and the judge threw the case out of court. The man was allowed to rejoin his family. It took two to three years to fight his case but by 2005 the man had permission to stay in the UK.

8.1.5. ST. ANTONY'S CHURCH, FOREST GATE

Sr. Mary Barrow lives in the parish of Forest Gate and has worked with RAMP for seven years. She told Sr. Anne that there were many different ethnic groups in Forest Gate parish – people from the Caribbean, India, Nigeria, Philippines, Ghana, China, Ireland, Scotland, England, the Congo, Uganda, Kosovo and a man from Australia and many people from Sri Lanka. In the area there were even many more nationalities represented including – Somali, Bangladeshi, Pakistani.

Sr. Mary said that it was hard to know how many people were recent arrivals in the parish. The recent NASS dispersal scheme meant that no one came directly to the area any more but people were dispersed to other parts of Great Britain. However one way or another they either found their way to Newham or back to Newham. She told how:

'One woman came here the other day from Glasgow. She had Indefinite Leave to Remain. She had been here about four years maybe less. Four children are here with her and three children are still in Somalia. She has twin boys aged sixteen. One she brought with her, the other she left behind and she left the younger children with relatives. She brought with her the twin who was sick and he's okay now but she has lost contact with his twin. She was badly persecuted and her husband shot. She comes to us for money to send home to her other children. We can't give her money but she really wants us just to listen to her and talk to her. It's hard.'

The predominant refugee arrivals in the area are from Somalia, Palestine, the Congo, Sri Lanka, Iran and very occasionally South American. Approximately 75% are families.

Among the people who came looking for help at RAMP they have had Colombians (illegally here) Sri Lankans, Somalians, Palestinians. They had one Iranian. He had been in the UK less than a year, been refused his application for asylum and then lost his appeal because he had not been told in time that he could appeal again against the decision. In February 2005 they still had Albanian/Kosovans coming for help although they were no longer arriving in the country. Sr. Mary stated:

> 'Unaccompanied minors are a major problem. They are supported in a foster family until they are eighteen and then are out on the streets. If they have been refused status they receive nothing. One young Somali came aged sixteen. She was refused asylum because the Home Office would not believe she was of the tribe. She had been given ELR for one year but the authorities had refused to renew it. She was still getting Income Support because the authorities hadn't noticed it should have ceased. When she becomes nineteen she will have to go onto Job-Seekers Allowance and will need to show her papers but she hasn't any.'

Sr. Mary told Sr. Anne about another unaccompanied minor (aged sixteen) who came from the Congo with her sister aged four. She was thrown on to the streets with no care and no money. Consequently she got into trouble with the police and her little sister was put into care. The probation officer was horrified that she was receiving no support.

Sr. Mary explained that a lot of asylum seekers were hidden, living in other people's houses and not known to authorities. At RAMP they give out food that has been donated to them by St. Antony's parishioners. Some people give them money for food. She said:

> 'It's very hard for people between status, when they transfer from NASS to Income Support. Many people get so excited when they hear they have been granted status they don't inform us so we can't arrange for the transfer to start. They have to wait until NASS terminates their payments before they can receive Income Support. It's getting the National Insurance Number that takes the time. They are not supposed to work but many work without telling us. Even when they receive their Income Support, they often continue working illegally. One lady told me that she was working as a cleaner illegally. She had used someone else's National Insurance card to get the job. Those working illegally are treated very badly by their employers because working illegally they are not protected by the law. If they had been allowed to work from the start that would never have happened. They often work in bad conditions for low pay and long hours. They don't complain because they would lose their jobs.'

The majority of people who came to RAMP for help were Muslims, the rest Christian, of whom some were Catholics. All the people who came wanted to talk about God and asked for prayer. Sr. Mary said: 'It is wonderful the faith that is there.' Sister said that she is 'just Mary to people who come but most know I am a sister and look for prayer, encouragement and conversation.' Sometimes she told the asylum seekers: 'the only way you are going to get this paper now is by prayer' and afterwards they came and thanked her. If she was aware that they were Catholics she tried to encourage and help the families to place their children in Catholic schools by using a bit of influence. However they always applied late.

Sister went on to explain that the requests for help were many and varied. A lot of people came because they were unable to sort out debts or to get in touch with Benefit offices. Others were unable to write a letter or make themselves understood. Sometimes they came for help with accommodation or for help negotiating with the landlord or Council. Sometimes they needed furniture and RAMP put them in touch with 'Home Store' (a second hand furniture store run very cheaply by the Quakers). RAMP provided food for those who had no food at all but money was rarely given. In the past RAMP used to give ten pounds emergency money but in 2005 that was no longer possible as RAMP found themselves in debt. However occasionally they gave money to pay fares to the solicitor or Home Office or if a family had run out of gas. They had a small clothes store with mainly baby clothes and a few children's clothes. Many refugees sent money home and that made it even harder for them to survive with little money.

Sr. Mary told the authors that many refugees came for help with documents and phoning. They had tried themselves but were not understood. Many asylum seekers needed counselling or help to get on to training courses. Newham had many English classes available as well as training courses in childcare etc with crèche facilities. Sr. Mary said that there were signs of hope among the younger refugees. While many of the older refugees were struggling with English the next generation, their children, were going to university or getting a job.

In RAMP they used to find people solicitors, but as Sr. Mary explained: 'It is more difficult now they have cut back on Legal Aid. In RAMP we have a few solicitors willing to see people once and then if they think their case is possible to take them on.'

While Sr. Mary did not work personally with children, RAMP helped families to register their children into school or for after school activities. Trinity Secondary School had a programme for older children and unaccompanied minors. There had been an art therapy group for children since early 2004. Stratford and Lister schools also ran art therapy classes for traumatised children.

Sr. Mary shared some of her personal experience of working with asylum seekers at RAMP. A Somali family – a mother with no English and five children, one a baby went to see Sr. Mary. They had nothing in the house but bunk beds. Sister had been given some food etc which she took round to them. She described what she saw:

> 'The children were sitting on a mat on the floor and the mother was most concerned that there was no carpet. They had no heating and the hot water when it came, it came in bursts and was boiling. The mother slept on the floor. There was no man. They had no furniture, just one plate and a cup. Going in to the house and seeing it [pause] that was.... [Sr. Mary found it difficult to put her feelings into words] I can't forget that woman. It haunts me.'

Another family that Sr. Mary knew well were from Zaire. They had an older son aged seven or eight and an autistic boy aged four born in the UK. They were French speakers and lived in Dagenham. They received no help with the boy. There appeared to be a tenuous relationship between the couple perhaps because of the situation they were in. The four year old screamed all the time. Sr. Mary said that she had just tried to be with that family. 'I tried to take them out for the day but they misunderstood and therefore did not turned up [pause]….. the hardship of having difficulty understanding.'

Sr. Mary knew another very educated couple from Zaire with five or six children. The father had been a dentist but could not get a job in the UK. He had psychiatric problems. They had just received status when he committed suicide by jumping in front of an express train. Sr. Mary said sadly: ' It's very hard to know how to help her (the wife).'

Amidst the tales of despair and desperation Sr. Mary was able to give some tales of hope. She told the authors how supportive the asylum seekers were for each other. A family from Bosnia, got off the lorry in Stratford and wandered around. Eventually they made their way back to the same spot as if it were a magic spot. A lady heard them speaking, took them home and got them settled. They had an eleven year old daughter, nearly twelve and a younger boy. They had been persecuted and driven out of Bosnia. The mother had lost a baby because she had been kicked in the stomach when she was pregnant. Their daughter was nineteen in 2005 and working as a volunteer mentor for asylum seekers. She had come through a great deal. However it had been a real struggle for the mother to learn English. The husband came later with his mother and became an alcoholic. Consequently he found it impossible to learn English or get a job. They had three daughters born in the UK.

In Sr. Mary's experience there was a lot of domestic violence among asylum seekers. The violence was caused partly by culture but also due to the men's lack of security. As we read in chapter four, many of the families had to destroy their documents and therefore lost any proof of their identity. The men found themselves in a new country, unable to communicate without a translator and not permitted to work. They had lost their role as the 'bread-winner' and had not as yet established a new role.

8.2. WHAT THE CHRISTIAN COMMUNITIES CAN DO TO HELP REFUGEES, ASYLUM SEEKERS

In 2005 Fr. Denis said that there had been an influx of refugees and asylum seekers over the previous ten years into London. On arrival the Catholic refugees had looked for the Church. They recognised the Religious service and could identify with the church structure so they felt at home. Symbols were extremely important to people, for example icons - African Christ, Indian Christ. Many lit candles and in St Stephen's Church the parishioners spent three hundred pounds a week on candles. In one way it was only something small but it meant a great deal to people to be able to do a familiar action when they were so far from home. The people recognised that even if they could not communicate in the same language they were united at a fundamental level. There were plenty of opportunities for the Church to help. Fr. Denis felt that it was important to be welcoming and to introduce people to other parishioners who could speak the same language or help to translate.

Fr. Denis explained that priests were not taught in the seminary what to do when they found themselves in a multi-ethnic parish. However deanery meetings were a support where priests could share their experiences. Working with so many ethnic groups helped one to appreciate all the continents and be aware of the global village. The bishop, Thomas McMahon had told Fr. Denis that visiting Newham was like 'going on the missions.' It had a very different feel to the rest of the diocese. Fr. Denis thought that three levels of support were needed: actual welcoming into the community; filling in forms - for housing etc. and knowing someone with the relevant information who could help.

When Sr. Joyce was asked: What do you think the Church can do to help refugees, asylum seekers? she immediately said: 'offer friendship'. She stressed how important it was to invite asylum seekers to events in the parish, to help them to feel welcome, to get someone to visit them and ask if they need help.

In Canning Town they had a good neighbourhood scheme in the parish whereby parishioners went out of their way to help asylum seekers who lived in their street either by inviting them to go shopping with them or inviting them in for coffee. The parish also held events like international evenings. They held that event every year and had international food to eat. The parish also collected and distributed clothes to refugees and asylum seekers.

To the question: What do you think the Church needs to do/ can do to help refugees, asylum seekers? Sr. Monica replied that she thought the most important thing was 'to raise awareness.' Parishioners need to be alert to people in their midst who need support and friendship. She went on to say that it was important 'to notice strange faces and talk to people. We have intuition and we can see by people's eyes if they are lonely and disengaged from normal life.' She added that once we have made contact then we can let people know about the resources available to them. She concluded: 'I'm proud of Britain, the services we extend to people in distress – both NHS and Social Services.'

Sr. Mary thought that the church could help refugees and asylum seekers by trying:
- to understand what it is actually like to be a refugee or asylum seeker and to take a positive approach, to be aware and not just rely on the media for knowledge
- to be a parish that cared and encouraged, that befriended and accepted refugees as fellow human beings
- to support with food and clothes etc
- to educate parishioners and young people.

She said:

> 'If people are aware of what people have suffered their attitude changes.' She told Sr. Anne that a group of Confirmandi (mostly born in Newham, although their parents had been born overseas) had been asked: 'What is an asylum seeker?' At first the young people had said: 'an illegal immigrant,' and 'a person who comes to take our jobs.' Eventually someone said: 'a person afraid of persecution.' Sister went on to say: 'Don't presume the young people know the plight of asylum seekers.'

Sr. Mary had found initially that no one wanted to know about asylum seekers so she spoke at Religious Services and found that more and more parishioners became interested. People brought food and clothes throughout the year to the church for RAMP. As she said: 'Nearly everyone in the parish has known at some time what it's like to have a hard life and are willing to help in any way they can.'

She also noted that many refugees needed help with 'parenting skills'. They had not got the benefit of an older generation in the UK to support them and pass on these skills. Parishioners could help by supporting, listening, encouraging.

When Fr. Ray was asked what he thought the Church could do to help refugees/asylum seekers he immediately responded with: 'Don't re-invent the wheel.' He added: 'In other words find out what support groups are already in your area and link in with them, talk to them, support them with food and offer yourself to help in whatever way you can. Be open to writing letters of support and challenge legislation.' Father continued:

> 'For example: Section 10 in the Asylum & Immigration Act which gives power to the Home Secretary to regulate the continuation of the provision of accommodation to failed asylum seekers, depending on their performance of community service. In practice it means that failed asylum seekers who cannot return home because of circumstances beyond their control, will have to take obligatory community service in order to have provision of accommodation. The local authorities will be expected to implement this forced labour. This is a breach of several articles of the European Convention of Human Rights (e.g. 4:2 prohibition of forced labour). All asylum seekers should have the choice to work and it is an irony that they are forbidden to work.'

Fr. Ray said that parishioners could be encouraged to support petitions, supply food and clothes. He suggested that parishioners could look for articles and passages of Scripture for spiritual reflection. These passages could possibly be reflected on in a justice and peace group or parish prayer group. He reminded the authors that 'Scripture was written by oppressed people for oppressed people. The Church has sanitised Scripture. We need to help people to read Scripture in a different way – speak about it, pray for oppressed people.'

Fr. Ray shared a reflection:

> 'Anyone whose faith is founded upon the Judaeo-Christian biblical traditions, the plight of refugees and asylum seekers should touch the very core of our being because our scriptures are largely written by refugees. The stories of Abram and Sarai, our parents in faith, tell of people who leave their own country. The Lord says, "Go from your country and your kindred and your ancestor's house to the land that I will show you" (Genesis 12:1). Can they ever claim it as their own? As a result of famine and war, Abram and Sarai have to continually move on. Abram even uses his wife as a passport for entry into the land of Egypt, much to the eventual embarrassment of his host

(Genesis 12:1). In his journey, Abram assumes a new name and a new identity (Genesis 17). But it was upon the death of his wife that we read of how a burial place became the mark of Abraham's residency (Gen. 23), but still only as a resident alien.

There were protocols for hosts and strangers in the tribal society of ancient Israel. The host was normally the father of the household in his own village. The practice was to offer an invitation to the stranger and then to repeat it. After the invitation is accepted the host would wash the stranger's feet to signify that he is a guest. The stranger would remain for an agreed-upon time which may be extended. He could ask for or covet his host's possessions and he would bless the host's household upon departing.

It was through constantly remembering their past, that the ancient Israelites were ever conscious of their obligations towards foreigners - "for you were once aliens in a foreign land." The law regarding resident aliens is contained in Deut. 24:17-18: "You shall not deprive a resident alien or an orphan of justice; you shall not take a widow's garment in pledge. Remember that you were a slave in Egypt and the Lord your God redeemed you from there; therefore I command you to do this." Resident aliens were protected by the people. They had right of free movement. However they had no right of granting hospitality to other visiting strangers.'

8.3. THE PARISH AND LONG TERM INTEGRATION

The authors asked Fr. Denis if he met any English people not happy with the influx of immigrants? He said that there had been some resentment from East Enders who saw immigrants apparently receiving so many opportunities in the way of grants and help when those born here had to struggle. However, he added that the East End had become so cosmopolitan that many had become tolerant. He had not come across anyone who was angry because the Church helped immigrants. There was a recognition that people were all one global community. In the past the community was settled East Enders and sometimes the immigrants were seen as threatening, and were blamed for crime but that time had passed. While some individuals might be unhappy with the situation, there was a general acceptance and it was very peaceful in Newham.

Fr. Denis said that the Church had a responsibility to encourage integration. In the parishes of Newham the immigrants sometimes had the opportunity to celebrate religious services in their own language, for example in Albanian or Tamil in Manor Park and Forest Gate had a Spanish Religious service for South Americans every month. It gave the refugees a sense of togetherness. However when a person came into church that person was first of all Catholic and then from Asia, Africa etc. There were some problems. Some groups found it quite difficult to mix, for example the Singalese and Tamils but many of the problems were lessened by the presence of so many nationalities.

Fr. Denis added that full integration took time and that the integration of the Muslim and Hindu population could take a long time. Father reminded the authors that it was only in 1850 that the Roman Catholics were allowed legally back into the UK after several hundred years. The English and Irish Roman Catholics had been in a ghetto and were looked down upon. The Roman Catholic community had quietly kept going over the years and eventually began to marry non-Catholics. It took a long time but hopefully the other faiths in the UK would become more integrated. There was already a little intermarriage but hopefully intermarriage would become more acceptable. The Catholic primary school helped considerably with integration. Father observed that children were much more accepting than adults and when you were in the school you were colour-blind. You just saw children.

The different ethnic groups were encouraged to celebrate their own unique liturgical customs in the UK. So the Eastern European families brought food in baskets to be blessed before Easter. The South American girls had a special ceremony in church when they celebrated their 16th birthday and the Kosovans brought their children to church to celebrate their first haircut when they were aged about 12-18 months. The Africans celebrated with their dancing and music, the Orientals with their costumes and in July 2005 the Sri Lankans brought their dancing. Every Christmas there was an international carol service in Manor Park.

Sr. Mary told the authors about a young refugee who ran clubs in art, drama and swimming etc for children in Forest Gate. They were mostly Kosovan. In her experience some ethnic groups found it difficult to mix with different ethnic groups. Integration was a problem. There was not enough mix of nationalities. She gave the example of a Nigerian student social worker on placement. RAMP had asked the young woman to go to the (Kosovan) Shpresa group for one week. She found it very difficult because she felt they really did not want her. The problem was simply that the children were exposed to different cultures but the parents were not exposed to the same extent. Sr. Mary explained: 'For integration to take place people need to be helped to mix with people who live in different ways. The immigrants need to ask themselves: What is our culture? What is it to be a Muslim? What is it to be British?'

CHAPTER NINE
DILEMMAS OF INTEGRATION POLICY

In this Chapter we will consider the basic concepts of integration; the refugees' integration policy; the lack of consistency in the UK asylum seekers' integration policy and we will review some elements of the UK integration policy in the light of the Kosovan families' experiences.

9.1. INTEGRATION - BASIC CONCEPTS

The word 'integration' is used in various contexts by researchers and policy makers, to explain the process through which newcomers on arrival in a country interact with the local inhabitants. According to Korac (2001) from 1996 onwards any research carried out regarding refugees in the UK was centred primarily on the practical or 'functional' aspects of integration.

The European Council on Refugees and Exiles (ECRE) considers integration to be a process of change that is dynamic and two-way as well as multi-dimensional, putting demands on both the host society and the newcomers involved. They need to be willing to adapt to their new surroundings. From a newcomers' perspective, integration requires a preparedness to adapt to the lifestyle of the host society without having to lose one's own cultural identity. However adaptation is not just on the part of the newcomers. The host society also is required to adapt if integration is to take place:

> 'From the point of view of the host society, it requires a willingness to adapt public institutions to changes in the population profile, accept refugees as part of the national community, and take action to facilitate access to resources and decision-making processes' (Schibel et al. 2002).

Obviously integration involves every level and sector of society, not just the newcomers, the local inhabitants of an area and the public, but also those involved in policy making, employers, service providers and so on. So integration involves both the informal and the formal sectors of society as Crete Brochmann (1996:112) stated in *European Integration and Immigration from Third Countries*: 'Integration must be a dialogue between two arenas: the formal official system in terms of rules and activities, and the informal processes which are partly invisible, yet nevertheless essential for the process of integration'. Integration is a process that can be successful only 'if the host society provides access to jobs and services, and acceptance of the immigrants in social interaction.' The aim of integration is for the minority newcomers while being free to keep their own culture and identity, to become equal partners in the society in which they live. Rainer Baubock (2003:42) concludes that full integration can take place only when the public culture reflects the fact of immigration and in response transforms its self.

Looking at integration from a psychological perspective the process is obviously also long term. It starts when the immigrant/refugee arrives at the destination country and finishes when that person becomes an active member of the host country's society.

The Refugee Council maintains that integration should be policy driven and defines integration as 'a process which prevents or counteracts the social marginalisation of newcomers and refugees, by removing legal, cultural and language obstacles and ensuring that refugees are empowered to make positive decisions on their future and benefit fully from available opportunities as per their abilities and aspirations' (Refugee Council 1999). However some social scientists question the term 'integration,' preferring to speak of 'inclusion' rather than 'integration' and look at the ways in which the newcomers are included in the various sectors of society – housing, welfare, education, work. Inclusion is seen as referring to the newcomers' access to, participation in and the benefits they derive from the society to which they belong. As inclusion helps agencies to be aware of their areas of specific responsibility, it is a useful concept for the formulation of policy. Other social scientists prefer to use the term 'participation' rather than either 'integration' or 'inclusion' as they ascertain that it implies a more active role for those involved (Home Office 2003f).

In her book, *The Migration and Settlement of Refugees in Britain* Alice Bloch (2002: 85), describing policies of receiving countries, cites Castles (1995) who presents four different ways in which host societies respond to the migration and settlement of migrants. The four models are total exclusion, differential exclusion, assimilation and pluralism.

Total exclusion means depriving migrants all rights, and obviously it's not acceptable in any of the highly developed countries. Differential exclusion means that the migrant is excluded from some aspects of society such as welfare or politics but is included in other areas, usually being given the right to work. For example in 2002 Germany had a policy of differential exclusion. Children born to migrant workers were not granted German citizenship so although they had some cultural and social rights they had almost no political rights. This put up barriers and caused segregation, preventing integration and thereby making total assimilation impossible (Bloch 2002: 82-83).

Assimilation literally means 'making similar.' In this modelimmigrants/minority groups abandon their original culture and societal norms in favour of adapting to the cultural norms of the host country. Therefore all minority groups disappear as they blend into society (Brochmann 1996: 112). Castles (1995:30) defined his third model as the assimilationist mode. In this model the process of settlement is one sided. Migrants are expected to adapt totally to their new society by giving up their own cultural identity in its entirety. This policy was prevalent in the UK until the late 1970s and has been changing slowly to pluralism and multiculturalism (Bloch, 2002: 88). Tariq Modood (2003:287) was able to write in 2003:

> 'The British, especially the English, are less open to their European neighbours but are less hostile than most Europeans to multiculturalism and to international exchange. This I think gives Britain and especially British multiculturalists a "mission" in Europe, that is to make Europe more open to the world and to multicultural situations, perhaps to be a bridge between Europeans and non-Europeans.'

9.2. IMMIGRATION AND REFUGEES' INTEGRATION POLICY

Although social processes are similar for all people entering a new society, there are some significant differences, one being the official status given to the newcomer according to their method of entry. The status given has an important effect on the 'pattern of integration' because it shapes the migrant's rights and opportunities: 'In fact all immigration countries have a range of policies for different groups: skilled immigrants, refugees, dependants of legal entrants, asylum seekers and undocumented workers. Group experiences and the long-term outcomes of settlement processes may differ radically' (Home Office 2003f). The authors of *Mapping the Field* have drawn up a list (Integration Matrix), that could be used to check each group of immigrants as an aid to identifying specific needs and problems encountered by each specific group, in order to plan the most beneficial refugee and migrant services (Home Office 2003f). The Integration Matrix has six areas for consideration:

- the 'Conditions of exit' - any factors regarding the situation in the migrant's country of origin, whether it be political dynamics or socio-economic factors that would include class structure and whether the area was a region of conflict or suffered from environmental ruin, as well as the level of poverty in the region;
- the 'Categories of entrant' or type of immigrant - whether they are skilled or unskilled, students, refugees, asylum seekers or undocumented or whether they are dependants of primary migrants;
- their 'Legal status'- their residence status, their right to work and their entitlement to provision by social services in the form of healthcare, accommodation etc;

- the 'Characteristics of entrants - age, gender, place of origin, nationality, ethnicity, presence of family members, English proficiency, educational background, religion, occupation and skill level, qualifications (recognised in the UK/unrecognised), migration experience (voluntary/forced, legal/illegal);'
- the 'Characteristics of ethnic community - number in UK, geographic distribution, segregation/concentration in specific areas, religion, ethnic community associations, leadership, social divisions, political divisions;'
- the 'Conditions of receiving context'- the degree of openness towards immigrants regarding the local population and government policies (such as access to various legal statuses, assistance, English language training, induction courses), available housing, degree of integration, nature of local labour market, educational provision, availability of advice, history of same or other ethnic group presence; public opinion - stereotypes, prejudice, discrimination and racism versus patterns of acceptance and co-operation.

The authors of *Integration: Mapping the Field* (Home Office 2003f) discuss separately, in their report the integration of immigrants and refugees because although most of the issues involved are the same they see two main differences. Firstly, voluntary migrants have usually planned and prepared for their migration and arrive with some resources while refugees are unable to plan or prepare and usually arrive with no resources at their disposal, and have suffered significant trauma during their journey to safety. Secondly, the immigration policies and the law in the host countries treats the two groups very differently even if the primary integration process is similar[4].

Joly and associates (1992)[5] identify five types of refugee in Europe. Firstly 'convention refugees': those who are recognised on the basis of the 1951 Geneva Convention[6]; secondly 'mandate refugees' who are recognised by UNHCR but not by their host government; thirdly 'humanitarian refugees' who have been granted the

---

[4] In demographic terms, anyone who crosses an international border with the intention of a long-term or permanent stay is an 'immigrant' or an 'international migrant'. 'Refugees' and 'asylum seeker' are technically sub-categories of international migrant. Other sub-categories include 'highly-skilled migrants', 'unskilled labour migrants', 'undocumented (or irregular or illegal) migrants', and 'dependants of primary migrants entering through family reunion'.

[5] As cited in Mapping the Field.

[6] Those who receive full Refugee Status receive automatically the right to special protection by the host state. This right includes help to settle and integrate and therefore allows access to social services, help with accommodation, education and retraining if necessary, access to work and help with learning the language of the host society.

right to stay on humanitarian grounds, then 'de facto refugees' who are refugees in practice, but for one reason or another have not sought Refugee Status; and last 'refugees in orbit', who move from one European country to another in search of a permanent status. Each category of refugees is regulated by different legal constraints and therefore is subject to different rights. The latter three groups - 'humanitarian', 'de facto' and 'in orbit' are constantly subjected to more and more restrictions and are denied some basic rights like the possibility of family reunification. As we stated in chapter one, as the UK governments made it harder for people to enter the UK legally as contract workers many had no option but to try to enter illegally or through seeking asylum. 'This creates the problem of blurred boundaries between economic migrants and refugees' (Home Office 2003f).

The UNHCR executive standing committee meeting in July 2004 discussed the problems of refugees[7] who find themselves 'in a long-lasting and intractable state of limbo' (five years or more), in a document entitled *Protracted Refugee Situations*. The Committee explained that while the refugees' 'lives may not be at risk, their basic rights and essential economic, social and psychological needs remain unfulfilled after years in exile. A refugee in this situation is often unable to break free from enforced reliance on external assistance' (Executive Committee 2004).

To allow a refugee to be self-reliant is not only more dignified for the individual concerned but is less costly for the host country and is a positive factor when it comes to possible repatriation. The essential elements of the UNHCR strategy are firstly the provision for all refugees of 'physical, legal and economic security,' secondly the removal of any barriers which prevent the refugee from being self-reliant and thirdly the creation of opportunities for the refugee (Executive Committee 2004). The UNHCR expressed concern that refugees not given these essential elements might feel the need 'to resort to negative coping mechanisms.' The UNHCR declared that it was the responsibility of the host Government to work at removing any barriers or legal obstacles to refugee movement or freedom to be employed (Executive Committee 2004).

Even if the refugee is allowed to train or re-qualify and work there is no guarantee that the person will actually be able to find work. Some refugees with excellent English find themselves as fully qualified professionals and yet 'socially excluded' by the host community. The refugees find themselves facing various barriers such as racism or the more insidious hostility towards newcomers or refugees which can be embedded in the psyche of some people and difficult to overcome. Sometimes

---

[7] There are - using the Joly and associates (1992) terminology - 'mandate refugees' who are recognised by UNHCR but not by their host government.

this hostility is due to racism but at other times it is due to negative ideas about refugees often gained from stereotyping by the media, or it can be simply that people are confused about the right of refugees to work (Section 8 of *the Nationality, Immigration and Asylum Bill* 2002). Even if the refugee manages to overcome all the barriers and become fully integrated into society, the question remains: 'Does this "integrated" refugee then become a full member of UK society or rather a member of an ethnic minority?' (Home Office 2003f).

However according to Morton Weinfeld (1997) before refugees can truly integrate into the wider society they need to consolidate their existing relationships firstly with their family and then their ethnic group. Only then can they integrate with other ethnic groups and with others in their neighborhood. Eventually they will integrate with the wider or national society. It is important that this process is recognised and acknowledged when it comes to policy because all policies will have an impact to a lesser or greater degree on each level of the nesting process of integration.

According to Glover (et al. 2001: 4,48) if refugees are truly to integrate in the host society, policies on migration must be integrated with all other governmental policies regarding the economy and social services. It is important that refugee groups are included from the start of policy planning and they must be considered when policy targets are set: 'Failure to integrate migrants into UK society and to allow them access to public services can lead to their being socially excluded in other respects, which can, in turn, cause personal and social problems.' Glover states that 'it is impossible to measure "a migrant's" experience of social exclusion [....]. However, lack of employment is the key cause of wider exclusion.' He states that it is necessary to give migrants access to:

-   employment;
-   health;
-   housing;
-   welfare services;
-   English language courses;
-   help in training or updating qualifications. Often migrants experience difficulties in obtaining employment due to the fact that their qualifications are not recognized in the UK;
-   necessary documentation. Many migrants are denied services – including access to child benefit, housing benefit and NHS treatment through lack of documentation that clarifies their entitlement. There are times when a lack of documentation also inhibits access to essential private services. It is impossible to open a bank account or be connected to essential utilities without the correct documents;

- help in acquiring citizenship. The actual acquisition of citizenship is considered an index of integration;
- help to combat racism. In a Home Office research study, Bloch (2000) states that thirteen per cent of refugees considered racism and discrimination a barrier to their successful settlement.

Similarly, Brian Ray wrote in 2002 that there are five ways in which any newcomer needs to integrate into the host society in order to be fully integrated:

- Linguistic – fluency and competency in language used both informally and formally;
- Labour Market – education, training, employment rates, mobility both social and professional, income;
- Civic/political – involvement with church and local groups, including political parties and unions, permission to vote and voting conduct;
- Educational - choice of school, performance and drop out rates, higher educational achievement, communication with students from host community and communication with teachers;
- Residential - mixed ethnic locality, size of accommodation for number of occupants, degree of housing mobility, rental discrimination, home ownership (Ray 2002).

9.3. ASYLUM SEEKERS' INTEGRATION POLICY

Glover and his associates (2001: 48) in the paper, *Migration: an economic and social analysis*, a Home Office consultation paper said that the Government 'has recognized the need to assist in the transfer from asylum to settled status: 'There is a weight of evidence that refugees find difficulties in making the transition from support to independence and fulfilling their potential for development and contributions to society [...] there is a need to invest early in integration to promote a quick move from dependency to self-value and sufficiency through work and inclusion in community and society.'

According to the UK Government's integration policy document *Integration Matters* Home Office (2004d):

'The new blood represented by refugees can be a real source of strength to Britain in our changing world. Many refugees have skills, talents and enthusiasm that can be real assets to Britain if we can help them make the most use of them. But to give of their best, they have to be able to integrate with the host society as quickly and smoothly as possible. Clearly the Government wishes to create a policy whereby British society is not only successful but truly integrated and its diversity is a cause for celebration'.

In the Government's document *Full and Equal Citizens* we read:

> 'For highly motivated and skilled people not to be fulfilling their potential in work is clearly a waste. Ensuring that refugees return rapidly to their former or related careers is in the best interests of themselves and their families, as well as the wider interests of the community in the UK' (Home Office 2003e).

However, when it comes to the integration of the asylum seekers in practice the Government draws a very strong distinction between refugees (people recognized as refugees according to the Geneva Convention) and asylum seekers (people whose claims are still under consideration, including those who have not been granted full Refugee Status but only given a limited period of protection - Discretionary Leave, Humanitarian Protection and Exceptional Leave to Remain). When the UK government speaks about integration, it refers to the process by which refugees (not asylum seekers) are: 'empowered to achieve their full potential as members of British society, to contribute fully to the community, and to become fully able to exercise the rights and responsibilities that they share with other residents'. This strategy is described in *Full and Equal Citizens 2000* (Home Office 2004d).

While the UK Government accepts that the experiences of asylum seekers whose asylum status is still being considered, is bound to affect their later integration, it still maintains that full integration cannot take place until a person has actually received Refugee Status because only then can they make plans for their future (Home Office 2004d, 1.6:10). The Government states that integration takes place when refugees are empowered to:

    a)   achieve their full potential as members of British society;
    b)   contribute fully to the community;
    c)   access the public services to which they are entitled.

The aim of this strategy is to support and enable refugees to integrate swiftly and to take up their place as full and equal citizens, while acknowledging that some may wish to return eventually to their country of origin (Home Office 2004d, 1.9: 1.10).

In the last couple of years extensive research has been carried out to discover the problems refugees have experienced when trying to gain language skills and job experience. The two issues run hand in hand. It is hardly surprising that many refugees find that their poor ability to communicate in English is the main obstacle to finding meaningful employment that would allow them to use their talents and skills to the full. Although refugees on average have better qualifications than the UK national average, they are six times more likely to be unemployed. On being granted Refugee Status they need prompt help to seek advice from Jobcentre Plus offices in order to make informed choices regarding training and employment options (Home Office 2004d).

Maybe the remedy to that problem could be achieved by changing the asylum seekers' policy? If the UK Government really believes what it stated in its document *Full and Equal Citizens* one might well ask – why are thousands of extremely skilled asylum seekers and refugees at present not allowed to work while waiting four or more years for official Refugee Status in the UK?

There are many critiques and suggestions regarding the UK government's integration policy. In 2004 the Asylum Rights Campaign (ARC) produced a report entitled *Providing Protection in the 21st Century* with the aim of putting Refugee Rights at the heart of the asylum policy. The report made forty-five recommendations to the government regarding the integration of asylum seekers and refugees. Recommendation 36 states:

> 'The government must develop a comprehensive strategy for the early integration and settlement of all those granted leave to remain in the UK. The strategy should be based on the premise that integration starts from the moment asylum seekers arrive. This should be reflected in the provision of English language teaching, vocational and professional training and the entitlement to take up paid or unpaid employment while awaiting a decision on their claim. These measures are, in any event likely to enhance their life if they return to their home country. Asylum seekers must be included within the scope and ambit of government social exclusion, community and race relations policy and legislation and ensure that the integration of asylum seekers is mainstreamed in the planning and delivery of relevant services' (ARC 2004).

The Refugee Council (which is a member of ARC) reiterated this recommendation in February 2005 stating in its own document regarding integration:

> 'Asylum seekers should be allowed to work while their asylum claim is being assessed. Asylum seekers do not want to be on state handouts, but they have no choice because the government will not let them work. Being able to work would restore pride and self-respect for asylum seekers and allow them to contribute to the economy and society' (Refugee Council 2005).

The Refugee Council went on to outline its own alternative plan to the government's asylum policy:

> 'At its heart is ensuring that the UK remains a safe haven for refugees fleeing violence, torture and persecution. To achieve this, the UK must continue to

welcome refugees, and have an asylum system that gives people a fair hearing, makes good quality decisions first time, and helps refugees who are allowed to stay to integrate fully into British society' (Refugee Council 2005).

It stresses the need to attain good quality, fair decisions on all asylum claims as quickly as possible, with 'proper legal advice …available from the start.' It reminds the government of the need for an efficient system stating that 'Poor initial decisions add to the length and expense of the system because they are often successfully challenged' and the faster permission is granted for people who are eventually allowed to stay in the UK, the more easily they can rebuild their lives.

The Refugee Council goes on to say that it is in the best interests of everyone in the country if refugees are allowed and helped to integrate as quickly as possible. They need some help at first to rebuild their lives, which have been shattered by their experiences but when given the opportunity refugees have always been great contributors to British society. Asylum seekers do not want to be reliant on the State for handouts. They want to work, to support their families and contribute to society and should be allowed to do so. 'Being able to work would restore pride and self-respect for asylum seekers and allow them to contribute to the economy and society' (UK Government Policy 2005).

Wondimu Yohannes, (2005) Director of Development and Integration, Refugee Action giving a key note presentation at a one day conference entitled '*A sense of Belonging*' in 2005 stated that:

'There has been debate about refugees needing to learn the language to become good citizens. But before they can be accepted as good citizens, there has to be inclusion – when people are included, they do not need rules for citizenship. Inclusion must come before exclusion. Refugee Action's stance was that integration should begin from the moment asylum seekers arrived in the UK not, as the Home Office integration strategy suggested, once applicants had been granted Refugee Status.'

Even though the Home Office has stated clearly, many times, that there is 'a need to invest early in integration to promote a quick move from dependency to self-value' (Dummett 2001: 41-42), and there are strong arguments to start the process of integration as soon as possible, in 2005 adult asylum seekers in the UK were still prevented from receiving formal education (apart from English lessons or voluntary courses) and were not allowed to partake in training or work while they awaited a decision on their status that could take several years. Yet over a third of all asylum seekers in the UK will eventually be granted some form of permission to remain in the UK. Such a lengthy wait must surely put their future careers at risk and prevent them from fulfilling their potential while denying them the right to contribute to the well being of the host nation.

9.4. INTEGRATION POLICY - KOSOVAN FAMILIES' EXPERIENCES

In the case of the fifty Kosovan asylum seekers' families, who were interviewed, the majority of them had arrived in the UK at least four to five years previously as illegal immigrants, with the help of smugglers. All those interviewed had left Kosovo with their young families after traumatic experiences and had young children, many born in the UK. We saw the families struggling to integrate while coping with frequent moves, and a deepening longing for stability. They found themselves with ever recurring and worsening health problems while they endeavoured to manage financially, and living with the ever-present fear of deportation. Even those who had been granted the Amnesty often found themselves in temporary emergency accommodation for weeks on end. Many also endured bad housing while others were frequently re-housed, which meant a move from their local support groups and for the children a change of schools. The Home Office's administration problems plus the interminable delays in the system meant that the Kosovans' process of application for Refugee Status was unending and many were still living in a state of limbo in spite of the Amnesty. The Amnesty was a very positive move by the Government but it had been somewhat lacking in organization and follow up. Nothing was put in place to help the asylum seekers to negotiate the endless form filling in order to transfer from NASS support to mainstream benefits and housing.

We included only some of the asylum seekers' traumatic experiences in this book. The asylum seekers travelled to the UK with young children in dangerous and extremely difficult conditions, i.e. locked in a lorry, without the right to leave the lorry even to use a toilet. It showed their extreme determination to escape and meant that their reasons were very strong. From personal contact with these families it was obvious (particularly from the humanitarian perspective) that it would not be right to return them to Kosovo. Even in 2005 there was still no peace there. It had been a very short time to achieve reconciliation between neighbours with different ethnic or national backgrounds.

From the various Home Office documents regarding integration we are aware that the UK Government appreciates the importance of integrating newcomers to Great Britain and has even set up a programme to help refugees to integrate. However, it is on the principle that the integration process starts after a person receives Refugee Status and not before. As a consequence asylum seekers are deprived of access to this process, as are the people who received the Amnesty. The government's motive might be logical because asylum seekers do not have permission to stay in the UK for good until they have Refugee Status, but practically the adults in Kosovan families, during several years in limbo, have missed many opportunities for integrating into the host society. That has had a negative effect not only on the adults but also on their children. Often in asylum seeking families there has been a reversal of roles with the parents dependent on their children for interpretation in many official and inappropriate situations. Therefore by the time the parents are able to function totally independently from their children, the children have lost a considerable amount of their childhood. Our survey showed that their children have been adversely affected by their parents' lack of security, inability to communicate and fully integrate.

In some ways the UK government did help the asylum seekers to integrate. They were treated well by the authorities, given housing, education for their children and free English lessons were available for the adults. However their integration was greatly hindered by two facts: that asylum seekers were not allowed to work and all major decisions were taken away from them. They could not work to support their families and therefore they had no contact with other ethnic groups in the work place. They tended to remain in ghettos, communicating almost totally, with their own ethnic group. They could not choose where to live or even whether to remain near friends or family. They became totally dependent on the State, their self-confidence was eroded and their ability to make choices reduced. The lack of freedom to choose, to make decisions about their own lives, created not only an unhealthy dependency but also caused unnecessary stress which resulted in depression and ill health.

Access to the labour market can make the integration process faster for new comers. Giving asylum seekers the right to work can be very beneficial for the social system and help the State. From our research we found that most of the asylum seekers did not want to be reliant on the state for money, they wanted to support themselves. If they were allowed to do so it could save the State many thousands of pounds every year. On the other hand (according to some politicians and authors) if asylum seekers receive too many privileges, the society of the host country might protest and if the country appears too welcoming to newcomers it might encourage many more to come and not only refugees, but also economic migrants, thus abusing the possibilities of applying for the status of refugee. The function of the international protection of refugees is to assure them safety and protection from persecution, and not to create better living conditions.

That view is held by the majority of countries and formulated in their asylum seekers' policies, but reality shows that the majority of asylum seekers will become citizens of the receiving country. Between 1993-2002 there were almost 526,000 applications for asylum in the UK, not counting dependents, and although the majority received a negative decision only 31,500 were deported. The government needs to take into account these facts in its asylum seekers' policy and to treat the asylum seeking family as a potential unit of the host society.

From our research we conclude that the process for application for asylum from families should be treated differently to other asylum seekers and full integration should be aided through speedier processing of their claims with permission to work and support their families from the moment of their arrival in the UK. This would encourage them to learn English and create a more normal and stable family setting for the children.

CONCLUSION

Our survey showed that there is a lack of consistency in the British integration policy regarding asylum seekers. The main problem is connected with the fact that in the UK, as in most countries, the integration policy is limited to people who have been granted Refugee Status and does not include people who are seeking asylum and awaiting status. Regardless how logical a government's arguments are, the experiences of the fifty Kosovan asylum seeking families in our survey, show that they and thousands others have been denied the possibility of fully integrating with the host society for several years by the present integration policy.

Even the families who came to the UK illegally were treated as potential receivers of Refugee Status and received accommodation, financial support, the possibility of learning English and education for their children. However the process of integration was hindered because of the following facts:

- The integration policy in the UK (2003-05) was aimed specifically at refugees not asylum seekers. Asylum seekers while encouraged to integrate were not encouraged to integrate fully until they had Refugee Status. In fact those who had been granted the Amnesty had given up the right to Refugee Status and although entitled to apply for British Citizenship would never qualify for the refugee integration programmes.

- The asylum seekers were denied the basic human right of work (sometimes for a few years) and were thereby forbidden from contributing to society and prevented from fully integrating. Receiving limited benefits the asylum seekers found themselves financially disadvantaged. They had the choice of either being poor and totally dependent on the State or working illegally. Unsure of their future in the UK, there was little incentive to learn English and with worsening health problems plus young children to care for, the women found difficulty accessing English classes

- There appeared to be a lack of clarity and a rather haphazard approach to Immigration policies in the UK. This has meant that the families' process of application for Refugee Status has been unending, resulting in a lack of stability and no sense of belonging.

- The Amnesty, although promising and in many ways beneficial, has lacked organization and follow up, proving that the UK Immigration policies of the past, and in particular the administration of those policies, has failed many of the genuine asylum seekers, forcing many families to suffer unnecessary stress and trauma.

As we saw above, the exclusion of the asylum seekers' families from the integration programmes (which apply only to refugees) affects the process of full integration of all those who will become future refugees as well. As the process of acquiring Refugee Status often takes years it seems to be too high a price for keeping the principle that 'integration in the full sense of the word can take place only when a person has been confirmed as a refugee.' It is necessary to recognize that the process of integration begins on the day of arrival in the host country.

The Convention on the Rights of the Child obliges all States to ensure the development of every child physically, mentally, spiritually, morally and socially (States Parties recognize the right of every child to a standard of living adequate for the child's physical, mental, spiritual, moral and social development, Art. 27.1).

Regarding the welfare dimension (Art.27.3) we can say that the UK policy towards asylum seekers in 2003-04 had many positive patterns. The UK government spent £15,000 a year supporting each asylum family with accommodation, health care and benefits for food and clothing which is indeed generous.

With regard to the educational dimension (Article 28) our survey showed that while the UK fulfilled its obligations, often the administrative decisions regarding housing and education did not take into account the interests of the children. Our survey of just fifty families showed that many children had been expected to move house and therefore change school on a frequent basis and consequently leave their friends and the teachers behind. Many parents told us that their children were upset at having to change school yet again just when they had settled in. In particular this proved to be very distressing and unsettling for primary school children and common sense tells us that it must have had an adverse effect not only on their levels of attainment in school but also on their general well-being.

Regarding the general well-being of the family, and child development (Preamble of the Convention on the Rights of the Child) the results of our survey showed that the asylum legislation in the UK did not always support this clause and other experiences show that this situation often arises[8].

To meet the Convention on the Rights of the Child (Article 2; Article 22; Article 39) a family must have stability, with a clear future perspective. Unfortunately many asylum seekers have no sense of stability. Until they receive status they do not

---

[8] For example in early June 2005 a refugee support worker contacted the authors. She was phoning on behalf of a young asylum seeker who had a six months old baby. They had been staying with friends but were now homeless. They were about to be deported and all benefits had been stopped. The local authority had offered to take the baby into care but had refused the mother any assistance.

know whether they will be allowed to stay in the host country, be deported or forced to move on[9].

The families have little stability and it is the children who suffer. Stability can only be reached by integrating the family into society. The UK Government appreciates the importance of integrating new comers to Great Britain, but on the principle that this process starts after a person receives Refugee Status. As a consequence asylum seekers are deprived access to integration programmes. The processing of asylum claims has been far too slow, often taking five years or more. Consequently the Kosovan families, along with many other asylum seekers who have recently been granted permission to stay indefinitely in the UK, have lost several years' opportunity for integration into the host society.

---

[9] For example in a case reported in the 'Guardian' newspaper in May 2005 by Helen Carter, a school in Manchester was appealing to the government on behalf of many asylum seekers' children who faced deportation along with their families. The school was appealing on the grounds that the international Convention for the Rights of the Child should offer the children some protection. The head teacher of St John's, Jed Morgan said that the recent deportation of a family had been as shocking as a death in the family: 'One minute they are here and the next minute they are gone. These children are victims and they are very vulnerable. Over the last three or four years they have become very settled and they have made good progress at school' (Carter 2005).

BIBLIOGRAPHY

Ahmed, K., (2003). *Refugees without papers face arrest*, 'The Observer' (UK), 26/10/2003.
Available from:
www.guardian.co.uk/Refugees_in_Britain/Story/0,2763,1071443,00.html.

Albanian News,(2003). Available from:
www.albanian.com/information/countries/kosova/index.html.

Amnesty International Report, (2003). *Prisoners in our own Homes* (29 April 2003). Available
from: www.amnesty.org/library/Index/ENGEUR700102003.

Association of Chief Police Officers of England, Wales and Northern Ireland (2000). *Asylum
Seekers Policing Guide*. Available from:
www.asylumsupport.info/publications/acpo/policing.pdf.

Baldaccini, A., (2004). *Providing Protection in the 21ˢCentury*, London: Asylum Rights Campaign
2004.

Baubock, R., (2003). *Public Culture in Societies of Immigration*, eds. R. Sackmann, B. Peters, Th.
Faist, *Identity and Integration Migrants in Western Europe*. Bremen: Ashgate Publishing
Limited.

BBC, (1999). News: *Albanian refugee camps 'to be cleared'* 11 May 1999. Available from:
www.news.bbc.co.uk/1/hi/world/europe/340554.stm.

BBC, (2004a). News: *Country profiles – Kosovo*. Available from:
www.news.bbc.co.uk/1/hi/world/europe/country_profiles/3524092.stm.

BBC, (2004b). News: *Kosovo's election*. Available from:
www.news.bbc.co.uk/1/hi/world/europe/3951763.stm.

BBC. (2004c). News: *Regions and territories: Kosovo*. Available from:
www.news.bbc.co.uk/1/hi/world/europe/country_profiles/3524092.stm.

BBC, (2004d). News: *Timeline: Kosovo*. Available from:
www.news.bbc.co.uk/1/hi/world/europe/country_profiles/3550401.stm.

Bloch, A., (2002). *The Migration and Settlement of Refugees in Britain*, Palgrave: Macmillan,
Houndmills, UK, New York US.

Brochmann, C., (1996). *European Integration and Immigration from Third Countries*, Oslo:
Scandinavian University Press.

Browne, D., (2004). Foreword. Home Office, *Integration Matters: A National Strategy for Refugee
Integration A draft for consultation*, July 2004, Available from:
www.ind.homeoffice.gov.uk/ind/en/home/laws___policy/refugee_integration0/a_natio
nal_strategy.Maincontent.0002.file.tmp/COI_NATI.pdf.

Bunting, M., (2001). *Haven't we been here before?* Special report 'Refugees in Britain' for 'The
Guardian', 23.05.2001.

Castles, S., (1995). *How nation states respond to immigration and ethnic diversity*, New Community, vol. 21,
no. 3: 293-308.

Census, April 1951 to 2001. Office for National Statistics. Available from: www.statistics.gov.uk/cci/nugget.asp?id=767.

Census, April 1951 to 2001. General Register Office for Scotland. Available form: www.statistics.gov.uk/cci/nugget.asp?id=767.

Census, April 1951 to 2001. Northern Ireland Statistics and Research Agency. Available form: www.statistics.gov.uk/cci/nugget.asp?id=767.

Commission of the European Communities, (2000). *Proposal for a Council Directive for minimum standards in giving Temporary Protection in the event of a Mass influx of Displaced Persons and on measures Promoting a balance of Efforts between Member States in Receiving such Persons and Bearing the Consequences thereof*, COM(2000) 303 final[2000/0127(CNS), Brussels 24th May 2000. Available from: www.europa.eu.int/eur-lex/lex/LexUriServ/site/en/com/2000/com2000_0303en02.pdf.

Dummett, M., (2001). On migration and Refugees, Routledge London and New York.

ECRE, (1999). *Position on the integration of refugees in Europe*. September 1999. Available from: www.ecre.org/positions/integ.shtml.

Elkes, P., (2003). *The Polish community in the Staffordshire Moorlands - a history*. Available from: www.bbc.co.uk/stoke/features/polish/polish_community.shtml.

Employability Forum, (2004). Refugee Teachers Task Force, Sept 2004. Available from: www.employabilityforum.co.uk/docs/ref_tea_up.doc.

ERP KIM Newsletter, (2005a). *Brussels reviews Kosovo 27 Jan 2005*. Available from: www.kosovo.com/news/archive/2005/January_27/1.html.

ERP KIM Newsletter, (2005b). *Italy's foreign minister in Kosovo for a visit 24 Feb 2005*. Available from: www.kosovo.com/news/archive/2005/February_24/2.html.

Executive Committee, (2004). of the High Commissioner's Programme, *Protracted Refugee Situations*. EC/54/SC/CRP.14. 10 June 2004. Available from: www.refugees.org/data/warehousing/docs/sc_prs.pdf.

Favell, A., (1998). *Philosophies of Integration: Immigration and the Idea of Citizenship in France and Britain*. London: Macmillan Press.

Ford, R., (2003). *Amnesty on asylum opens door to 50,000*, 'The Times' (UK), 25/10/2003. Available from: www.timesonline.co.uk/newspaper/0,,125-867276,00.html.

Gibney, M.J., (1999). *Kosovo and beyond: popular and unpopular refugees*,
'Forced Migration Review', Issue 5, August Pub: Refugees Studies Programme. http://www.fmreview.org/text/FMR/05/10.htm.

Glover, S., (2001). *Migration an economic and social analysis*, Home Office Report. Available from: www.homeoffice.gov.uk/rds/pdfs/occ67-migration.pdf.

Goble, F., (2003). *Asylum Seekers behind the Headlines*, A report on asylum seekers in the United Kingdom, the East of England region and the European Union, compiled by the office of E. McNally MEP. Available from: www.erylmcnallymep.org.uk/asylum_seekers_in_the_uk.htm.

Bibliography

Greicevci, B., (2003). *Kosovo my Home*. Available from: www.tol.cz/look/BRR/article.tpl?IdLanguage=1&IdPublication=9&NrIssue=1&NrSection=5&NrArticle=9798.

Guild, E., (1998). *Fairer, Faster, Firmer: A Modern Approach To Immigration and Asylum*, Cmnd 4018, White paper, The Stationery Office 27th July 1998.

Guild, E., (1999). Britain must take in 5,000, 'Daily Telegraph' 18th April 1999.

Guild, E., (2000). *Kosovar Albanian Refugees in the UK*. J. van Selm, ed. *Kosovo's Refugees in the EU*. London, Pinter, New York 2000: 67-90.

Hailbronner, K., (2000). *Immigration and Asylum Law and Policy of the European Union*, The Hague, London, Boston: Kluwer Law International.

Hamilton, M., (2003). *Interview by authors*, Manor Park, London, Feb. 2003.

Heath, T., Jeffries, R., and Lloyd, A., (2003). *Asylum Statistics 2002 UK*. Research Development Statistics. Available from: www.homeoffice.gov.uk/rds/pdfs2/hosb803.pdf.

Heffernan, E., (2004). *Interview by authors*, Manor Park, London, Sep. 2004.

Hein, C., (2000). *Italy: Gateway to Europe, but not the gatekeeper?* J. van Selm, ed. *Kosovo's Refugees in the European Union*, Pinter, London, New York: 139-161.

Home Office, (1999). *Change of Policy in respect of citizens from the Federal Republic of Yugoslavia* 277/99 Press Release: 13th September 1999.

Home Office, (date unknown). *Population by ethnic group and age 1989-1999. Social trends 30.* National Statistics United kingdom, Labour Force Survey.

Home Office, (2002a). *Secure Borders, Safe Havens – Integration with Diversity in Modern Britain*, February 2002a (White Paper).

Home Office, (2002b). *Asylum Statistics, United Kingdom*, London.

Home Office, (2002c). *Control of Immigration Statistics United Kingdom*, 2001, London.

Home Office, (2003a). *Asylum Statistics: 3rd Quarter 2003 in United Kingdom*, London.

Home Office, (2003b). Department for Constitutional Affairs document, 27 October 2003.

Home Office, (2003c). *Asylum in the United Kingdom, London*, Home Office, 23 November 2003.

Home Office, (2003d). *Fairer, Faster & Firmer – an introduction to the UK Asylum system*, London.

Home Office, (2003e). *Full and equal citizens. A strategy for the integration of refugees into the United Kingdom*, www.homeoffice.gov/ind/hpg.htm.

Home Office, (2003f). *Integration: Mapping the Field*. Report of a Project carried out by the University of Oxford Centre for Migration and policy Research and Refugee Studies Centre. December 2002, Home Office Online Report 28/03.

Home Office, (2004a). *Asylum Statistics: 4th Quarter 2003, in United Kingdom*, London.

Home Office, (2004b). *Asylum Statistics: 1st Quarter 2004, in United Kingdom*, London.

Home Office, (2004c). *Asylum Statistics: 3rd Quarter 2004, in United Kingdom*, London.

Home Office, (2004d). *Integration Matters: A National Strategy for Refugee Integration A draft for consultation,* July 2004. Available from: www.ind.homeoffice.gov.uk/ind/en/home/laws___policy/refugee_integration0/a_natio nal_strategy.Maincontent.0002.file.tmp/COI_NATI.pdf.

Home Office, (2005a). *Asylum Statistics: 4th Quarter 2004, in United Kingdom,* London.

Home office, (2005b). *Sizing the unauthorized (illegal) migrant population in the United Kingdom in 2001.* Available from: www.homeoffice.gov.uk/n_story.asp?item_id=1323.

Human Rights Watch, (2001). *War crimes in Kosovo.* Available from: www.hrw.org/reports/2001/kosovo/.

ICAR, (2004). *Community Impact, Information Centre about Asylum and Refugees in the UK.* Media Image, July 2004, commissioned by the Mayor of London. Available from: http://www.icar.org.uk/pdf/mici003.pdf.

Immigration and Nationality Directorate Department for Constitutional Affairs (IND 2003) Press Release 24 November 2003.

Janowski, K., Out There News. Available from: www.megastories.com/kosovo/map/intro.htm.

Kirk, R., (2004). *Skills Audit of Refugees.* Home Office on line Report 37/04. Available from: www.homeoffice.gov.uk/rds/pdfs04/rdsolr3704.pdf.

Korac, M., (2001). *Cross-ethnic networks, self-reception system, and functional integration of refugees from former Yugoslavia in Rome,* Italy. 'Journal of International Migration and Integration,' 2 (1): 1-26.

KTV, (2004). *Oneworld : Kosovo has not many reasons to be proud of Tolerance.* Available from: www.oneworld.net/article/search/.

Modood ,T., (2003). *New Forms of Britishness: Post-Immigration Ethnicity and Hybridity in Britain,* R. Sackmann, B. Peters, Th. Faist, eds. *Identity and Integration Migrants in Western Europe.* Bremen: Ashgate Publishing Limited: 77-90.

Moss, P., (2003). *Report from Kosovo.* BBC Radio 4. Article=9798 broadcast Sept/Oct 2003.

National Asylum Support Service. Available from: www.getrights.co.uk/nass_support.htm.

Nationality, Immigration and Asylum Bill 2002. Available from: www.parliament.the-stationery-office.co.uk/pa/cm200102/cmbills/119/2002119.pdf.

National Statistics UK Online, (2001a). Available from: www.statistics.gov.uk/cci/nugget.asp?id=767.

National Statistics UK Online, (2001b). Available from: www.statistics.gov.uk/CCI/nugget.asp?ID=455&Pos=4&ColRank=2&Rank=1000.

Nowicki, M., (2005a). *Kosovo: When Being the 'Good Guy' Is Not Enough Ombudsperson of Kosovo.* 4 Feb 2005. Available from: www.tol.cz/look/TOL/#author.

Nowicki, M., (2005b). *Taking a Hard Look, Ombudsperson of Kosovo*. 23 February 2005. Available from: www.tol.cz/look/TOL/article.tpl?IdLanguage= 1&IdPublication=4&NrIssue=104&NrSection=2&NrArticle=13612.

Pack, D., (2005). *No Solution For Kosovo Possible Without Or Against Serbia*. Available from: www.kosovo.com/news/archive/2005/January_27/1.html.

Partos, G., *World's unease over new Kosovo PM*, BBC (2004e). News. BBC's south-east Europe analyst 4 Dec. 2004. Available from: news.bbc.co.uk/1/hi/world/europe/4067579.stm.

Peach, C., UK: *A Country with Long Experience of Immigration*. Available from: www.europa.eu.int/comm/employment_social/eoss/downloads/helsinki_peach_en.pdf.

Polish Community. Available from: www.multicultural-matters.com/polish_community.htm.

Portes, A., Zhou, M., (1993). *The new second generation: Segmented assimilation and its variants*. Annals of the American Academy of Political and Social Sciences, 530: 74-96.

Portes, A., (1998). *Divergent Destinies: Immigration, the Second Generation and the rise of Transnational Communities*. P. Schuck, R. Munz, eds. *Paths to inclusion : the integration of migrants in the United States and Germany*. Migration and refugees series, v.5. New York and Oxford: Berghahn Books and American Academy of Arts and Sciences: 33-57.

Ray, B., (2002). *Immigrant Integration: Building to Opportunity*. Migration Policy Institute, October 1, 2002. Available from: www.migrationinformation.org/Feature/display.cfm?id=57.

Refugee Council, (2004a). 'Inexile' - the magazine on refugee rights, Issue 30.

Refugee Council, (2004b). *The Amendments at a glance - UK News Roundup*, 'Inexile', Issue 32:2

Refugee Council, (2004b). *Home Office revises Section 55 procedures*, 'Inexile' Issue 32:4

Refugee Council Info Centre: Support and Entitlement. Available from: www.refugeecouncil.org.uk/infocentre/entit/sentit001.htm.

Refugee Council (2005). *UK Government Policy on Integration & Suggestions for Policy from Refugee Council*. Refugee Council Documents Re Integration. 4 February 2005. Available from: www.refugeecouncil.org.uk/news/2005/feb05/relea189.htm.

Refugee Council On-Line, (2005). *Press myths-the facts Feb 2005*. Available from: www.refugeecouncil.org.uk/news/myths/myth001.htm.

Salesians Offer Formation for Teachers and Youths in Kosovo - Pristina , (2003). Serbia, Oct. 14, 2003 Zenit.org.

Schibel, Y., Fazel, M., Robb, R., and Garner, P., (2002). *Refugee integration: Can research synthesis inform policy?* Feasibility study report Free University of Berlin, Department of Political Science. Home Office On-line Report 13/02. Available from: www.homeoffice.gov.uk/rds/pdfs2/rdsolr1302.pdf.

Seddon, D., Fitzpatrick, P., Chatwin, M., (2002). *Migration and Social Security Handbook*, London: Child Poverty Action Group.

Shah, A., (2001). *The Kosovo Crisis*. Available from: www.globalissues.org/Geopolitics/Kosovo/WhatNow.asp.

Shields, M. A., Price, S.W., (2003). *The labour market outcomes and psychological well-being of ethnic minority migrants in Britain.* Home Office Online Report 07/03. Available from www.homeoffice.gov.uk/rds/pdfs2/rdsolr0703.pdf.

Stalker, P., (2001). *No Nonsense Guide to International Migration.* Oxford: New International Publications.

Stalker, P., (2005). *Stalker's guide to international migration.* Available from: www.pstalker.com/migration/mg_about_guide.htm.

The Press Association, (2003a).*15,000 families granted asylum.* October 24, 2003. Available from: www.guardian.co.uk/Refugees_in_Britain/Story/0,2763,1070434,00.html.

The Press Association, (2003b).*Blunkett unveils Asylum Clampdown.* October 27, 2003. Available from: www.guardian.co.uk/Refugees_in_Britain/Story/0,2763,1072024,00.html.

TOL Week in Review, (2005). *Too Early To Discard Inclusiveness.* 18-24 January 2005. Available from: www.tol.cz/look/TOL/article.tpl?IdLanguage=1&IdPublication =4&NrIssue=99&NrSection=2&NrArticle=13377.

Total Number of Asylum applications submitted by country of destination (United Kingdom) 1980-2001. Available from: www.migrationinformation.org/GlobalData/countrydata/data.cfm.

United Nations, (2004). Security Council. *Report of the Secretary-General on the United Nations Interim Administration Mission in Kosovo.* S/2004/613, 30 July 2004, paras. 24 and 7 respectively. Available from: http://daccessdds.un.org/doc/UNDOC/GEN/N04/446/69/ IMG/ N0444669.pdf?OpenElement.

UNHCR, (1997). *Background paper on refugees and asylum seekers from Kosovo.* Available from: www.jurist.law.pitt.edu/kosovo.htm.

UNHCR, (2001). Statistical Yearbook 2001 Annex C.1 and C.2, Available from: www.ecre.org/factfile/FAQfiles/annexes01.pdf.

UNHCR, (2002). *Asylum Applications Lodged in Industralized Countries: Levels and Trends 2000-2002.* Available from: www.ecre.org/factfile/FAQfiles/unhcrind02.pdf.

UNHCR, (2003a). *Asylum Trends In Industrialized Countries, February 2003.* Population Data Unit/PGDS Geneva, 3 April 2003. Available from: www.unhcr.ch/cgi-bin/texis/vtx/statistics/opendoc.pdf?tbl=STATISTICS&id=3e8d7fb34

UNHCR, (2004a). *Asylum Applications Lodged in Industrial countries: Levels and Trends.* Jan – Jun 2004. Available from: http://www.unhcr.ch/cgi-bin/texis/vtx/statistics/opendoc.pdf?tbl=STATISTICS&id=4199cfce4.

UNHCR, (2004b). Population Data Unit/Pgds, 2003 Global Refugee Trends UNHCR Geneva. 15 June 2004. Available from: http://www.unhcr.ch/cgi-bin/texis/vtx/statistics/opendoc.pdf?tbl=STATISTICS&id=40d015fb4.

UNHCR, (2004c). *Basic facts – Refugees by Numbers,* July 2004. Available from: www.unhcr.ch/cgi-bin/texis/vtx/basics/opendoc.pdf?tbl=BASICS&id=416e3eb24.

Bibliography

UNHCR, (2004d). *Document Position on the Continued International Protection Needs of Individuals from Kosovo.* Aug 2004. Available from: www.unhcr.se/se/Protect_refugees/pdf/Aug_Kosovo2.pdf.

UNHCR, Population Data Unit: Governments, Available from: www.migrationinformation.org/DataTools/asylumresults.cfm.

van Selm, J., (2000a). *Introduction.* J. van Selm, ed. *Kosovo's Refugees in the European Union.* Pinter, London, New York 2000: 1-23.

van Selm, J.,(2000b). *Appendix 2.* J. van Selm, ed. *Kosovo's Refugees in the European Union.* Pinter, London, New York 2000:226.

van Selm, J., (2003). Refugee protection and security issues. E. Newham and J. vanSelm, eds. *Refugees & Forced Displacement – International security, human vulnerability, and the state.* United Nations University Press, New York, 66-92.

Watson, M., McGregor R., (1999). *Asylum Statistics in the United Kingdom 1998* (London: The Stationery Office), issue 10/99, 27 May 1999. Available from: www.homeoffice.gov.uk/rds/pdfs/hosb1099.pdf..

What now global issues: Kosovo. Available from: www.globalissues.org/Geopolitics /Kosovo/WhatNow .asp

Wright, G.J., (2004). *Navigation Guide to Resettlement Programmes and the UK, ICAR.* Available from: www.icar.org.uk/pdf/ngo005.pdf.

Yohannes, W., (2005). *Refugees, Asylum seekers and community integration,* **Director** of Development and Integration, Refugee Action, key note presentation at Conference - A Sense of Belonging. Available from: www.creativexchange.org/html/library/ASOB_Conf_Rep_08_02.pdf.

TABLES AND FIGURES

APPENDIX

QUESTIONNAIRE - MIGRANTS   Reference No. [   ]

<u>1.PROFILE</u>

A. Informant

1.Country of origin: [   ]

2.Did you live in a City [   ]   Town [   ]   Village [   ] ?

3.Informant: Man [   ]   Woman [   ]

4.I am aged:

14-16 years		31-40 years		Over 60 years	
16-20 years		41-50 years			
21-30 years		51-60 years			

5.What is your marital status –

I am	
Married	
Living with a partner	
Divorced	
Separated	
Widow/widower	
Single	

6. Nationality of partner/wife/husband [   ]

B. Children

7.Have you children   Yes [   ]   No [   ]   8. How many ? [   ]

9.Please list your children with their age/s

CHILD	Age	Boy/ Girl
1		
2		
3		

10.Where are your children ?

CHILD	With me	In this country	In home country	In another country
1				
2				
3				

C. Household

11.List other members of your household.

Relationship to you	Number of persons	Relationship to you	Number of persons
Wife/husband		No relation	
Your mother		Your partner's mother	
Your father		Your partner's father	
Your brother/s		Your partner's brother/s	
Your sister/s		Your partner's sister/s	

2.EDUCATION

12.How long were you in education in your country of origin?

Education	Number of Years
Yours	
Your partner's	

3.OCCUPATION

13.What was your occupation in your country of origin?

Occupation	Mine	My Partners	Occupation	Mine	My Partners
In full time education			Government worker		
Not working			Business person		
Shop owner			Teacher		
Teacher			Hospital		
Engineer			Doctor		
Military service			Social worker		
Working bank			Electrician		
Lorry driver			Plumber		
Agriculture			Shop assistant		
Other			Not disclosed		

4.RELIGION

14.Do you belong to any Faith group ?

Christian	My	Partner's
Roman Catholic		
Church of England		
Free Church – Methodist		
Baptist		
Pentecostal		
Greek Orthodox		
Russian Orthodox		
Other -		
Other Faiths		
Muslim		
Judaism		
Hinduism		
Buddhism		
Other		
No religious affiliation		

5.MOTIVATION TO LEAVE COUNTRY OF ORIGIN

15.When did you decide to leave your own country?

Month [   ]   Year [   ]

16.Why did you choose to leave?   (Tick no more than five)

In my own country -		Comment:
There was a war		
Religious persecution		
Political persecution		
People being killed		
Houses burnt down		
Own house burnt down		
It was unsafe		
Death threat		
People assaulted		
Women raped		
Famine		
Poverty		
People arrested		
Natural disaster - flood		
Volcanic eruption		
earthquake		
Hope for a better life in another country		
Other-		

17.Did you leave any of your family at home ?   Who?

Relationship to you	Number in home country	Number who have fled abroad
Mother		
Father		
Mother in law		
Father in law		
Wife / partner		
Husband/ partner		
Children		
Your sister/s		
Your brother/s		
Partner's sister/s		
Partner's brother/s		

18.Have any of your family come to join you in England?   Yes ☐   No ☐

Relationship to you		Relationship to you	
Mother		Mother in law	
Father		Father in law	
Wife / partner		Husband/ partner	
Children			
Mother's sister/s		Father's sister/s	
Mother's brother/s		Father's brother/s	

6.CHOOSING THE UK

19.Why did you choose to come to England rather than another country?

I chose England:	
By chance	
For economic reasons	
Because it is easier to get permission to stay	
Because I have relatives already in England	
For political reasons	
Because it's a free country	
Other -	

20.Did you consider other countries?   Yes [ ]   No [ ]

I considered going to:		I considered going to:	
Canada		Italy	
France		U.S.A	
Germany		Other -	

7.ENTRY PROCESS

21. Did you arrive legally?   Yes [ ]   No [ ]

22. a) Have you a passport?   Yes [ ]   No [ ]

b) Is it a British Passport?   Yes [ ]   No [ ]

c) If 'No' what Nationality is on your passport?   [ ]

23.How did you travel to England?

(please indicate the order of different forms of travel used)

I travelled by:	1	2	3	4	5
Plane					
Small boat					
Ship					
Cross channel ferry					
North Sea Ferry					
Lorry					
Car					
Other					

Comment:

24.Which was your port of entry?

Dover	
Folkestone	
Harwich	
Heathrow	
Portsmouth	
Stansted	
Other	

25. Did you have to apply for asylum?   Yes [ ]   No [ ]

If 'yes' - Did you know you would have to apply for asylum when you arrived in England?

[ ] Yes   [ ] No

26 What happened when you arrived in England?

a) I registered in	
Croydon	
Dover	
Harwich	
Heathrow	
Portsmouth	
Stansted	
Other	

b) I registered -	
immediately	
Next day	
After 2 days/ 3days	
After 4days/ 5 days	
After 6 days/ a week	
After 2 weeks	
After 3 weeks or more	
Never registered	

c) On registration I was given -	
Identity	
Food	
Accommodation	
Money	
Other -	

d) On registration I was sent to –	
London	
Southend	
Other -	

7. How were you treated by the Authorities (police, immigration officials)?

Very well	
Well	
okay	
Badly	
Very badly	

28. What papers have you received from the Home office?

Ind - Identity	
Passport	
Refugee status	
Temporary residence	
Exceptional leave to remain	
Permanent residence	
Awaiting decision from Home Office	
Other -	

Comment :

29. Has the Christian community/ your Faith group helped you to settle here?

Helped by/with:	
Spiritual support	
Friendship	
Work	
Correspondence with authorities	
Placing your child in a school	
Advice	
Money	
Other -	

30.How are you treated by other people in London?

Welcomed as friends	
Ignored as strangers	
Made to feel unwelcome	
As scroungers	
As terrorists	
Other -	

8.ASSIMILATION

A. English Lessons

31. a Did you need English lessons?   Yes ☐   No ☐

b. If 'Yes' - Was it easy to get English lessons immediately? Yes ☐ No ☐

32.Are you attending English lessons now?   Yes ☐   No ☐

Where ? ☐

How often? ☐

33.How did you find English lessons?   (Please tick only one)

I was helped to find English lessons by -	
A friend took me to lessons	
My child's school helped me find lessons	
The Church helped me find lessons	
A relative helped me find lessons	
other	

34.What did you have to do to receive English lessons?   (Tick no more than two answers)

Go to a centre/school any day	
Go to a centre/school on a particular day	
Just turn up for a lesson	
Fill in a short form with my name and address	
Fill in a form asking for details about my knowledge of English	
Fill in a long complicated form in English	
Other	

B.Children's School

35.Was it easy to get your child/children places in school? (Tick only one)

It was:	
Very easy	
Fairly easy	
Difficult	
Very difficult – child still not in school	

C. Accommodation

36.What did you have to do to get a house/flat to live in?

When I/we first arrived in England I was/we were placed in

A detention centre		A good hotel	
Bed and breakfast		A poor hotel	
An excellent hotel		Other	

208

After [ ] weeks I was/we were moved to: (Tick only one)

A council house	
Bed and breakfast	
Privately owned rented flat/house	
Social housing belonging to a Housing Association	
A good hotel	
A poor hotel	
Other -	

37. If you were in a hotel, how long were you there? [ ]

38. Where do you live now?

A council house	
Bed and breakfast	
Privately owned rented flat/house	
Social housing belonging to a Housing Association	
A good hotel	
A poor hotel	
Other -	

39. How long have you been in this accommodation? [ ]

40. How many flat/houses have you lived in since you arrived here?

41. a) How have you found your present accommodation ?   (Tick only one)

The accommodation is:		The accommodation is:	
Very good		Fair	
Good		Poor	
Adequate		Terrible	

b) How many rooms has your present accommodation? (please include living rooms, kitchen, bathroom and bedrooms) [ ]

D. Medical care

42. How long was it before you found medical care ?

Doctor			Dentist	
One week		(please tick	One week	
2--8 weeks		two)	2– 8 weeks	
2--6 months			2– 6 months	
more			more	

E. Legal care

43. Have you an immigration solicitor?   Yes [ ]   No [ ]

44. How many immigration solicitors have you had?

What has their advice been like?

Solicitor	Very good	Good	Adequate	Fair	Poor	Useless
1.						
2.						
3.						
4.						

45.How did you find an Immigration solicitor?   (Tick only one)

I found a solicitor:	
Through a relative	
Through a refugee charity	
Through social services	
Through the Home Office	
Other -	

46. Have you a housing solicitor?   Yes ☐   No ☐

47. How many housing solicitors have you had?   ☐

What has their advice been like?

Solicitor	Very good	Good	Adequate	Fair	Poor	Useless
1.						
2.						
3.						
4.						

48. Have you had to change any solicitor due to their incompetence?   Yes ☐   No ☐

Comment:

9. LINKS WITH HOME COUNTRY AND FUTURE INTENTIONS

49.Do you often meet other people here from your own country?

I meet people from my own country:	
Every day	
A few times a week	
Every week	
Once a month	
Now and again	
Other	

50.What contact do you have with friends and family in your own country?

I have contact with my own country:	
Directly by letter	
Directly by phone	
Through other relatives and friends	
Other -	

51.a) Would you like to return to your own country to live?   Yes ☐   No ☐

b) If yes, why do you want to return home?

I want to return home because:	
Miss family	
Miss friends	
Homesick	
Prefer life style in home country	
Prefer culture in home country	
Prefer climate at home	
Find language a problem in England	

.Other -	

52. If you would like to return home – what has prevented you from returning to your own country?

I cannot return home because:	
Of war	
Of religious persecution	
Of political persecution	
Of death threats	
Of family commitments here	
I couldn't afford to move home	
Of my work / occupation	
Readjustment would be too difficult	
Other -	

53. Have you permission to stay in England indefinitely? Yes ☐ No ☐

54.

a) I have permission to work in this country:	Yes		No	
b) I have a National Insurance number:	Yes		No	
c) My partner has a National Insurance number:	Yes		No	

55. a) Have you got a job at present? Yes ☐ No ☐

b) Has your partner got a job at present? Yes ☐ No ☐

c) If 'Yes' our jobs are:

	My job	My partner's job
Legal		
Illegal		
Part time		
Full time		

56. What kind of job do you have? (please tick)

Occupation	Mine	My Partners
In full time education		
Not working		
Shop owner		
Teacher		
Business person		
Government worker		
Working in a hospital		
Engineer		
Military service		
Work in a bank		
Lorry driver		
Electrician		
Social worker		
Doctor		
Shop assistant		
Mechanic		
Agriculture		

Other -		

57. What job would you like to do?

Occupation	Mine	My Partner's	Occupation	Mine	My Partner's
In full time education			Teacher		
Government worker			Business person		
Shop owner			Hospital		
Mechanic			Doctor		
Engineer			Social worker		
Military service			Electrician		
Working bank			Plumber		
Lorry driver			Shop assistant		
Agriculture			Other		

58.What do you like about England?

I like:	
Freedom	
Law	
Culture	
Climate	
Language	
Other -	

Comment:

59.What don't you like about England?

I don't like:	
Freedom	
Law	
Culture	
Climate	
Language	
Other -	

Comment:

WELL-BEING

60.What have you found most difficult about coming and living in England?
What has been your greatest problem here?

Language	
Different customs	
Health	
Self esteem	
Lack of occupation	
Housing	
Dealings with Immigration /Home Office	
Other –	

2.Have you or any of your family had any health problems since you came here?

Yes ☐ No ☐

61. Are you or any of your family suffering from any of the following?

	You	Partner
Unable to sleep		
Lack of appetite/ excessive appetite		
Feeling of tension/ irritable		
Feeling constantly tired		
Disinterest in life		
Palpitations		
Panic attacks		
Headaches/ migraines		
Aches and pains/ abdominal pain		
Heart problems		
Depression		
Bad dreams		
Other -		

62. a) I regularly attend

I regularly attend		My partner regularly	
Counselling		Counselling	
Hospital		Hospital	
Psychiatrist		Psychiatrist	

b) How often? [   ]

63. Have your children been affected in any particular way by your family's lack of stability /change of situation? Please explain:

	Child 1	Child 2	Child 3	Child 4
Unable to sleep				
Lack of appetite				
Getting into trouble at school				
Getting into trouble at home				
Silent/withdrawn				
Depressed				
Extremely noisy				
Over-active				
Other -				

Comment:

64. What do you think is the main problems which caused your stress and anxiety?

What are you most afraid of life?

(please choose no more than 5 answers)

Serious illness	
Losing health, disability	
Unsuccessful life	
Unsuccessful marriage	
Broken family	
Losing someone close	
Worsening of material situation	
Worsening of housing situation	
Poverty, misery , unemployment	
Feeling loneliness	
Lack of friends	
Dull and boring life	
Finding at the end of life it has been empty and wasted	
Lack of success in carrying out plans concerning education or work	
Abandoning certain ideals and plans that used to be important	
Humiliation	
Forced repatriation	
Lack of stability	
I'm not afraid of anything	
Other fears -	

65. How did you and your family live five years ago when compared to how you live now?

In the next year:	
You will live much better	
You will live somewhat better	
Nothing will change	
You will live somewhat worse	
You will live much worse.	

66. Do you think that in the next 12 months you and your family will live better than today, or worse?

In the next year:	
You will live much better	
You will live somewhat better	
Nothing will change	
You will live somewhat worse	
You will live much worse.	

67. Are you in contact with any Asylum-Seekers / Refugee / State/ voluntary or faith help groups?

Yes ☐   No ☐

If 'Yes' - Please tick the groups you are in contact with:

I am in contact with /receive help from –	I am in contact with /receive help from	
Children's Society , Manor Park	NCRP , Harold Road Centre	
Didsbury centre, East Ham	Outreach Programme, Canning Town	
Froud Centre, Romford Road	Redbridge Refugee Forum, Ilford	
Harmony House, Dagenham	Refugee Arrivals Project	
Horizon Project	Sure Start, Manor Park	
Newham Refugee Centre, Romford Road	Others – (please specify)	

Comment:

68.If you are not already a British citizen -Would you like to apply to become British citizens?

Yes ☐   No ☐

69.What would you suggest regarding an Immigration policy?

I would suggest:	
On reception of identity given the right to work	
Quicker processing of claims	
Asylum status granted within one year	
On arrival – short term support centres – accommodation, medical, interpretation and language courses offered	
Other –	

Comment:

70. What do you think the Christian Communities/Faith groups could do to help Immigrants?

QUESTIONNAIRE UPDATE MARCH 2004

1. Status

Documentation from Home Office	March 2004
Temporary residence	
Permanent residence	
Exceptional leave to remain	
Granted humanitarian protection	
Granted discretionary leave	
Refugee status	
Awaiting decision from home Office	
Awaiting deportation	
Appealing against Home Office decision	
Case closed	
October 2003 Amnesty- Questionnaire	
Passport	
Travel document	
Granted Amnesty	

2. Have you ever had Exceptional Leave to Remain?   Yes ☐   No ☐

For how long?   one year ☐   two years ☐   longer ☐

Any change to your situation since the Spring of 2003?

3. I have moved house: Yes ☐   No ☐

4. I have changed my immigration lawyer ... Yes ☐   No ☐
If yes, why?

5. My children have had to change school/s ...   Yes ☐   No ☐
   Why?

5. Children.
We have had a baby in the last year....   Yes ☐   No ☐
The baby is a : girl ☐   boy ☐

The baby is now ☐ months old.

We need help with:	Yes / no
Baby clothes	
A baby bath	
A pram/ pushchair	
A cot	

6. Benefits

We receive the following benefits:	Amount each week	Yes
Housing benefit		
Child benefit		
Child Tax credit		
Job seekers allowance		
Income support		
Council tax benefit		
Working tax credit		
NHS tax credit – free prescriptions		
Asylum support / NASS		
Free school meals		
Please write down any other Benefit you receive		

7. Have you ever been without benefits?   Yes ☐   No ☐

	Once	2 times	3 times	more
We have been without benefits:				

8. Have you ever had any problem obtaining your benefits?   Yes ☐   no ☐

We were without benefits?	2 weeks	1 month	2 months	3 months	4 months	longer
1st time						
2nd time						
3rd time						

UPDATE OCTOBER 2004　　　　Ref. Number ☐

STATUS

I arrived in the UK on ..../.......... (month / year)

2) I have been granted the Amnesty.　Yes ☐　　No ☐

　　I have Refugee Status.　Yes ☐　　No ☐

3) I now have Exceptional Leave to Remain (ELR) in the UK.　Yes ☐　No ☐

4) I am still awaiting the decision of the Home office　Yes ☐　　No ☐

5) I am appealing against the Home Office's negative decision　Yes ☐　　No ☐

SECTION A -to be answered by those who have received the Amnesty

6) I was granted the Amnesty on ..../............./ 2004 (day / month/ year)

7) I receive the following benefits

Income support	Yes		No	
Job seekers allowance	Yes		No	
Child benefit	Yes		No	
Child tax credit	Yes		No	
Family tax credit	Yes		No	
Housing benefit	Yes		No	
Free prescriptions	Yes		No	
Other (please give name of benefit)	Yes		No	

8) Were you ever without benefits at any time when you transferred from Social Services/ NASS to Mainstream benefits? Yes ☐　　No ☐

9) I was without benefits for:

1 week		2 weeks		3 weeks	
1-2 months		3-4 months		longer than 4 months	

HOUSING

10) My home

I now live in:	
A council flat	
A council house	
Private rented flat	
Private rented house	
Rented flat belonging to Housing association	
Rented house belonging to Housing association	
Other	

11) My home has ☐ rooms (not counting the bathroom, Kitchen and hall)

12) The condition of my home is:

Very good	Good	Adequate	Fair	Poor	Very poor

13) I would like to move because ....
....
....

14) I have to move because:

my tenancy agreement has ended   Yes ☐   No ☐

my landlord wants me to move out   Yes ☐   No ☐

c. other ....

15) Did you have any problems when you moved from Social Services/NASS to housing provided by local Council?   Yes ☐   No ☐

Yes, I was evicted from my home and had to go to the Homeless Unit. ☐

What happened?

The Homeless Unit sent me to emergency accommodation   Yes ☐   No ☐

      and

I had to stay in bed and breakfast / hotel accommodation

for   ☐   weeks

Please describe the emergency accommodation:

I am still in emergency accommodation   Yes ☐   No ☐

I was moved to temporary accommodation after   ☐   weeks

16) Have you applied for British citizenship for any children born in England? Yes ☐ No ☐

17) Have you applied for a passport?   Yes ☐   No ☐

18) Have you applied for travel documents?   Yes ☐   No ☐

If yes, what happened:

19) How would you describe your present quality of life?

Very poor	Poor	Good	Very good

20) What is your top concern at present?

Health	Housing	Money	Depression	Loneliness	Poor English	No work	No travel document

Please explain which of the above is your top concern and why:

21) Have you any relatives living in the UK?   Yes ☐   No ☐

22) Which of members of your extended family live in the UK?

Mother/ mother in law	Father/ Father in law	Brother/s	Sister/s	Aunts/ uncles	Cousins

Where do your relatives live?

East London	South London	South England	Midlands
West London	North London	North England	Scotland

Is there anything else you would like to tell us:

SECTION B -To be answered by those who have not got the Amnesty

6) I receive the following benefits:

Income support	Yes		No	
Job seekers allowance	Yes		No	
Child benefit	Yes		No	
Child tax credit	Yes		No	
Family tax credit	Yes		No	
Housing benefit	Yes		No	
Free prescriptions	Yes		No	
Other	Yes		No	

7) Have you ever been without benefits ?   Yes ☐   No ☐

8) I was without benefits for:

1 week	2 weeks	3 weeks	
1-2 months	3-4 months	longer than 4 months	

HOUSING

10) My home

I now live in:	
A council flat	
A council house	
Private rented flat	
Private rented house	
Rented flat belonging to Housing association	
Rented house belonging to Housing association	
Other :	

11) My home has ☐ rooms (not counting the bathroom, Kitchen and hall)

12) The condition of my home is

Very good		Good		Adequate		Fair		Poor		Very poor	

13) I would like to move because:

14) I have to move because:

my tenancy agreement has ended   Yes ☐   No ☐

my landlord wants me to move out   Yes ☐   No ☐

other :

15) Have you ever had any problems with your housing?   Yes ☐   No ☐

Yes, I was evicted from my home and had to go to the Homeless Unit.   ☐

What happened ?

The Homeless Unit sent me to emergency accommodation   Yes ☐   No ☐

                    and

I had to stay in bed and breakfast / hotel accommodation

for   ☐   weeks

Please describe the emergency accommodation:

I am still in emergency accommodation   Yes ☐   No ☐

I was moved to temporary accommodation after ☐ weeks

16) How would you describe your present quality of life?

Very poor	Poor	Good	Very good

17) What is your top concern at present?

Status	Health	Housing	Money	Depression	Loneliness	Poor English	No work

Please explain which of the above is your top concern and why:

18) Have you any relatives living in the UK?   Yes ☐   No ☐

19) Which of members of your extended family live n the UK?

Mother/ mother in law	Father/ Father in law	Brother/s	Sister/s	Aunts/ uncles	Cousins

20) Where do your relatives live?

East London	South London	South England	Midlands

West London	North London	North England	Scotland

ISBN 141207403-7

9 781412 074032